W9-BRC-887

Regional Institutions and Governance in the European Union

Edited by
José M. Magone

Westport, Connecticut
London

Library of Congress Cataloging-in-Publication Data

Regional institutions and governance in the European Union / edited by
  José M. Magone.
    p. cm.
  Includes bibliographical references and index.
  ISBN 0-275-97617-3 (alk. paper)
    1. Regionalism—European Union countries. 2. Decentralization in
  government—European Union countries. I. Magone, José M. (José
  María), 1962–

JN34.5 .R45 2003
341.242'2—dc21   2002070950

British Library Cataloguing in Publication Data is available.

Library of Congress Catalog Card Number: 2002070950
ISBN: 0-275-97617-3

First published in 2003

Praeger Publishers, 88 Post Road West, Westport, CT 06881
An imprint of Greenwood Publishing Group, Inc.
www.praeger.com

Printed in the United States of America

The paper used in this book complies with the
Permanent Paper Standard issued by the National
Information Standards Organization (Z39.48-1984).

10 9 8 7 6 5 4 3 2 1

In memory
of the
unforgettable
Vincent Wright,
a true gentleman researcher

Europe is not just about material results, it is about spirit. Europe is a state of mind.

—Jacques Delors
The Independent
May 19, 1994

Contents

List of Tables and Figures

TABLES

FIGURES

List of Abbreviations

AEFR	Association of European Frontier Regions
AER/ARE	Assembly of European Regions (Association des Regions Européennes)
BIC	British Irish Council
CAP	Common Agricultural Policy
CBI	Confederation of British Industry
CCR	Comissão de Coordenacão Regional/Commission for Regional Coordination
CDHN	Community Development and Health Network
CEA	Committee of European Affairs
CEMR	Council of European Municipalities and Regions
CiU	Convergència i Unió/Convergence and Union
CLRA	Congress of Local and Regional Authorities
CoR	Committee of the Regions and Local Authorities
COREPER	Committee of Permanent Representatives
COSLA	Convention of Scottish Local Authorities
CPMR	Conference of Peripheral Maritime Regions
CSF	Common Support Framework
CSG	Consultative Steering Group
EC	European Community
ECOSOC	European Economic and Social Committee
EEC	European Economic Community
EMU	Economic and Monetary Union

ERDF	European Regional Development Fund
ERPII	Economic and Regional Policy Division
ESDP	European Spatial Development Perspective
ESF	European Social Fund
ETUC	European Trade Union Confederation
EU	European Union
EURES	European Employment Service
GATT	General Agreement on Tariffs and Trade
GDP	Gross Domestic Product
GREMI	Groupe de Recherche Européen sur les Milieux Innovateurs/European Research Group on Innovative Milieus
IGC	Intergovernmental Conference
ITUC	Interregional Trade Union Council
LGIB	Local Government International Bureau
MEP	Member of European Parliament
MFP	Member of Flemish Parliament
MLG	Multilevel Government
MP	Member of Parliament
MSP	Member of Scottish Parliament
NICVA	Northern Ireland Council for Voluntary Action
NIEC	Northern Ireland Economic Council
NISRA	Northern Ireland Statistics and Research Agency
NPC	Nieuwe Politieke Cultuur/New Political Culture
NUTS	Nomenclature des Unités Territoriales
OMC	Open Method of Coordination
PP	People's Party (Spain)
PSEP	Physical and Social Environment Program
PSOE	Spanish Workers' Socialist Party
RDA	Regional Development Agency
RETI	Association of Industrial Regions in Decline
ROM	Ruimtelijke Ordening en Milieubeheer/Spatial Planning and Environmental Care
RPG	UK Regional Planning Guidance
SDP	Single Development Programme
SEM	Single European Market
SME	Small- and Medium-Sized Enterprise
SNG	Subnational Government
SNP	Scottish National Party
SPD	Single Programming Document
TEU	Treaty of the European Union
TNC	Transnational Corporation
TUC	Trade Union Congress
WDA	Welsh Development Agency

WEC	Wales European Center
WO	Welsh Office
WTO	World Trade Organization

Preface

The origins of this book go back to a workshop titled "European Public Policy for Regional Policy Makers" held at the Staff House of the University of Hull September 15–16, 2000. The workshop was funded by the Intensive Program subsection of the Socrates program and its purpose was to bring together scholars and students to discuss the recent devolution processes in the United Kingdom in a comparative perspective. Several Ph.D. and M.A. students from our partner institutions were invited to take part in this workshop. Alison Woodward, Linze Schaap, Karen Celis, and Wouter-Jan Oosten became important contributors to this volume. I want to thank them for their continuing support.

Eight of the chapters collected in this volume are high-quality versions of papers presented at the workshop at Hull. The chapters by Elisa Roller and Amanda Sloat comparing Scotland and Catalonia and by Susan Hodgett and Elizabeth Meehan on Northern Ireland were included at a later stage and were written specifically for this volume.

I am also grateful for the academic support of Charlie Jeffery, who made the effort to come to Hull during a period when the United Kingdom had to cope with the fuel crisis and was close to a standstill. He not only encouraged the participants to take part in the England Social Research Council (ESRC) Devolution program, of which he is the director, but he also presented an interesting paper at the workshop. Barry Jones, Graham Pearce, Norman O'Neill, Alex Wright, and Charlie

Jeffery provided enthusiastic discussion on the UK devolution process. I want to thank them for their lively contributions during the workshop.

This book is intended to be a contribution to the conceptualization and empirical study of regional governance within the framework of the European Union multilevel governance system. As such it is only a drop of water in the ocean, but I believe an important one.

I want to thank all the contributors for their enthusiastic participation throughout the entire project.

Last, but not least, I want to thank Elisabetta Linton from Greenwood Publishing Group for supporting this project from the proposal stage to today's volume.

Introduction: The Role of the Regions in European Union Multilevel Governance

José M. Magone

The difficulties of defining the term "governance"[1] were partially over-come when the European Commission decided in July 2001 to come up with its own definition. The European governance white paper defines governance as follows:

> It means rules, processes and behaviour that affect the way in which powers are exercised at European level, particularly as regards to open-ness, participation and accountability, effectiveness and coherence. (Euro-pean Commission, 2001b, 8)

In this sense, the European Commission attempts to reposition its role within the future of the European Union. It clearly wants to strengthen its role as the motor of European integration by emphasizing that the Community Method is still the main mode of governance, although naturally seconded by other methods such as the Open Method of Coordination (OMC) adopted in the Extraordinary Council of Lisbon in March 2000. The European governance white paper is certainly part of the always existing strategy of the European Commission to remind other institutions such as the Council and the European Parliament about its place and their place in the institutional setting.[2] This initiative clearly tries to gain enough democratic legitimacy by linking it to the need to increase the involvement of all possible actors in this process. Such a strategy has been pursued in the past, and it will be at the heart of the European Commission's agenda-setting capacities and repertoire of multiple strategies (Cram 1997, 37–39; Schmidt 2001). Criticisms leveled at the white paper related to the issue of whether the Commission defending its interests within the institutional framework is useful (Wincott 2001), because in reality the period of creeping competence and incrementalism led to a very messy and disorganized establishment of governance particularly during the Commission presidency of Jacques Delors. The rhythm of creeping competence slowed down only in the mid-1990s (Pollack 1994; 2000). The emphasis on the definition of boundaries between layers of governance, even if they will become softer and softer with time, is an important exercise.

If one looks at the report on consultations to the Commission elaborated by the Governance Team—a special task force set up in 2000 and assigned to coordinate and organize the consultation process toward the definition of European governance—one can recognize a strong commitment of the European Commission to get as many views as possible about the reality of European governance. Regions and local authorities are strongly committed to the whole process.

> The regional and local players are indisputably those who have proved to be the most numerous, spontaneously with the most insistent messages. The institutional part has been played as from December 2000 by the Committee of the Regions [CoR] with the adoption of an own-initiative opinion. The Presidents of the German Länder and also the LGIB [*Local Government International Bureau*] had, for their part, established contact even earlier. Substantial contributions will follow in the form of position papers from Eurocities, the CEMR [*Council of European Municipalities and Regions*], ARE [*Association of European Regions*], the CRPM [*Conference of Peripheral Maritime Regions*], the Austrian Länder, the Association of German Towns and Municipalities, the Association of European Border Regions, and the Scottish Executive and COSLA [*Convention of Scottish Local Authorities*], plus the contributions from local authorities (e.g., Landstinget Sörmland), not counting the multitude of players who have responded to requests via the Internet or by mail. (European Commission 2001a, 4)

This process toward redefinition of European governance, the Constitutional Convention process chaired by Giscard D'Estaing (*The Economist*, December 12, 2001; August 15, 2001, p. 31), and the discussion on the future of the European Union are all interlinked. They all want to bring the whole European integration process closer to the citizens of the European Union. More than that, it is in the interest of political elites to empower citizens, to give a sense of ownership of the whole process. According to the report on the consultation, over 500,000 people took part in some way in the process. In this long-term project, regional and local authorities are quite crucial to strengthening the democratization of European Union governance (European Commission 2001a, 3–4).

Here already, we can see that the definition and clarification of European governance must be followed by clarification and definition of what national, regional, and local governance are and entail. In a multilevel governance system, each tier has its own logic of governance that needs to be assessed and looked at internally and externally. Although an internal definition and clarification of the corresponding level of governance are quite easy to do, it becomes more complex and difficult when we try to assess linkages to other levels in European Union governance. Some hierarchy of norms and rules will emerge eventually, but flexible informal linkages may emerge as well. In a globalized world, the regional multilevel governance system of the European Union may be challenged by direct linkages of the subaltern tiers to the global governance system. In the long-term perspective, the dynamics of the different levels of the EU multilevel governance system may fuse and create a coherent whole (Maurer, Mittag, and Wessels 2000). As long as there is no attempt at definition, the process of fusion and integration will be messy and difficult (Figure I.1).

This so-called transition from government to governance will entail a blurring of the boundaries between public and private, leading even to fusion between them, and between civil society and state actors. This naturally completely complicates the picture. Elements of a Luhmannian autopoietic (self-organizing) system may be useful to characterize the dynamics of governance in relation to the more top-down hierarchical governmental approach (Sbraglia 2000; Knill 2000; Luhmann 1998, 65; see chapter 8 by Linze Schaap in this volume).

In this sense, it is important to differentiate analytically what is happening at each of the tiers of the EU multilevel governance system. In this book, a team of scholars tries to assess what is regional governance within the EU multilevel governance system. Regional assertiveness and consciousness increased considerably in the past forty years. According to Stein Rokkan and Derek Urwin a revivalism of the regions across western Europe can be found in the early 1970s (Rokkan and Urwin 1983, 118; Harvie 1994). This is also the late phase of the welfare state and the beginning of a complete restructuring of the west European nation-states into competition states (Cerny 1990; Scharpf 2000). Thatcherism and Reaganomics clearly contributed to processes of economic and political decentralization including the United Kingdom. The development toward regional governance is parallel to the transformation of both the nation-state and the European Union toward governance. Until then a more rigid structure of decision making and policy making based on principles of government were quite dominant.

Figure I-1 A sketch of European Union Multilevel Governance

With the new technologies, decentralization, and complexity of society, there was a silent transformation toward governance. This new concept implied a more flexible, less hierarchical and multiform system of decisionmaking, which allowed for the inclusion of civil society. It was a transformation from government based on a rigid hierarchical system to governance based on a flexible network (Blatter 2001, 207–208; Marks, Hooghe, and Blank, 1996).

The new structure of opportunities created by governance led to the establishment of a stronger role for the European Commission. In alliance with the regions, it was able to change the role of national governments in the whole framework. Indeed, undefined governance at the European level led to diffusion of governance to the national level and the regional level (Tömmel 1998). By the mid-1990s, the governance system of the European Union had to be conceptualized as a pendulum swinging between the supranational level (European Commission, Parliament) and the national level (Council, European Council) (Wallace 2000b, 46). The hope of the regions to become more strongly involved in the whole process of decision making as an independent third level did not materialize. Instead, a Committee of the Regions and Local Authorities with merely advisory powers was established. In spite of that, regions were able to gain some importance at the national level by moving toward cooperative federalism in some countries such as Germany, Spain, Belgium, and Austria. Regional governments tried to use all possible access points to influence the European integration process on their behalf. Latecomers to the whole process just had to internalize this process from government to governance at a faster rate. Since the second half of the 1990s we have been observing a strong commitment of both Swedish and Finnish governments as well as some regions to develop more flexible regional development arrangements as a response to the EU governance system in general and the European regional policy instruments in particular. The whole process of regional partnerships in all twenty-one Swedish regions and in the northern and eastern regions of Finland show that there is a diffusion of the multilevel governance system from the center to the periphery (Svensson and Östhol 2001; Arter 2001).

This transition from government to multilevel governance probably will lead to problems of coordination among the different levels, due to time pressures, different rationales of governance, and structural adjustments. Mismatching interfaces among the levels may be one of the outcomes in a transitional period. It takes time to adjust different rationales within a new multilevel framework (Magone 2001, 36–37; Scharpf 1994). The case of the Italian region of Marche may be used as an example. Throughout the 1990s, Italy had to cope with major domestic transformations that were intended to strengthen the autonomy of the regions in the overall process toward political reform. Already in 1988, a Council State-Regions was established to ensure better information to the regions of the overall process of European public policy formulation, making, and implementation. In spite of the major changes, Italian regionalization has had to deal with difficulties of coordination among the different levels, including the European one.

One positive aspect is that with time the coordinating skills have improved (Ciaffi 2001, 115–121).

The contributors to this volume concentrate their study on regional governance as part of a European Union multilevel governance system and address the issues presented here.

The first two chapters contextualize the whole process toward regional governance within the European Union multilevel governance system from two distinctive perspective. In Chapter 1, José Magone gives an account of the relationship between the European Union and the regions and how the new structure of opportunities was used by regional actors. He discusses aspects of the internalization of the European integration process in the logics of regional governance. In Chapter 2, Norman O'Neill is more interested in looking at the processes of regional development and linking to the European and global level. Both chapters provide the framework for the case studies examined in this volume.

Half of the book is dedicated to the very important devolution process that is taking place in the United Kingdom. All five chapters are geared toward analyzing both the internal dynamics of new governance systems as well as their linkages to other levels of governance.

In Chapter 3, Graham Pearce and Steve Martin discuss the transition of the United Kingdom as a unitary state with two levels of governance (national and local) to the new system of asymmetrical devolution with new elected tiers in Wales and Scotland as well as Northern Ireland. Their study clearly shows the problems of reconstructing national governance within the EU multilevel governance system.

Chapters 4 and 5 are dedicated to Scotland. Elisa Roller and Amanda Sloat (Chapter 4) compare the Scottish and Catalan cases in terms of governance. Alex Wright (Chapter 5) is interested in the external dimension of governance. Roller and Sloat show how decentralization may lead to a stronger involvement of actors in the whole regional governance system and their linkages with the European Union. In the two regions, one can find strong regionalist nationalist parties that put the established national parties under pressure. Roller and Sloat are interested in assessing how civil society perceives the European dimension as fostering their regional interests. Alex Wright concentrates on regional executive-legislative relations as well as the linkages to other levels, including the international level. Questions of the limits of paradiplomacy are addressed in this interesting chapter.

According to J. Barry Jones in Chapter 6, the Welsh devolution process did not substantially change the linkages to Brussels. He clearly states that, on the contrary, there is continuity to policies adopted before devolution. What happened is a kind of a refinement of the relationship. The linkage to the national governance system is still characterized by asymmetrical interdependence. J. Barry Jones's contribution shows that the establishment of a strong regional governance system may take longer than expected in some cases.

Susan Hodgett and Elizabeth Meehan (Chapter 7) bring to the fore an excellent presentation on what is happening in Northern Ireland at the grassroots level. This very difficult case of UK devolution is also characterized by positive efforts by local communities. Whereas the whole process of devolution at the political level is characterized by interruptions, the European Commission has always been interested in overcoming the long-standing historical dispute between Unionists and Republicans. It seems that the European integration process may be, in the end, the key to solving the long-standing division of the island.

Chapters 8, 9, and 10 are dedicated to other recent developments toward regional governance in other countries. Linze Schaap's case study on the Rotterdam city-province project (Chapter 8) makes us aware that in some countries, the unitary structure is not challenged at all. The Dutch case shows that there is a transformation from government to governance going on, but this is not affecting the very territorial structures of the political system. As Schaap states, maybe it is better to avoid any further reform of the territorial organization, but to improve the governance mechanisms of the existing system.

Chapter 9 is dedicated to how new institutions related within the region and how they are linked to other levels. Karen Celis and Alison Woodward have done an excellent job in studying the first legislature of the new Flemish parliament. From the beginning, there is a wish to create a new political culture that will be distinct from the discredited national one. Aspects of gendered representation and differences in style of representation are discussed in detail. Linkages to the European governance tier are not relevant at this stage of the creation and internalization of principles of Flemish regional governance.

Wouter-Jan Oosten undertakes a case study on the emerging Euroregion of Gent-Terneuzen in Chapter 10. Cross-border cooperation is an emerging further element in the repertoire of regional governance. It not only blurs the boundaries between nation-states, it brings regions together and creates larger spaces of cooperation. They may be considered as "islands of advanced European integration." The European Union program Interreg is an important strategic device to strengthen this aspect of regional governance.

Chapter 11 is a collective effort to come to some conclusions related to regional governance within the European Union. This volume does not intend to be comprehensive and final; it is merely a contribution to the present discussion on the nature of governance within the European Union. As such, it should serve as a catalyst for more research on regional governance.

NOTES

1. Here is not the place to discuss thoroughly this new heuristic concept. It is sufficient to mention that the origins of the concept go back to the Greek *kybernan* (to pilot; to steer), and it was used for the first time metaphorically by Plato to characterize the phenomenon of governing people. It was in common use in most Latin languages up to the French Revolution. The recent emergence of the term "governance" goes back to the early 1990s, when several Anglo-Saxon scholars used the term to characterize the art or way of governing by international institutions (including the EU) (Barata n.d). Rhodes (1996) provides a good summary of the development of governance in contrast to hierarchies and markets.

2. The Community Method gives primacy to the European Commission as the motor of European integration and reduces the powers of the European Parliament and the Council to mere legislative bodies. Since the 1950s, the European Union as a polity in the making has become so complex that even the proliferation of specialized agencies established throughout the 1980s and 1990s watered down the powers of the European Commission in certain areas. The white paper wants to rebalance the power of each institution. Other modes of governance were added in the past fifty years to the Community Method, such as the regulatory approach, intensive transgovernmentalism, policy coordination and benchmarking, and the open method of coordination (for a brief discussion, see Wallace 2000a).

REFERENCES

Arter, D. 2001. Regionalization in the European peripheries: The cases of northern Norway and Finnish Lapland. *Regional and Federal Studies* 11, no. 2, (summer): pp. 94–114.

Barata, M. de. Oliveira. n.d. Étymologie du terme "gouvernance." At http://www.europa.eu.int/com/governance.html

Blatter, J. 2001. Netzwerkstruktur, Handlungslogik und politische Räume: Institutionenwandel in europäischen und nordamerikanischen Grenzregionen. *Politische Vierteljahresschriften* 42 (2): 193–222.

Cerny, P. G. (1990). *The changing architecture of politics: Structure, agency and the future of the state.* London: Sage.

Ciaffi, A. 2001. Multi-level governance in Italy: The case of Marche. *Regional and Federal Studies* 11 (2): 115–46.

Cram, L. 1997. *Policy-making in the European Union: Conceptual lenses and the integration process.* London: Routledge.

European Commission. Governance Team. 2001a. Consultations conducted for the preparation of the white paper on democratic European governance. Report to the Commission. SG 8533/01, June.

European Commission. 2001b. European governance. White paper, July 25, 2001, COM(2001), 428 final.

Harvie, C. 1994. *The rise of regional Europe.* London: Routledge.

Knill, C. 2001. Private governance across multiple arenas: European interest associations as interface actors. *Journal of European Public Policy*, 8, no. 2 (April): 227–46.

Luhmann, N. 1998. *Die gesellschaft der gesellschaft.*Vol. 1. Frankfurt a. M.: Suhrkamp.

Magone, J. M. 2001. *Iberian trade unionism: Democratization under the impact of the European Union.* New Brunswick, N.J.: Transaction.

Marks, G., L. Hooghe, and K. Blank. 1996. European integration from the 1980s: Statecentric *v* multi level governance. *Journal of Common Market Studies* 34 (3): 341–78.

Maurer, A., J. Mittag, and W. Wessels. 2000. Theoretical perspectives on administrative interaction in the European Union. In *Committee governance in the European Union,* edited by T. Christiansen and E. Kirchner, pp. 21–44. Manchester: Manchester University Press.

Pollack, M. 1994. Creeping competence: The expanding agenda of the European Community. *Journal of Public Policy* 14 (2): 95–140.

———. 2000. The end of creeping competence? EU policy making since Maastricht. *Journal of Common Market Studies* 38 (3): 519–38.

Rhodes, R. A. W. 1996. The new governance: Governing without government. *Political Studies* 44, no. 4 (September) 652–67.

Rokkan, S., and D. W. Urwin. 1983. *Economy, territory, identity: Politics of west European peripheries.* London: Sage Publications.

Sbraglia, A. M. 2000. Governance, the state, and the market: What is going on? *Governance* 13, no. 2 (April): 243–50.

Scharpf, F. W. 1994. Community and autonomy: Multi-level policy-making in the European Union. *Journal of European Public Policy* 1 (2): 219–42.

———. 2000. The viability of advanced welfare states in the international economy: Vulnerabilities and options. *Journal of European Public Policy,* 7, no. 2 (June): 190–228.

Schmidt, S. K. 2001. Die einflussmöglichkeiten der Europäischen Kommission auf die europäische politik. *Politische Vierteljahresschriften* 42 (2): 173–92.

Svensson, B., and A. Östhol. 2001. From government to governance: Regional partnerships in Sweden. *Regional and Federal Studies* 11 (2): 25–42.

Tömmel, I. 1998. Transformation of governance: The European Commission's strategy for creating a "Europe of the Regions." *Regional and Federal Studies* 8 (2): 52–80.

Wallace, H. 2000a. The Institutional Setting: Five Variations on a Theme. In *Policy making in the European Union,* 4th ed., edited by H. Wallace and W. Wallace, pp. 3–37. Oxford: Oxford University Press.

———. 2000b. The policy process: A moving pendulum. In: *Policy making in the European Union,* 4th ed., edited by H. Wallace and W. Wallace, pp. 39–64. Oxford: Oxford University Press.

Wincott, D. 2001. The Commission and the reform of European governance. *Journal of Common Market Studies* 39, no. 5 (December): 897–911.

The Third Level of European Integration: New and Old Insights

José M. Magone

INTRODUCTION: THE IMPACT OF EUROPEAN PUBLIC POLICY IN THE REGIONS

The importance of European public policy for the European Union member-states has increased in the past fifteen years. Particularly, the relationship between national and subnational government has changed considerably. The emergence of the "Europe of the Regions" is no longer a catchword, but an important reality in the European Union. Indeed, the European Commission found in the regional governments an important ally in promoting the Single European Market (SEM) and by doing so, it softened the resistance of many of the national governments to implementing the SEM and Economic and Monetary Union (EMU). This alliance continues to be the pillar of European regional policy (Tömmel 1998, 53–54). In this chapter, I want to make people aware of the past achievements of this transformation of EU territorial politics, which is further supported by the growing number of networks of interactions among actors of the different member-states and the regions. The main aim of the territorial politics of the European Union is to achieve even development throughout the territory. For this to be achieved, long-term structural, industrial, and social policies have to be implemented. European spatial development is based on three main principles:

- Economic and social cohesion
- Sustainable development
- Balanced competitiveness in the European Union

These three principles have to be regarded as interacting ones. To single out one of them would lead either to the failure of achieve the goal of social and economic development or to a decline of competitiveness. The coordination of European and national spatial policies are essential for the successful implementation of an integrated multisectoral indicative strategy (European Commission 1997a, 5 and 7). All these efforts go back to the *Europe 2000+* document of the European Commission, which clearly emphasized this need for convergence of economic and social conditions in creating a more competitive space that can cope with the challenges of globalization (European Commission 1995). To understand the silent revolution of thinking in relation to European spatial development, one has to look more closely at how subnational regional policy makers and institutions react to it. In the end, it is this level of policy formulation, making, and implementation that will lead to the likely success of the SEM.

In this sense, this chapter intends only to share some thoughts on the past, present, and future developments of this quite challenging new stage of European integration. Here we are going beyond a mere political science approach. Indeed, the transformations can only be noticed through a combination of approaches taken from sociology, anthropology, environmental sciences, geography, and economics.

The following pages deal with the territorial politics of the European Union and the impact on the territorial organization of the member-states, a short discussion of the presence of the regions at supranational level, the creation of the Committee of the Regions, and the growing regionalization of European union politics and policy. Some conclusions are presented to close this chapter.

SINGLE EUROPEAN MARKET AND THE TERRITORIAL POLITICS OF THE EUROPEAN UNION: FROM TWO- TO MULTILEVEL GAME

Since the mid-1980s the European integration process has entered a new stage, which clearly can be labelled the development toward a multilevel governance system. Until the mid-1980s the two main actors of the European integration process were the nation-states and the supranational institutional framework. Within the latter, an institutional tandem Council and Commission dominated the decision-making process. The leadership of Jacques Delors of the European Commission between 1985 and 1995 changed this decision-making process toward a multilevel governance system, which today is still in the making (Ross 1995). The regions became important players in pushing the European integration process and developing strategies to enhance their role in the decision-making structures of the European Community (EC)/European Union (EU) (H. Wallace 1996a). This two-level–game thesis of Robert Putnam, comprising the supranational and national actors as the sole players, became obsolete in the 1990s (Putnam 1988), when regional governments of Belgium, Germany, and Austria achieved some representation in the Council of the European Union after the adoption of the Maastricht Treaty. They were able to successfully influence decisions that may concern social and economic cohesion (Keating and Hooghe 1996, 221). The creation of a Committee of the Regions in 1993 made it possible to channel most of the already existing diffuse representation of regional governments at the supranational level.

The main vehicle of the transformation of the relationship of the regions within the EU territory was the enhancement of the role of the structural funds in promoting economic and social cohesion, so that even development and equal access to the SEM could be achieved in the long-term perspective. The importance of the structural funds in transforming the rationale of the European Union cannot be overemphasized. They contributed to a more long-term coordinated program approach in the EU policy process, overcoming the uncoordinated efforts at single programming in European regional policy before 1988, which were not driven by inspiring mid- to long-term programs such as the SEM and EMU. The most salient aspect of this transformation was naturally the emergence of a coherent EU territorial politics rationale that was related to the principles mentioned earlier and coordinated with national regional development strategies. The reform of the structural funds in 1988 emphasized new buzzwords such as *partnership* among supranational, national, and subnational actors and *subsidiarity*. Although the process of decision making was still dominated by the nation-states, which had to submit long-term regional development plans, the regions in the past fifteen years had more opportunities for influence through monitoring mechanisms and other channels. There was also a learning process going on in the past decade related to implementation and coordination of funds. Since 1998, the *Agenda 2000* document reduced the original five (after 1994, six) objectives to three objectives, thus making for a more efficient and concentrated use of the funding. Between 1994 and 1999, 67.6 percent of the structural funds were directed toward objective 1 (lagging behind) regions; the remainder was distributed among the other objectives (Armstrong 1989; European Commission 1996, 14–15; 1997b, 22–24; 1999).

The transformation of the rationale was informed also by the expansion to southern Europe that took place in the 1980s. After the accession of Greece in 1981 and Portugal and Spain in 1986, the European Community was no longer a cohesive homogenous economic space; it had become more heterogenous and uneven, as their economic structures were much weaker than those of the rest of the European Union. This naturally led to a transformation of the rationale of European public policy. For the first time, the European Community had to introduce economic and social development strategies to improve the access of the southern European citizens to the SEM. According to Lord Cockfield (1994), the approval of the SEM by the southern European member-states was made dependent on the flow of additional funding to restructure and modernize their economies. This naturally should have remained an essential element in pushing the importance of European regional policy on the EU agenda throughout the 1990s. The southern European alliance became even more cohesive in the Edinburgh summit of December 1992, when the Delors II package led to a doubling of the structural funds available for the Common Support Framework 2 (CSF2, 1994–1999). Indeed Belgium, Portugal, and Ireland vetoed any change or watering down of the economic and social cohesion of the structural funds. The unanimity voting was therefore used in this particular instance not to reduce the power of the supranational organizations but, on the contrary, to strengthen the supranationalization of regional policies against the wish of the larger countries to renationalize it (Hooghe and Marks 2001, 98). By the mid-1990s, 40 percent of the EU budget was assigned to the structural funds and European regional policy (Hooghe and Keating, 1996). Part of the funding came from the continuing half reforms of the Common Agricultural Policy (CAP). At this stage, more countries were receiving large amounts of structural funds, such as Ireland and Germany. European regional policy will continue to play a major role in strengthening regional governments as actors in their own right and contributing to even development and equal access to the SEM. Although the 1999 discussions on the finances of the European Union did not lead to an upgrading of the overall volume of funding for the structural funds, it led to rationalization in terms of objectives (from six to three). The forthcoming expansion to Central and Eastern Europe will certainly call for a reform of the structural funds, but by no means its disappearance.[1]

If one looks at the gross domestic product (GDP) per capita in relation to the EU average, the cohesion countries (Portugal, Spain, Greece, and Ireland) were able to make considerable progress in the past decade of structured common support framework programs. By 1999, Greece achieved 69.3 percent of the EU GDP per capita average, Portugal 71.8 percent, Spain 79.6 percent, and Ireland 105.1 percent. The cohesion countries achieved an average 78.2 percent. This means that the gap between the poorest and richest countries narrowed by 13 percentage points between 1986 and 1996 (see Figure 1.1).

Although there is a considerable gap between north and south, this is less when compared between western Europe and eastern Europe. In 1999, the average GDP per capita of all thirteen candidates together to EU membership in relation to the average EU15 is 44.15 percent with Cyprus (82 percent) and Slovenia (71 percent) having the highest, and Bulgaria (23 percent) and Turkey (29 percent) the lowest. More problematic is a comparative study between the regions within the southern European countries and those in comparison to northern European regions (Table 1.1).

One can see that the differences in the GDP per capita remained almost the same. The difference between the poorest and richest regions, in spite of a decade of structural funds, remained almost the same. In 1986, Hamburg was five times richer than Alentejo in Portugal; this was reduced to three times in 1996. In spite of that, other regions, particularly the islands and ultraperipheral regions of the European Union, continue to be five times poorer than Hamburg.

Although some homogeneity was achieved among richer and poorer member-states, structurally the wealth differences among the regions are still pretty much the same. Probably policy instruments and territorial organization are important factors in narrowing these differences. But the crucial point here is that the dynamics introduced by the structural funds created a myriad of formal, semiformal, informal, permanent, and provisional institutions that made the system more complex over time. From CSF1(1989–1993) to now CSF3 (2000–2006), a dense network of people who are interested in pushing forward the European integration process has been established, which involves an ever-increasing number of actors. Through European public policy, flexible bridges were built between the different levels of governance. The growing number of experts, civil servants, and members of organized civil society involved in European public policy are actors of European integration (Tömmel 1998, 64–71; Pires 1998; Magone 2000a; Paraskevopoulos 1998; Lang, Naschold, and Reissert 1998; and Lang and Reissert, 1999; Keating 1998, 182–183).

The transformation of the European public policy rationale in the past sixteen years is related to this reconstruction of the territorial organiza-

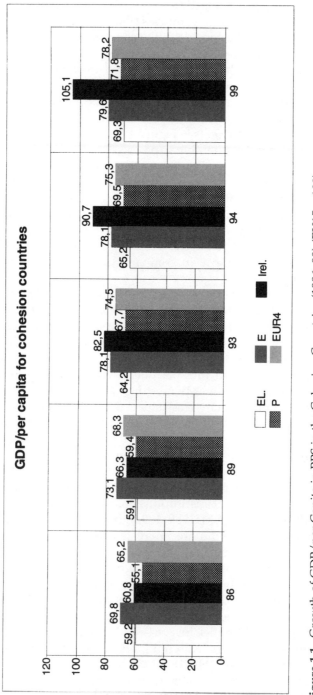

Figure 1.1 Growth of GDP//per Capita in PPS in the Cohesion Countries (1986–99) (EU15 = 100)

Source: Graph based on data from European Commission, *Sixth Periodic Report on the Social and Economic Situation and Development of the Regions of the European Union* (Luxembourg: Office of the Official Publications of the European Communities 1999), p. 199.
EL: Greece; **E:** Spain; **Irel:** Ireland; **P:** Portugal; **EUR4:** Cohesion countries

TABLE 1.1 GDP Per Capita in PPS in the Cohesion Countries (1986–1999)

1986 Regions	GDP/capita	Rank	1996 Regions	GDP/capita	Rank
Hamburg(D)	185	1	Hamburg(D)	192	1
Reg.Bruxelles Cap.(B)	163	2	Reg.Bruxelles Cap.(B)	173	2
Ile de France(F)	162	3	Darmstadt(D)	171	3
Darmstadt(D)	152	4	Luxembourg(Grande Duché)	169	4
Wien(A)	148	5	Wien(A)	167	5
Greater London(UK)	148	6	Ile de France(F)	160	6
Bremen(D)	144	7	Oberbayern(D)	156	7
Stuttgart(D)	143	8	Bremen(D)	149	8
Oberbayern(D)	141	9	Greater London(UK)	140	9
Luxembourg(Grand-Duché)(L)	137	10	Antwerpen(B)	137	10
Highest 10	**153**		**Highest 10**	**158**	
Stockholm(S)	133	11	Stuttgart(D)	135	11
Ahvenanmaa/Aland(FIN)	132	12	Groningen(NL)	134	12
Lombardia(I)	132	13	Emilia-Romagna(I)	133	13
Uusimaa(FIN)	129	14	Lombardia(I)	132	14
Valle d'Aosta(I)	129	15	Valle d'Aosta(I)	131	15
Berlin(D)	128	16	Uusimaa(FIN)	129	16
Emilia-Romagna(I)	125	17	Trentino-Alto Adige(I)	128	17
Mittelfranken(D)	124	18	Grampian(UK)	126	18
Antwerpen(B)	124	19	Friuli-Venezia Giulia(I)	126	19
Karlsruhe(D)	123	20	Karlsruhe(D)	126	20
Düsseldorf(D)	122	21	Veneto(I)	124	21
Grampian(UK)	122	22	Berksh.,Buckinghams.,Oxf.(UK)	124	22
Noord-Holland(NL)	117	23	Mittelfranken(D)	123	23
Köln(D)	117	24	Stockholm(S)	123	24
Piemonte(I)	117	25	Salzburg(A)	121	25
Highest 25	**138**		**Highest 25**	**143**	
Guyane(F)	37	1	Guadeloupe(F)	40	1
Guadeloupe(F)	37	2	Ipeiros(EL)	44	2
Alentejo(P)	37	3	Reunion(F)	46	3
Acores(P)	40	4	Guayne(F)	48	4
Madeira(P)	40	5	Acores(P)	50	5
Reunion(F)	40	6	Voreio Aigaio(EL)	52	6
Centro(P)	42	7	Martinique(F)	54	7
Voreiio Aigaio(EL)	44	8	Madeira(P)	54	8
Extremadura(E)	44	9	Extremadura(E)	55	9
Algarve(P)	44	10	Dessau(D)	55	10
Lowest 10	**41**		**Lowest 10**	**50**	
Ipeiros(EL)	47	11	Andalucia(E)	57	11
Martinique(F)	49	12	Dytiki Ellada(EL)	58	12
Dytiki Ellada(EL)	49	13	Magdeburg(D)	58	13
Norte(P)	51	14	Peloponnisos(EL)	58	14
Ionia Nisia(EL)	52	15	Calabria(I)	59	15
Andalucia(E)	53	16	Alentejo(P)	60	16

TABLE 1.1   continued

1986			1996		
Regions	GDP/ capita	Rank	Regions	GDP/ capita	Rank
Castilla-La Mancha(E)	54	17	Centro(P)	61	17
Galicia(E)	55	18	Anatoiki Makedonia.Thraki(EL)	61	18
Thessalia(EL)	55	19	Thüringen(D)	61	19
Anatoiki Makedonia.Thraki(EL)	56	20	Mecklenburg-Vorpommern(D)	61	20
Kriti(EL)	57	21	Dytiki Makedonia(EL)	62	21
Dytiki Makedonia(EL)	58	22	Ionia Nisia(EL)	62	22
Kentriki Makedonia(EL)	58	23	Norte(P)	62	23
Calabria(I)	59	24	Thessalia(EL)	63	24
Peloponnisos(EL)	61	25	Galicia(E)	63	25
Lowest 25	**52**		**Lowest 25**	59	

Source: European Commission, *Sixth Periodic Report on the Social and Economic Situation and Development of the Regions of the European Union* (Luxembourg: Office of the Official Publications of the EC 1999), p. 200.

tion within the member-states and as a consequence in the European Union as a whole.

Since the 1970s, the global economic system has been in transformation. Apart from the fact that in the 1970s industrialized countries reached the limits of mere mass consumption economies, new technologies and working organizations were introduced that led to a major restructuring of these economies. The transition is only now in the new millenium coming to its end. In the past thirty years, member-states experienced a decline of control over their economic decisions to private nongovernmental transnational organizations. Moreover, worldwide economic competition between countries became even more intense in the 1980s. The European integration process reflects the will of member-states to move toward a regime of shared sovereignty that will attenuate the effects of globalization and competition (W. Wallace 1999, 509–12).

The whole SEM and EMU projects are designed to create a larger market and establish economies of scale, so-called European champions to compete against the United States and an Asia-wide Economic Community (Hayward 1995). The competition state (Cerny 1990) of the 1980s had to be replaced by a more or less integrated nation-state within the European Union. Although some countries hesitate in taking part in the myth of the "EU super-state," in reality the economic, social, and political trends are toward the creation of such a European-wide market with a more or less coordinating political structure.

The globalization thrusts clearly were an important factor in pushing decentralization and deconcentration of national territories onto the agenda. The main reason is that the region as such was perceived as a more adequate and flexible unit to attract foreign investment and adjust rapidly to a changing global economy. The discussion on location factors—such as infrastructures, education of the working force, cultural life, social capital, and government performance in the regions—that may influence transnational corporations (TNCs) to bring in investment was regarded as quite crucial for the establishment of a more appropriate economic organization of the territory (European Commission 1993). Some highly centralized countries such as France, Italy, Greece, the Netherlands, Portugal, and the United Kingdom introduced only reluctantly some form of decentralization or devolution.

Meanwhile, all member-states are pursuing decentralization, deconcentration, or devolution of the administration of their territories in view of democratizing the decision-making process and making policy implementation more efficient. Apart from Portugal and Greece, all member-states have made considerable efforts in creating a more flexible territorial structure. This new structure of opportunities is an excellent occasion for regional actors to enhance their role within the EU multilevel governance system. The United Kingdom is naturally the latest development in this process. The devolution of some legislative powers to Scotland, Wales, Northern Ireland, and London may be only the beginning of a complete regionalization of the United Kingdom. Although resistance is still quite widespread, the English regions may become part of this process sooner than later. This naturally may lead to a more interesting and fascinating way of doing politics in the United Kingdom (Jones 1997; Mitchell 1997; Elcock 1997; Martin and Pearce 1999; Griffiths 2000).

The discussion about matching European funding with government funding in Wales, which is defined as an objective 1 region, clearly showed that the European Union, the SEM, the EMU, and globalization are important factors in this equation. Indeed, the United Kingdom is moving very quickly toward a new constitutional framework,[2] which may end up being very similar to the German cooperative federalism or the Spanish state of autonomies. This naturally is changing the role of national governments, which will probably concentrate their efforts in coordinating and supervising the actual formulation, making, and implementation of policy done at the regional level.

The growing importance of regional governments can be seen in the representation at the Council of Ministers of the European Union. Belgium, Germany, Austria, Spain, and more recently the United Kingdom are increasingly conceding more powers to the regions at the supranational level. Naturally, the case of Belgium illustrates that the process of decision making has to be coordinated and consensual so that, in the end, all the actors are able to recognize themselves in the decision-making process (Kerremans 2000). This means that Belgian regions and the national government have to be very flexible and open channels for fast-track decision making throughout the whole process. In spite of a long tradition of cooperative federalism, still today German coordination of all the actors is not at all optimal, as Wolfgang Wessels and Dietrich Rometsch (1997) express. This may be a lesson both for Spain (Morata 1998, 395–99) and for the United Kingdom (Kassim 2000, 33), which are newcomers to this more complex process of decision making. A culture of cooperation can only become reality after a lengthier period of interaction. A crucial factor is the perception of the population of a country toward European integration. In the case of Belgium, the experience is that Belgian national and regional governments have been quite keen to promote the European integration process, so the decision-making process is always bound to be pro-European. Liesbet Hooghe expresses that without being a member of the European Union Belgium would have collapsed by now. The European Union is one of the factors fostering integration in the highly fragmented and federalized Belgian political system (Hooghe 1994, 322–23). A quite similar pro-European position can be found in Spain and Germany. Both national and subnational levels are pro-integrationist. In this sense, clashes can be ironed out and transformed into consensual solutions. In contrast to all these countries, the majority of the population in the United Kingdom is very euroskeptic. In spite of all that, the regional political elites tend to have a more positive attitude and a less reserved position toward the European Union. This means that clashes between regional and national government representatives may become a reality in the future. Such clashes could be seen in relation to the European funding discussion, which led to the resignation of Welsh first minister Alun Michael. Such a situation may erupt in the decision-making process at the EU level in the future and the United Kingdom, which is a newcomer to this more complex process of decision making. (See Table 1.2).

In sum, the emergence of the regions as actors in their own right not only has made the politics of the individual member-states more diverse and interesting but also must be set in the context of reorganization of the economic space and democratization of decision making. The strategic role of the structural funds gave a new impetus and importance to regional actors. Although Greece and Portugal are the two countries lagging behind in this process, the pressure for decentralization and deconcentration will continue to grow from below. The need to mobilize regional civil societies for the creation of new projects will be one of the reasons for this transformation of attitude.

TABLE 1.2 Typology of States and Regional Organizations in the European Union

Type of State	States	Political Regions	Administrative Regions (Planification)
FEDERAL	Austria	Länder(9)	
	Belgium	Communautés(3); Regions(3)	
	Germany	Länder(16)	
UNITARY REGIONALIZED	Italy	Regioni ordinarie(15); Special Regioni speziali(5)	
	France	Régions(21)	
	Spain	Comunidades Autonomas(17)	
	United Kingdom	Scotland, Wales, Northern Ireland	Standard English regions
UNITARY DECENTRALIZED	Denmark	Faröe Islands	Amter Groups
	Finland	Aaland Islands	Counties
	Netherlands	Rijnmond Region	Provinces(13)
	Sweden		Regional administrative organs(21)
UNITARY CENTRALIZED	Greece		Regions(13)
	Ireland		Regional authorities(8)
	Luxembourg		
	Portugal	Madeira island region and Azores islands region	Comissoes de Coordenação Regional(5)

Source: Adapted and extremely simplified from Loughlin, John, *La autonomia en Europa ocidental: un estudio comparado.* In: Letamendia,Francisco (coord.), *Nacionalidades y Regiones en la Unión Europea* (Madrid: Editorial Fundamentos 1998), pp. 144–45.

FROM DIFFUSE TO ORGANIZED INTEREST GROUP REPRESENTATION

One of the most important factors leading to the salience of a third level of European integration is the growing representation of regional governments at the supranational level.

In the past fifteen years one could see a considerable increase of regional offices. At present there are 149 regional government offices represented at the EU level (see Figure 1.2).

Since 1999, the Netherlands allows the direct representation of their thirteen provinces in a common building. This shows that even traditional centralized states are providing more opportunity for their regions to influence the decision-making process. The first offices were established by the United Kingdom (1984), Germany (1985), Spain

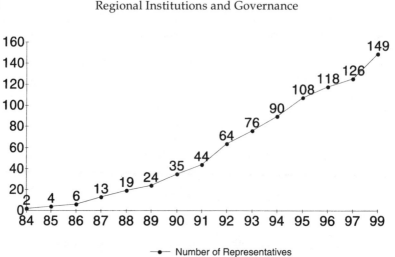

Figure 1.2 Increase of Regional and Local Government Offices (1984–1999).

Source: Smets, Isabelle, Les Régions Se Mobilisent-Quel "Lobby Régional" À Bruxelles? In: Claeys, Paul-H., Gobin, Corinne, Smets, Isabelle, Winand, Pascaline (eds.), *Lobbyisme, Pluralisme et Intégration Européenne* (Brussels: European Interuniversity Press 1998), p. 322; updated to 1999.

(1986), and France (1986). All other regional governments were established in the 1990s (Figure 1.3).

The main idea of representation at the supranational level is to enhance the lobbying possibilities. In the end, the regions are interested in pursuing a multiple crack strategy, which means the strategic exploitation of multiple points of access. It naturally documents that there are still gray areas of interest representation that are not regulated and structured and may lead to advantages in information gathering and networking (Marks, Nielsen, Ray, and Salk 1996, 45; Smyrl 1997; Bomberg and Peterson 1998; Jeffery 2000).

The very fragmented decision-making process, which has been constantly under review since 1986, makes it possible for the regions to find new opening gates and try to gain advantage for their constituencies. This aspect of the continuous search for opportunities of influence is certainly related to the fact that the institutionalization and constitutional enshrinement of regional representation is still lagging behind. Indeed, one aspect that has to be highlighted is that the European Union so far has been a constant process of review of treaties. This naturally is changing the relationships among the main institutions and any new institutions that may emerge in the process. This allows a very short time for institutions to gain a new institutional equilibrium. Within a

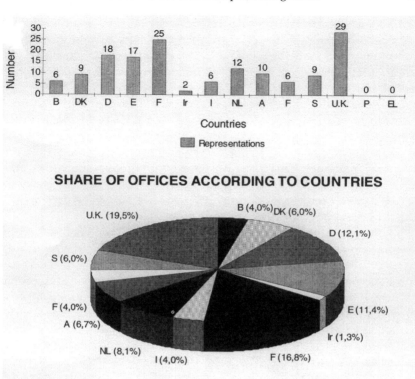

Figure 1.3 Regional Representations at the EU Level (1999).

Source: Based on data from *The Directory of EU Information Sources,* 10th revised edition (Brussels: Euroconfidentiel 1999), pp. 34–39.

five-year period they are again under review and have to readjust their interfaces to the new structural changes. This so-called "treatyism" (Schuppert 1995) is naturally an advantage for the increasing importance of regional presence at the supranational level. The constitutional convention under the chairmanship of Giscard D'Estaing established in the European Council of Laeken under the Belgian presidency may contribute to a simplification and rationalization of such a process of treatyism.

The creation of the Committee of the Regions and Local Authorities (CoR) in the Treaty of the European Union in 1993 and its functioning since 1994 originally led to a major euphoria among regional politicians. From the very beginning, regional politicians were among the members of the new committee, which clearly had nothing more than advisory powers. The organization of the committee according to Euro-party membership gave a different dynamics to the committee in comparison to the consensual nature of the Economic and Social Committee, which was organized along functional groups. Although the regions were an important actor in the new committee, local authorities were also represented. This was quite essential so that unitary states could be represented in this committee. This still gives very much power to the nation-states, which in some cases, such as France and Portugal, have the right of appointment of the delegates to the CoR. Meanwhile, the big expectations of the CoR were lowered. It is now regarded as an institutionalized channel to get access to EU information, parallel to more informal ones. This naturally shows that the regional authorities still have to look at other possibilities of influence if they want to achieve greater importance at the European Union level (Munoa 1998; Calussi 1999; Loughlin 1996; Bassot 1993).

In spite of all the criticisms, the CoR is already a big achievement in comparison to the diffuse opportunities of influence by the regions in the 1980s. Only in 1988 did the European Commission create a Consultative Assembly for Regional and Local Authorities so that subnational government could be consulted on aspects related to the reformed structural funds. This naturally shows how important it was for the European Commission to mobilize the subnational level. Other European-wide associations such as the Assembly of European Regions (AER), Conference of Peripheral Maritime Regions (CRPM), Association of the European Frontier Regions (AEFR), Union of Capital Regions, La Diagonale Continentale, and other function-oriented associations were important forums where regional governments could create common agendas in relation to the European Union. These associations are quite important to raise regional consciousness and create spaces of decentralized democracy. Although symbolic in many ways, the collective action of regional authorities is a major contributing factor in shaping the institutions of the European Union (Balme 1999, 76 and 86–87). Ambition, for the more conscientious regions, does not end here.

Indeed, one can speak already of a paradiplomacy of regional governments, which, although inconsistent, is reinforcing this process of the regional dimension of European integration. The best example is naturally the Four Motor Europe consisting of the regions of Baden-Württemberg, Lombardy, Catalonia, and Rhone-Alps, which still today has mere symbolic importance, but may transform in the long-term perspective into a technological and scientific motor of the Europe of the Regions. This naturally makes us aware of the importance of the regions for the continuing process of treaty reform in the European Union. The third level was able to gain more institutional power since the Single Europe Act (SEA), the Treaty of the European Union (TEU), and the Amsterdam Treaty. Such institutionalization of the third level may go further in the future, but it is a slow process. In any case, regions are interested in shaping the European integration process from below, and this may be regarded as a form of democracy enhancement in the continuing discussion about the final European Union institutional design. In fact, most of the candidates for membership in Central and Eastern Europe are already involved in cross-border or interregional frameworks of cooperation with EU member-states and are adjusting their structures to a multilevel governance system. This naturally shows that decentralization of structures continues to be on the agenda for the next decade. This follows the rationale imposed by globalization to develop more flexible territorial structures (Keating 1999a; Aldecoa 1999).

According to a recent contribution by Beate Kohler-Koch, the network approach will continue to gain relevance in the European integration process. This has been one of the main characteristics of the present development of the SEM, which clearly is being structured and organized by the European Commission. Although the European Commission is labeled by its critics as technocratic, Kohler-Koch argues that the European Commission was supposed to be only the guardian of the treaties and implement the agreements (Kohler-Koch 2000, 31–32; Bach 1999, 38–59).

This naturally can only be revised in the long-term perspective. Any institutional reform has to take into account the legitimacy of the decision-making process. Indeed, the main problem of the present Euro-Polity is that it is still only government for the people, whereas government by the people or of the people is still largely underdeveloped or nonexistent. It is an output-oriented polity, not a democratic input-oriented polity (Scharpf 1998, 6–28).

Kohler-Koch (2000) proposes, therefore, that institutionalization of direct democracy devices such as European-wide referenda should assure more democratic legitimacy for the process. In this context, she pleads for the possibility of a regional and a functional veto in case decisions may affect either the third level of European integration or the function-specific policy area. For this she proposes a steady enhancement of the European Parliament, which should take over an intermediary role in the creation of the European Union. The European Commission should be a mere secretariat of policy coordination. Naturally, Kohler-Koch regards the European Union as a political system *sui generis*, which cannot be compared or cannot replace the nation-states. This means that diversity and flexibility have to be regarded as important elements in a consensus-based redesigned European Union along the lines of the Swiss model (Kohler-Koch 2000, 37; Christiansen 1997; Macmullen 1999; H. Wallace 1996b). This proposal of Kohler-Koch is just one among many, but it clearly follows a trend that may enhance the role of the regional populations in the long-term perspective. The regional veto and functional veto based on referendum overcome the elitist temptation to reproduce the present domination of European integration not only by the national political elites but by regional and functional elites as well (Kohler-Koch 2000, 34–35).[3] The proposal is naturally feasible due to the fact that the technological capacities to organize Europe-wide referenda have improved considerably with the new information technologies. It may also reduce the still existing gap between national *demoi* and create a new Europe-wide *demos*. Acknowledging the diversity and the multiplicity of identities clearly helps to strengthen the legitimacy of a Euro-Polity in the making (Weiler 1996, 526; Schmitter 1996).

According to *Eurobarometer* data, people feel attached primarily to town/village, region, and the country of origin. Attachment to Europe (abstract or concrete) is always a distant identity (Figure 1.4). This naturally means that the region can become a political unit that may enhance the role of the European Union in improving the quality of life of citizens. Moreover, European integration processes, both territorial vertical and horizontal as well as functional among the different tiers of governance, will certainly increase the legitimacy of the European integration process. For this to happen, the process of institutional restructuring of regional cooperation and European involvement in it must continue for a long period of time. Nevertheless, some progress has already been made in the area of cross-border and interregional cooperation that may be supportive of the highly utopian project of Beate Kohler-Koch.

INSTITUTIONAL TRANSFORMATION: FROM DOMESTICATION TO REGIONALIZATION OF EUROPEAN UNION POLITICS

Michael Keating once made the point that the recent developments of territorial restructuring across Europe are related to the fact that the homogeneous nation-state was always a myth that had to be secured by policies of homogenization of the particular territory. In the past thirty years we have been witnessing a process of reconstruction of national government within an integrated Europe. This has not led to the demise of the nation-state, but it has created a multitude of institutional regimes that contributed to an easing of the rigidity of national politics that was quite common up to the 1970s. This is particularly evident in multinational states such as Belgium, Spain, and France, but also seen in Germany, Austria, and Italy. The outcome is an asymmetrical configuration of a government. The present European Union itself

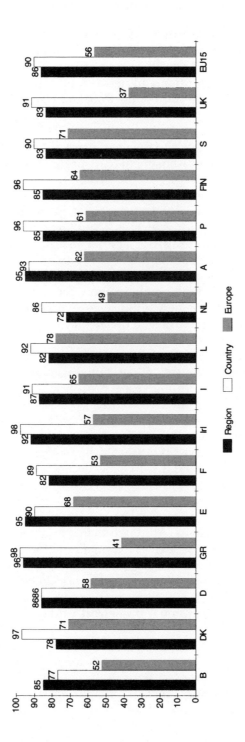

Figure 1.4 Attachment to Region, Country, and Europe.

Source: Own graph based on data from *Eurobarometer*, Spring 1999, 51:B. 10-12.

is an incomplete project that is very asymmetrical in its institutional development. In some parts of the European integration process, one can find a high level of density and organization, yet in other parts the whole process of institution and network building is taking place at a much slower pace. We are bound to acknowledge that the different nation-states and subnational governments are responding to this process in different ways, according to their level of institutional development. This naturally leads to the emergence of aspects of ambiguity in the transformation and adjustment of institutions within the multilevel governance system (Keating 1999b, 74–82).

This is why, after almost a decade of studies of subnational mobilization at a supranational level, the interest in the role of subnational government at the national level is being targeted more and more by European integration specialists. The domestication of European Union politics is leading to a parallel study of the regionalization of European Union politics. This means that the complex European Union governance system is still in the making and offers a huge opportunity for regions to shape it. The new political system *sui generis* will probably enhance aspects of decentralized democracy and accountability, which will strengthen ambitions of subnational governments. Although between the different levels there are still many mismatching interfaces that prevent more efficient cooperation, this may be overcome in the long-term perspective through aspects of social learning.

The best example is the cross-border cooperation between Spanish and Portuguese regions. The different regional political systems in the two countries were major obstacles slowing the decision-making process for common projects. Whereas Portuguese regions are highly centralized and represented by five deconcentrated Commissions for Regional Coordination (*Comissões de Coordenacao Regional*—CCRs), the Spanish regions are more flexible in their decision-making process, due to the fact that they have decentralized regional governments within regional political systems. Although there are differences in the levels of competence of regions such as Extremadura (low) and Galicia (high), in comparison to Portuguese regions they are better equipped to make decentralized decisions. This problem was slowly overcome in the 1990s, although there is still a long way to go to establish more compatible cross-border institutional frameworks (Magone 2000c, 157; 2001, 259–80).

The Iberian case is completely different from those of Germany and Austria, where presently there is discussion about aspects of stronger regionalization of European politics. In the case of Germany, the regional parliaments, the *Landtage*, recognized that the new developments in European Union politics have led to a loss of importance in the framework of cooperative federalism (*politikverflechtung*). The creation of similar European-affairs committees in the Landtage is clearly transforming the discussion about the involvement of subnational actors. Referring to the resolution of the German federal Constitutional Court related to the Maastricht Treaty and the importance of enshrining the role of national parliaments in the TEU, the Landtage are aiming to achieve the same for themselves. One of the main arguments is that an enhancement of the European Union discussion at the subnational level would improve the deteriorating perception/image of European Union politics among the German population. The regional level is also regarded as a more appropriate level to create a more democratic discussion about the future of the European Union. Here again one can see that the regionalization of European Union politics is still very asymmetrical. Some Länder have a stronger involvement of the Landtage in the process of European integration than others. This involvement becomes even more important if we take into account that the Bundesrat consists of regional government representatives and not of members of the Landtage (Lenz and Johne 2000: 20–29).

In Austria, several measures were undertaken to assure that EU membership would not deteriorate the position of the nine Austrian *Bundesländer* in the overall process of EU national policy coordination. In practice, Gerda Falkner (2000) comes to the conclusion that in spite of a liaison office in Vienna, the regional governments and regional parliaments, the Landtage, have difficulties coping with the growing number of decisions to be taken within the Committee of Permanent Representatives (COREPER). Although in the Austrian case the Landtage representatives are in the Bundesrat, EU national policy coordination would make it too difficult to come to a final decision on time. This means that the decision-making process has to be centralized around representatives of the Bundesländer in Brussels, which are sent for approval to the Vienna liaison office (Falkner 2000). The Austrian case may be related to the fact that new members have to learn a lot and be flexible in adjustment to the new demands of the European multilevel governance system. For a small state, this may even take longer than for larger countries, such as the Portuguese 1986 or the Swedish 1995 cases have shown (Ekengren and Sundelius 1998; Magone 2000b, 143–44).

The Austrian case is more complex that those mentioned ealier, because of the strength of the subnational government. This naturally makes a case for the establishment of direct interfaces between the supranational and the subnational levels, which would enhance the role of parliamentary institutions across the EU territory. This would naturally contribute to the regionalization of European Union, with regional policy makers as an essential part of it.

The asymmetrical nature of government in Europe today is related to the more or less dense institutionalization of civil societies. In some parts of Europe there is a move toward the creation of cross-border regional societies and institutions, but in other parts regional civil societies are still lagging behind newly created institutions (Sodupe 1999; Cochrane 1993).

In the first category we can locate the Saar-Lorraine-Luxembourg Euroregion, which recently has reinforced their cooperation and cross-border institutionalization. Furthermore, the Belgian Walloon, the Belgian German-speaking community, and Trier-Rheinland-Pfalz have become part of the process, thus creating a Grand Region. Last year, the first interregional economic and social committee was founded, which intends to create a Euro-region–wide institution for this cross-border regional society. The process of interregional integration started as far back as 1956 (Lerch 1999, 401–5; Wirtschafts- und Sozialauschuß der Europäischen Gemeinschaften 1999; Wolters 1993). Recently, a cross-border right to question (*fragerecht*) was introduced, which was supported by the Interregional Council of Parliamentarians. This allows for cross-border regional interventions in national politics and vice versa (*Frankfurter Allgemeine Zeitung*, June 9, 2000, p. 3).

Similarly, since the early 1990s, French and Spanish regions are making efforts at integration. The best known processes are two projects affecting the Mediterranean regions. These are led by two rival Catalan politicians. The project led by Pascual Maragall, the mayor of Barcelona, is bringing together six administrative capital cities. The so-called C-6 project includes the cities of Barcelona, Montpellier, Palma de Mallorca, Toulouse, Valencia, and Zaragoza. The main idea is to create motors of technological development in this western Mediterranean region. It covers a surface of 180,623 square kilometers (8 percent of the EU surface) and 16.4 million people (5 percent of the EU population). The more modest Euro-region project led by *Generalitat*, the Catalan government, president Jordi Pujol consists only of the three regions of Catalonia, Languedoc Roussillon, and Midi-Pirénnées. It covers 104,619 square kilometers (4.65 percent of the EU territory) and 10.6 million people (3.24 percent of the EU population). A high level of institutionalization through working groups has been achieved in the two projects, but it is still early in the day to make an evaluation about a process which has been dominated thus far by political and economic elites (Morata 1995, 121–27; 1997).

A further project of integration between Spanish and French regions is the *Diagonale Continentale*. The diagonale continentale is still an unknown project. It was founded by Spanish and French regional economic and social committees on November 24, 1995. The following twelve regional economic and social committees are integrated in this project: Extremadura, Madrid, Castilla-LaMancha, Castilla y Leon, La Rioja, Navarra, Aragon, Midi-Pirénées, Limousin, Auvergne, Bourgogne, Centre. It comprises 445,000 square kilometers (20 percent of the EU territory) and has 21 million inhabitants. The group was formed to prevent further regional imbalances of these peripheral regions in relation to other parts of Europe such as the historical densely populated Blue Banana region between northern Germany and Lombardy (La Diagonale Continentale 1995; Committee of the Regions 1997; Seiler 1999: 163–72).

Similar horizontal efforts of integration have been taking place between Spain and Portugal since the early 1990s. In this case, the main factor of thrust was naturally the *Interreg* program of the European Union. The process of creating compatible institutions is still going on. In spite of all that, some progress has been made in creating the beginnings of a cross-border regional civil society. The best example is the Interregional Trade Union Councils (ITUCs), which are contributing to the establishment of cross-border regional economic integration and thus pushing the process of SEM. The ITUCs are promoted by the supranational European Trade Union Confederation (ETUC). One of the main tasks of the ITUC is to support legally and socially migrant workers who are moving from one country to another. One of the big achievements of the integration of the cross-border regions was to create the first European Employment Service (EURES) in the cross-border region of North Portugal and Galicia. EURES are financed by the European Union and are designed to help migrant workers with legal advice and at the same time coordinate efforts for the development of civil society projects so that the living quality of workers and the economic prospects of these underdeveloped regions can be improved. Meanwhile there are thirty-eight ITUCs and eighteen EURES placed in the Euregios across the European territory. This naturally is still just a beginning of institutional presence of the supranational level, but quite an important development (Magone 2001, 270 and 274).[4]

A more recent development that has captivated the economic actors across the European Union are the territorial employment pacts promoted both by the regions as well as the European Union with the objective of creating new innovative small- and medium-size enterprises. In spite of the fact that territorial employment pacts began appearing only since 1996, by 1999 there were eighty-nine pacts in place (Figure 1.5).

This naturally further smoothes the process of cross-regional integration and transforms the relationship between subnational and national governments in the respective countries. One can see, for example, not only a vertically defined relationship between national governments and subnational governments, but also transnational horizontal inte-

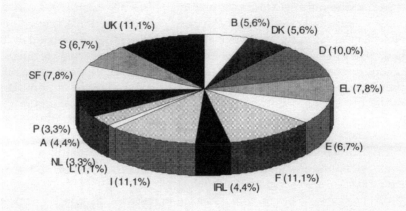

Figure 1.5 Distribution of Territorial Employment Pacts (1999).

Source: European Commission, *Territorial Employment Pacts: 61 Operational Tools* (Brussels: Office of the Official Publications of the European Communities 1999), p. 13.

gration of regions, not only for economic advantage but also to create a more permanent relationship. The creation of such interregional institutions probably allows for a faster regionalization of European Union politics. Transnational regional societies are European in nature, so they may contribute to the creation of European civil society. These so-called islands of European civil society give further evidence of the asymmetrical nature of the European integration process (Magone 2000d, 238).

This perspective of the third level of European integration will remain the most attractive one in the future. This will also in some way respond to the critique that Helen Wallace brought forward some years ago, which clearly complained about the lack of studies on integration processes per se.[5] It is the interfaces among the different levels of the governance system where European integration may be measured quantitatively and qualitatively.

CONCLUSION: RECONSTRUCTING THE EUROPEAN INTEGRATION PROCESS

In the past fifteen years, the European integration process regained its vitality. It is no longer a merely elitist project, but it is shaping daily the lives of European citizens across the European Union. This is particularly visible at the regional level, where the implementation of structural funds and other policy areas is leading to a regionalization of European Union politics. For the moment, one has to assess realistically that the European integration process is in a transition process from a two-level to a multilevel governance system. Multilevel governance as well as the third-level approach are only heuristic devices to highlight the importance of the subnational level of governance. In reality, all levels are in permanent transformation due to the continuing implementation of the SEM, the EMU, and institutional reform. This characteristic of the political system *sui generis* advises us to be cautious about the final institutional design of the European Union. The silent revolution is one of transregional and transnational cooperation between regional and local authorities. It takes time to develop more salient and important institutions of cooperative behavior in the third level of the EU governance system.

A research agenda for the twenty-first century will have to include more studies about concrete integration processes than general overviews of the state of the art. This will lead to studies in regional parliaments, regional civil societies, and cross-border regional institutions. The slow but certain internalization of the European Union politics rationale by regional authorities and localities will make the whole process more democratic and accountable. The Spanish example clearly shows that the dynamics of decentralization become more important with the growing interdependence of regions among each other. It is in this context that the discussion of Europe of the Regions, in general, and the devolution process in the United Kingdom and other countries, in particular, ought to be studied and analyzed. All these processes are contributing to a reconstruction of European politics, which will certainly be reinforced even more strongly by future expansion to Central and Eastern Europe. Moreover, it also affects the present discussion on the "Charter of Fundamental Rights of European Citizens" and the prospects of a European constitutional process, initiated at the Laeken European Council in December 2001. Regional and cross-border regional civil societies may be among the ones to gain most from it.

NOTES

1. Apart from pre-accession aid, the prospective budget of the European Union agreed to in the Berlin summit has taken into account this future expansion. Slowly the structural funds for the cohesion countries and other member-states are being reduced and channelled toward Central and Eastern expansion (Chevalier 2000; see also Jakoby 1999 and Jessen 1999, 167–75).

2. According to a survey, people in the United Kingdom are more content with their constitution today than they were in 1995. However, support for the European Union continues to be very low (The *Times*, August 25, 2000).

3. Compare with Radaelli (1999): 770–71:
   Democratic control and accountability are concepts in search of new meanings even at the national level. The proliferation of non-majoritarian

institutions and networks of private and public actors points towards post-parliamentary governance. The EU constitutes a peculiar accentuation of this trend. This situation requires a leap forward, rather than a journey back to the past of parliamentary control. In perspective, the increasing role played by politicization over expertise is indicative of a positive maturation of the EU. Politics generates conflict, structures cleavages, and polarizes public opinion but at the same time frees policies from the trap of technocracy and makes room for a more benign utilization of expertise. Democracy is all about conflict, and perhaps a certain degree of inefficiency in the policy process is the price that has to be paid for a wider participation and a more mature debate, as the case of media ownership regulation typifies. . . . Politicization, in short, aids the maturation of the EU as a polity, and perhaps will make it less different from national political systems. . . . *The conclusion is not that technocracy has disappeared in the EU, nor that depoliticization is feasible and desirable, but that expertise is operating in an increasingly politicized environment.* (770–71) [emphasis added]

4. Apart from Catalonia, Basque Country, and Galicia, Spanish regional civil societies are still quite marginalized in the decision-making process of structural funds. For the case of Valencia, see Held and Sanchez-Velasco 1996, 236–46.

5. See H. Wallace (1997):

Political and other social scientists are unsure of what political and societal convergence might mean and how either might relate to the feasibility of integration. An enormous amount of literature has been published over the past decade ostensibly about European political integration. But actually most of it has been about the politics of the EC/EU and how it works, but not about integration. We are well informed about institutional processes and about patterns of political activity at the national level, as well as at the supra- and infra-national levels. We also know a great deal about particular forms of policy-integration in the field of regulation especially, just as we know much about the politics of bargaining and new opportunity structures provided by EU resource transfers. (224)

REFERENCES

Aldecoa, F. 1999. Towards plurinational diplomacy in the deeper and wider European Union (1985–2005). In *Paradiplomacy in action: The foreign relations of subnational governments,* edited by F. Aldecoa and M. Keating. Special issue of *Regional and Federal Studies* 9, no. 1 (Spring): 82–94.

Armstrong, H. 1989. Community regional policy. In: *The European Union and the challenge of the future,* edited by J. Lodge, pp. 167–85. London: Pinter.

Bach, M. 1999. *Die Bürokratisierung Europas: Verwaltungseliten, experten und politische Legitimation in Europa.* Frankfurt/New York: Campus.

Balme, R. 1999. Las condiciones de la acción colectiva Regional. In *Nacionalidades y regiones en la Unión Europea,* coordinated by F. Letamendia, pp. 69–91. Madrid: Fundamentos.

Bassot, E. 1993. Le Comité des Régions: Regions Françaises et Länder Allemands face à un nouvel organe communautaire. *Revue du Marché Cummun et de l'Union Européenne,* no. 371 (September–October): 729–39.

Bomberg, E., and J. Peterson. 1998. European Union decision making: The role of subnational authorities. *Political Studies* 46, no. 2 (June): 219–35.

Calussi, F. B. 1999. The Committee of the Regions: In an atypical influential committee? In *EU committees as influential policymakers,* edited by M. P. C. M. Van Schendelen, pp. 225–49. Aldershot: Ashgate.

Cerny, P. G. 1990. *The changing architecture of politics: Structure, agency and the future of the state*. London: Sage.

Chevalier, J.P. 2000 (in two parts). L'accord interinstitutionnel du 6 Mai 1999 et les perspectives financières 2000–2006: De nouvelles ambitions pour l'Union Européenne? *Revue du Marché Commun et de l'Union Européenne.* Part I in no. 440 (July–August): 441–60; Part II in 441 (September): 524–32.

Christiansen, T. 1997. Tensions of European governance: Politicized bureaucracy and the multiple accountability in the European Commission. *Journal of European Public Policy* 4, no. 1 (March): 73–90.

Cochrane, A. 1993. Beyond the nation-state? Creating Euro-regions. In *Die Politik der dritten Ebene: Regionen im Europa der Union*, edited by U. Bullmann, pp. 393–405. Baden-Baden: Nomos Verlaggesellschaft.

Lord Cockfield. 1994. *The European Union: Creating the single market*. Chichester: Wiley Chancery Lane.

Committee of the Regions and Local Authorities (CoR). 1997. Avis du Comité des Régions du 18 Septembre 1997 sur "La Diagonale Continentale: Un espace de coopération pour assurer la cohésion de l'amenagement du territoire Européen."

La Diagonale Continentale. 1995. *La force d'une cooperation. Espagne, Region de Castille et Leon*. Valladolid, November 24, 1995.

Ekengren, M., and B. Sundelius. 1998. Sweden: The state joins the European Union. In *Adapting to European integration: Small states and the European Union*, edited by K. Hanf and B. Soetendorp, pp. 131–48. London: Longman.

Elcock, H. 1997. The north of England and the Europe of the Regions, or, when is a region not a region? In *The political economy of regionalism*, edited by M. Keating and J. Loughlin, pp. 422–35. London: Frank Cass.

European Commission. 1995. *Europe 2000+: Cooperation for European territorial development*. Brussels: Office of the Official Publications of the European Community.

———. 1996. *Europe at the service of regional development*. Luxembourg: Office of the Official Publications of the European Community.

———. 1997a. *European spatial development perspective*. First official draft, presented at the informal meeting of ministers responsible for spatial planning of the member-states of the European Union, Noordwijk, June 9–10, 1997.

———. 1997b. Agenda 2000: For a stronger and wider union. *Bulletin of the European Union*. Supplement 5/97.

———. 1999. *The structural funds in 1997*. Ninth Annual Report. Brussels: Office of the Official Publications of the European Community.

European Commission/Netherlands Economic Institute. 1993. *New location factors for mobile investment in Europe*. Luxembourg: Office of the Official Publications of the European Community.

Falkner, G. 2000. How pervasive are Euro-politics? Effects of EU membership on a new member-state. *Journal of Common Market Studies* 38, no. 2 (June): 223–50.

Griffiths, D. 2000. Writing on the margins: Welsh politics. *The British Journal of Politics and International Relations* 2, no. 1 (April): 124–34.

Hayward, J. 1995. International industrial champions. In *Governing the new Europe*, edited by J. Hayward and E. Page, pp. 346–73. Oxford: Oxford University Press.

Held, G., and A. Sanchez-Velasco. 1996. Spain. In *Policy networks and European structural funds*, edited by H. Heinelt and R. Smith, pp. 227–56. Aldershot: Avebury.

Hooghe, L. 1994. The dynamics of constitution building in Belgium. In *Contemporary Political Studies 1994*, edited by P. Dunleavy and J. Stanyer, pp. 314–24. Belfast: Political Studies Association.

Hooghe, L., and M. Keating. 1996. The politics of European Union regional policy. *Journal of European Public Policy*, 1 (3): 367–93.

Hooghe, L., and G. Marks. 2001. *Multi-level governance and European integration.* Lanham: Rowman and Littlefield.

Jakoby, H. 1999. Reform der EU-Strukturfonds: Handlungsbedarf in den Ländern für die neue Programmperiode 2000–2006. *WSI-Mitteilungen* 6: 407–14.

Jeffery, C. 2000. Subnational mobilization and European integration: Does it make any difference? *Journal of Common Market Studies* 38, no. 1 (March): 1–23.

Jessen, C. 1999. Agenda 2000: Das reformpaket von Berlin, ein erfolg für gesamteuropa. *Integration* 22 Jg., 3/99, pp. 167–75.

Jones, B. 1997. Wales: A developing political economy. In *The political economy of regionalism*, edited by M. Keating and J. Loughlin, pp. 388–405. London: Frank Cass.

Kassim, H. 2000. The United Kingdom. In: *The National Co-Ordination of Eu Policy: The Domestic Level*, edited by H. Kassim, B. G. Peters, and V. Wright, pp. 22–53. Oxford: Oxford University Press.

Keating, M. 1998. *The new regionalism in Western Europe: Territorial restructuring and political change.* Cheltenham: Edward Elgar.

———. 1999a. Regions and international affairs: Motives, opportunities and Strategies. In *Paradiplomacy in Action: The Foreign Relations of Subnational Governments*, F. Aldecoa and M. Keating. Special issue of *Regional and Federal Studies* 9, no. 1 (Spring): 1–16.

Keating, M., and L. Hooghe. 1996. By-passing the nation-state? Regions and the EU policy process. In *European Union: Power and policymaking*, edited by J. Richardson, pp. 216–29. London: Routledge

———. 1999b. Asymmetrical government: Multinational states in an integrating Europe. *Publius: The Journal of Federalism* 29, no. 1 (winter): 71–86.

Kerremans, B. 2000. Determining a European policy in a multilevel setting: The case of specialized coordination in Belgium. *Regional and Federal Studies* 10, no. 1 (Spring): 36–61.

Kohler-Koch, B. 2000. Regieren in der Europäischen Union: Auf der Suche nach demokratischer Legitimität. *Aus Politik und Zeitgeschichte*, B6: 30–38.

Lang, J., F. Naschold, and B. Reissert. 1998. Reforming the implementation of European structural funds: A next development step. Paper of the Wissenschaftszentrum Berlin. Fs Ii 98–202.

Lang, J., and B. Reissert. 1999. Reform des Implementationssystems der Strukturfonds: Die neuen Verordnungen vor dem Hintergrund der Leistungsfähigkeit des bisherigen Systems. *WSI-Mitteilungen* 6: 380–89.

Lenz, A., and R. Johne. 2000. Die Landtage vor der herausforderung Europa: Anpassung der parlamentarischen Infrastruktur als Grundlage institutioneller Europafähigkeit. *Aus Politik und Zeitgeschichte*, B6: 20–29.

Lerch, W. 1999. Neu in Europa: Der interregionale Wirtschafts- und Sozialausschuß der Großregion Saar-Lor-Lux. *WSI-Mitteilungen* 6: 396–406.

Loughlin, J. 1996. Representing regions in Europe: The Committee of the Regions. *Regional and Federal Studies* 6: 147–65.

Macmullen, A. 1999. Fraud, mismanagement and nepotism: The Committee of Independent Experts and the fall of the European Commission 1999. *Crime, Law and Social Change* 32: 193–208.

Magone, J. M. 2000a. EU territorial governance and national politics: Reshaping marginality in Spain and Portugal. In *Margins of European integration*, edited by N. Parker and B. Armstrong, pp. 155–77. Basingstroke: Macmillan.

———. 2000b. Portugal. In *The national co-ordination of EU policy: The domestic level*, H. Kassim, B. G. Peters, and V. Wright, pp. 141–60. Oxford: Oxford University Press.

———. 2000c. The transformation of the Portuguese political system: European regional policy and democratization in a small EU member-state. In *Europeanization of southern European political systems*, edited by K. Featherstone, and G. Kazamias. Special issue of *South European Society and Politics* 5 (2): 119–40.

———. 2000d. La costruzione di una società civile Europea: Legami a più livelli tra comitati economici e sociali. In *Il comitato economico E sociale nella costruzione Europea*, edited by A. Varsori, pp. 222–42. Venice: Marsilio.

———. 2001. *Iberian trade unionism: Democratization under the impact of the European Union*. New Brunswick, N.J.: Transaction Publishers.

Marks, G., F. Nielsen, L. Ray, and J. Salk. 1996. Competencies, cracks and conflict: Regional mobilization of the European Union. *Governance in the European Union*, edited by G. Marks, F. W. Scharpf, P. C. Schmitter, and W. Streeck, pp. 40–63. London: Sage.

Martin, S. and G. Pearce. 1999. Differentiated multi-level governance? The response of British subnational governments to European integration. *Regional and Federal Studies*, 9 (2): 32–52.

Mitchell, J. 1997. Scotland: The Union state and the international environment. In *The political economy of regionalism*, edited by M. Keating and J. Loughlin, pp. 406–21. London: Frank Cass.

Morata, F. 1995. L'Eurorégion et le réseau C-6: L'Émergence du suprarégionalisme en Europe du sud? *Pole Sud*, no. 3 (Autumn): 117–27.

———. 1997. The Euro-region and the C-6 network: The new politics of subnational cooperation in the western Mediterranean. In *The political economy of regionalism*, edited by M. Keating and J. Loughlin, pp. 292–305. London: Frank Cass.

———. 1998. *La Unión Europea: Procesos, actores y politicas*. Barcelona:Ariel.

Munoa, J. M. 1998. El Comité de las Regiones y la democracia regional y local en Europa. In *Nacionalidades y regiones en la Unión Europea*, coordinated by F. Letamendia, pp. 51–68. Madrid: Fundamentos.

Paraskevopoulos, C. J. 1998. Social capital and the public/private divide in Greek regions. *West European Politics* 21, no. 2 (April): 154–77.

Pires, L. M. 1998. *A politica regional Europeia em Portugal*. Lisboa: Fundacão Calouste Gulbenkian.

Putnam, R. 1988. Diplomacy and domestic politics. *International Organization* 42: 427–61.

Radaelli, C. M. 1999. The public policy of the European Union: Whither politics of expertise? *Journal of European Public Policy* 6, no. 5 (December): 757–74.

Ross, G. 1995. *Jacques Delors and European integration*. Oxford: Oxford University Press.

Scharpf, F. W. 1998. *Governing in Europe: Effective and democratic?* Oxford: Oxford University Press.

Schmitter, P. C. 1996. Some alternative futures for the European polity and their implications for European public policy. In *Adjusting to Europe: The Impact of the European Union on National Institutions and Policies*, edited by Y. Meny, P. Muller, and J. L. Quermonne, pp. 25–40. London, New York: Routledge.

Schuppert, G. F. 1995. On the evolution of a European supra-state: Reflections on the conditions and prospects for a European constitution. In *Constitutional policy and change in Europe*, edited by J. J. Hesse and N. Johnson, pp. 329–368. Oxford: Oxford University Press.

Smyrl, M. E. 1997. Does European Community regional policy empower the regions? *Governance* 10, no. 3 (July): 287–309.

Sodupe, K. 1999. La Unión Europea y la cooperación interregional. In *Nacionalidades y regiones en la Unión Europea*, coordinated by F. Letamendia, pp. 13–50. Madrid: Fundamentos.

Tömmel, I. 1998. Transformation of governance: The European Commission's strategy for creating a "Europe of the Regions." *Regional and Federal Studies* 8 (2): 52–80.

Wallace, H. 1996a. Politics and policy in the European Union: The challenge of governance. In *Policy-making in the European Union*, edited by H. Wallace and W. Wallace, pp. 3–36. Oxford: Oxford University Press.

———. 1996b. Integration von verschiedenheit. In *Das Europaische Mehrebenensystem*, edited by T. König, E. Rieger, and H. Schmitt, pp. 29–45. Frankfurt a. M.: Campus.

———. 1997. Pan-European integration: A real or imagined community? *Government and opposition* 32 (2): 216–33.

Wallace, W. 1999. The sharing of sovereignty: The European paradox. *Political Studies* 48: 503–21.

Weiler, J. H. H. 1996. European neo-constitutionalism: In search of foundations for the European constitutional order. *Political Studies* 44 (3): 517–33.

Wessels, W., and D. Rometsch. 1997. German administrative interaction and European Union: The fusion of public policies. In *Adjusting to Europe: The impact of the European Union on national institutions and policies*, edited by Y. Meny, P. Muller, and J. L. Quermonne, pp. 73–109. London: Routledge.

Wirtschafts- und Sozialauschuß der Europäischen Gemeinschaften (In Zusammenarbeit mit dem Wirtschafts- und Sozialrat des Großherzogtums Luxemburg, dem Wirtschafts- und Sozialauschuß der Großregion und der Luxemburgischen handwerkskammer). 1999. *Europa der Bürger-Großregion: Debatte.Berichte Von Der Konferenz Am 29.3.1998 in Luxembourg*. Luxembourg: Office of the Official Publications of the European Community.

Wolters, M. 1993. Euregios along the German border. In *Die politik der dritten ebene: Regionen im Europa der Union*, edited by U. Bullmann, pp. 407–18. Baden-Baden: Nomos Verlaggesellschaft.

2

Regional Business Development and the European Union

Norman O'Neill

Underpinning the process of regionalization throughout the European Union (see Magone, and Pearce and Martin in this volume), is an increasing belief (but it is only a belief) that successful economic development in a region is functionally related to its institutions, in terms of the network of associations supposedly supporting business innovation. The reality is that what constellation of factors effectively contributes to regional business development remains an open question, requiring a great deal more comparative empirical research. Even so, what is also true is that the main institutions of governance—whether the European Commission itself, member-states, or the regions within them—*behave* as though business development is in general functionally related to the network of regional institutions. The explanation for this has probably more to do with the political history of the Commission than it has to do with social scientific research. In any event, the influence of the European Commission on all aspects of regional policy has been clearly evident for some years (see Tömmel 1998), and especially more recently in the European Spatial Development Perspective (ESDP), which was formally agreed upon by the Council of Ministers in May 1999. The European Commission requires all applications for structural fund programs to take account of its principles. The ESDP sets out three spatial planning objectives:

- A more balanced pattern of spatial development and a new urban-rural relationship
- More equitable access to physical and new communications networks, and improvements in the fostering of innovation
- Sustainable management of resources—natural built and cultural heritage

Each of these forms part of the UK Regional Planning Guidance (RPG). Similarly, the four pillars of the European Guidelines on Employment—Employability, Entrepreneurship, Adaptability, and Equal Opportunities—agreed upon at the Helsinki Conference in 1999, have set the framework for the UK government's own National Employment Action Plan, which adopts exactly the same four. These in turn have been the focus of the business development strategies adopted by the UK's Regional Development Agencies.

The social scientific literature lending credence to the supposed relationship between successful business development and regional institutions, tends—as perhaps one would expect—to be associated with technological revolution, globalization, new forms of management and information systems, and changes in the international division of labor.

Castells and Hall (1994), in their worldwide analysis of successful regions, argue that the planned hi-tech industrial centers called technopoles "explicitly commemorate the reality that cities and regions are being profoundly modified in their structure, and conditioned in their growth dynamics, by the interplay of three major, interrelated historical processes": technological revolution (information technology and genetic engineering), globalization (a global economy operating in world-wide space for the factors of production and markets), and new forms of management systems (based on the generation of knowledge).

Globalization involves both production and consumption. In the sphere of production there is an evident global division of labor in which the components of commodities are frequently manufactured in different parts of the world. Recent advances in technology and communications enable a clear decomposition of production processes in which, for example, in the semiconductor industry (which underpins much of the revolution in electronics and communications) it is commonplace for components to be manufactured in Japan, assembled in southeast Asia, and then finally processed and packaged in (say) France or Ireland (Foster-Carter 1985, 35). Accordingly, the competitiveness of any one nation or region in this global market is coming to depend less upon the performance of particular firms, and more on the functions they perform—the value they add—within the global economy (and the value-added frequently corresponds to forms of agglomeration of the kind epitomized in Castells and Hall's description of a technopole).

The pace of technological change is so great that even official categories of job descriptions are inadequate to gauge the extent of economic transformation. Robert Reich (1992) has identified three broad categories of work: routine production services, in-person services, and symbolic-analytical services (174). These are perhaps more usefully defined in terms of routine operations embracing both traditional manufacturing (in decline)—involving repetitive tasks and undertaken mostly by unskilled men—and retail services (which are on the increase) such as checkout operations in supermarkets and elsewhere (undertaken largely by unskilled women), person-to-person services (such as hairdressing, domestic plumbing, nursery provision, etc.) that cannot be exported, and knowledge workers such as research scientists, systems analysts, software engineers, investment bankers, architects, design engineers, and the like, whose operations involve problem solving, problem identifying, and strategic brokering, and who are engaged in a global trade in symbols (data, words, oral and visual representations, and so on).

Correspondingly, in the sphere of consumption we can identify the formation of what might be called global regional markets. A broad comparison of the postwar period and what has happened over the past two decades illustrates the point. After 1945, world trade was regulated through the General Agreement on Tariffs and Trade (GATT) on the basis that in the context of an expanding global market reciprocal agreements offered some protection to home markets. But when GATT was reshaped in the form of the World Trade Organization (WTO), there was an implicit recognition that the world is divided into global regional markets—such as the North American Free Trade Association, the European Union, and developments taking shape in the Pacific Rim—each of which, for the most part, operates internally. Multinationals therefore seek a presence in each of these regional markets.

In theory then, each of these regions should be able to access its own domestic market on more favorable terms in relation to transportation costs, speed of delivery, and economies of scale.

These ideas have informed a large part of the Delors white paper on growth, competitiveness, and employment, and appear to have shaped much of the subsequent thinking within the European Commission.

Regions are therefore perceived as being both internal (a "Europe of Regions") and external (the "European Single Market") to nation-states, and whatever their theoretical propensities, economists have been encouraged to re-examine the significance of the region in economic development.

It is notable that other social scientists, particularly sociologists (in the tradition of Marx and Weber), have been very reluctant to conceptualize the region as something other than territorial space, rather than as a fundamental category in socioeconomic analysis, comparable in utility to representations of social realities such as social class, social status, the family, the capitalist enterprise, the community, the labor market, and the commodities market. What has tended to refocus attention on the region in the last two decades has been the spectacular economic success in places such as Silicon Valley, Orange County, and Route 128 in the United States; Toyota City and Sakaki in Japan; the cité scientifique, Toulouse in France, Baden-Württemberg in Germany, and Emilia-Romagna in Italy.

It was clearly believed that in studying the pattern of technological innovation and business growth in these successful regions, something could be learned that could perhaps be applied elsewhere so that other regions may, by imitation—so to speak—"get a piece of the action." In most of these cases, technological innovation (both process and product) has been significant, often with universities playing an important role, and the production systems concerned have been in stark contrast to the postwar domination of "Fordism," characterized in terms of large-scale automation, involving a semiskilled workforce and standardized products.

The difference is thus frequently presented in terms of customized production in contrast to standardized production, quality against quantity, segmented (*niche*) markets compared with large undifferentiated markets, multichanging and flexible tasks compared with repetitive and inflexible tasks, skilled labor in contrast to semiskilled and unskilled labor, a participatory (matrix) model of management rather than an authoritarian (military) style of management, and small batch production in contrast to a mass production system.

It was not very long before these transformations came to be conceptualized in terms of a "manifestation of the resurgence of the region as the centre of post-Fordist, flexible, learning-based production systems" (Storper 1995, 192).

To what extent, then, can it be argued that the region—however its social and cultural properties are conceptualized—is a locus for economic success or failure, rather than success or failure being explained more simply in terms of the introduction and application of new technology? After all, economic development has always occurred in time and place, and therefore how are the examples given above any different from previous patterns of localization? In what sense is the region to be understood in terms of the coordination of the most advanced forms of economic activity in the modern world?

There is much conceptual confusion in which regionalism is conceived either as a consequence of globalization (regions seeking to protect themselves against the vicissitudes of the market and to counter the power of international capital) or as its opposite, and in consequence, an improbable development. The reality is that regionalism is an integral part of globalization, representing both its positive and negative features. Recognition of its positive features is a focus that links technological innovation, supply chains, organizational behavior, and the circulation of elites with collective action through a public-private partnership to improve competitiveness and the creation of wealth and employment. Thus, increasingly the European Commission regards European Regional Development Fund (ERDF) funding more in terms of stimulating structural innovation and less in terms of compensation for poor economic performance.

In an extensive review of the literature on regionalism, Michael Storper (1995) suggests that there are three main schools: "those interested in institutions, those focusing on industrial organisation and transactions, and those who concentrate their attention on technological change and learning" (192). He proposes that there is "good reason for including the region as an essential level of economic co-ordination in capitalism." But, he insists, no one has arrived at an accurate formulation as to why this is the case, and his solution is to offer the concept of "untraded interdependencies between actors"— which, according to him, generate "specific material and non-material assets in production."

Other authors have defined these so-called "untraded interdependencies" in terms of a "regional production culture" (see, for example, Schwartz and Romo 1993), whereas MacLeod and Goodwin (1999, 704) focus on "institutional thickness" and argue that

> securing local economic success is not solely determined by a narrow set of economic factors and/or financial inducements. Instead, the capacity to territorally "embedded" global processes in place is now increasingly conditioned upon a plethora of social, cultural and institutional forms and supports.

Successful regions are those that effectively underpin these interdependencies and which allow actors to generate technological and organizational change.

This formulation is useful because it moves beyond the analysis of production systems *per se* (especially of the input-output variety) and refocuses our attention on contrasting cultural factors such as those emphasized by Max Weber (1991) in his analysis of the role of ideas in promoting economic activity. The emphasis on sociotechnical systems in a wider cultural setting or on a framework of norms (although Storper himself expresses it differently) is also important because, like ideology, it assumes institutional forms, such as the creation of public-private partnerships, arenas of public consultation, economic development fora, and a whole host of organizations designed to assist business growth, particularly in relation to small- and medium-size enterprises.

Initially, however, the focus among Europeans, in particular, was on niche marketing and flexible production systems. In Italy, Bagnasco (1977) talked about the "Third Italy" corresponding to the northeast center of the country (including Emilia Romagna), which Piore and Sabel (1984) were subsequently to theorize into a model of "flexibility plus specialization." Generalizing from this theoretical and empirical work, they echoed sentiments that had been expressed by Giacomo Becattini (1978) in his studies of the wool-making districts adjacent to Florence.

Becattini's Florentine colleagues drew a parallel between what was occurring in parts of Tuscany with Alfred Marshall's (1919) notion of industrial districts in late-nineteenth-century England in which externalities were linked to the internal division of labor, and where corresponding sociocultural support promoted various forms of interfirm linkages.

Even those who criticized the flexible specialization approach, such as Leborgne and Lipietz (1992), nevertheless still entertained the notion of a "mode of regulation," with an emphasis on input-output relations, relating large firms to SMEs through supply chains, characterized in France as the *partenariat* (Storper 1995, 195). Thus, their model of competition is similarly based upon and reflected in labor market norms, interfirm dependencies, and geographically specific politics and institutions.

Even so, there are many conspicuous examples of competitive success in the absence of either regional supply chains and local downstream investment or active support for enterprise and innovation by business agencies, underpinned by a strong sense of regional identity. All the will in the world by local politicians, chambers of commerce, and public-private partnerships to encourage economic development cannot conjure up success when the requisite material factors are absent.

The model is therefore appropriate in some cases of regionalization, but not in all. It is, for example, conceivable that quite different forms of input-output relations will coexist within a single region and can alternatively be explained in terms of scale versus scope, profit versus operating margins, and so on and so forth. What is beyond doubt, though, is that post-Fordist forms of production and distribution are almost universally defined in terms of flexibility plus specialization, with a focus on regional development, where a variety of networks (material and social) help sustain business growth.

Agglomeration tends to occur where transaction costs are minimalized through both traded and untraded interdependencies—the latter being defined in terms of tacit knowledge or where face-to-face contact is required in commercial transactions (such as the preparation of customized products or even with software, where commercial secrecy is an important issue).

Once these local supply chains become established, economies of scale occur, and more firms are encouraged to move into the region. Some firms will undoubtedly fail, but the net effect will be to increase employment as the supply of skilled labor is absorbed by those expanding and profitable firms still in business.

The material, institutional, and normative factors combining to promote success in high-tech agglomeration are aptly defined by Castells and Hall (1994). They are usually planned developments—some private, but often involving partnership between the public and private sectors, and they are promoted by central, regional, or local government, often in association with universities. Their function is to generate the basic materials of the informational economy (Castells and Hall 1994, 1).

Not surprisingly, Silicon Valley is regarded as the prototype, where the link between Stanford University and startup companies is well documented, as indeed is the case also in relation to MIT and Route 128. This may not have been true in the past. After all, it was not the case, for example, in relation to aircraft production in the 1920s, where as Storper (1995) among others points out, "no research universities were strongly present in the leap forward of Los Angeles" (202). But it is certainly true today in relation to information technology and the biotechnology industries, where innovation is strongly formal science–based, as indeed was the case in the early years of semiconductors.

That said, there are of course many research-led universities (both public and private) corresponding with several public and private advocates of partnership, but there are far fewer Silicon Valleys.

The success of Silicon Valley probably has less to do with sociotechnical networks than with the fact that its early entrepreneurs were able to attract investment associated with the American military-industrial complex, and in this, the Stanford connection was probably crucial: an innovations multiplier having its origin in research and development for the military. Not that the southern California aerospace industry stemmed from the Cold War. On the contrary, its roots were in the early success of the Douglass Aircraft DC 3 in the 1930s; but this does not in the least detract from the main thread of the argument. A. R. Markusen and colleagues have illustrated how very effective regional coalitions can be in transferring high-technology resources from the military-industrial complex to high-technology manufacturing (Markusen, Hall, and Glasmeier 1986; Markusen, Cambell, and Deitrich 1991).

In the European experience, it is, above all, members of GREMI—the *Groupe de Recherche Européen sur les Milieux Innovateurs* (Aydalot and Keeble 1988)—who have introduced the region as a focus of economic analysis. For them, the *milieu* is the context in which business decisions are taken: the locus of development that channels innovative agents to form material and social networks promoting economic activity. Essentially, the *milieu* is a territorial version of what Mark Granovetter (1985) has termed the "embeddedness of economic and social processes." It is conceived as the network of regional institutions that supports innovation, the network being the principal metaphor involving a circulation of elites (Pareto 1974; Mosca 1939), consisting of entrepreneurs, politicians, local government officers, academics, and so on. For others, a network is less comprehensively conceived, consisting merely of input-output relations, integrating those involved in transactions, within a territorially defined space—a key theme being the aforementioned Marshallian notion of industrial districts in which innovation occurs more effectively than elsewhere

As Maillat and Vasserot have pointed out (see Aydalot and Keeble 1988, 164), although contemporary definitions of "creative regions" do not usually correspond with the profiles of old industrial districts, many of the latter continue to display several of the features—particularly those defined by Andersson (1985), such as high skill and knowledge levels, good communication networks, and university-industry links—that can be successfully developed to adapt to, and facilitate innovation in, new technology. They argue, for example, that this has been evident in the "cradle of the Swiss watch-making industry" (Maillat, Schoepfer, and Voillat 1984; Maillat 1984) as well as in the Franche-Comté, Alsace, Rhône-Alpes (Pottier 1984), Saint-Étienne (Peyrache 1986; Thomas 1986) and Nord Pas de Calais (Cunat 1986). The example cited as typical is initial specialization in machine tools, which facilitates a "transition to the manufacturing of numerical control machines and robots" (Maillat and Vasserot 1986, 165).

Despite much description—and indeed repetition—GREMI has not, however, succeeded in clearly defining the sociological conditions that facilitate innovation. As Storper (1997, 17) has poignantly emphasized, "There is a circularity: innovation occurs because of a *milieu*, and the *milieu* is what exists in regions where there is innovation" (emphasis in original).

Moreover, despite the fact that those associated with GREMI focus repeatedly on the properties of a *milieu*, nowhere do they adequately indicate why some regions are successful and others are not. There is little comparative analysis of the kind engaged in by Max Weber, for example, who posited normative systems as being significant in the emergence of what his long-deceased adversary Karl Marx had designated the capitalist mode of production. Nevertheless, some significant challenges have been directed toward economic theory. Perrin (1993), in particular, has been influential in suggesting the abandonment of some of the basic precepts in neoclassical economics: notably, equilibrium theory and the paradigm of rational action, to be replaced by a frame of reference that embraces the active creation of knowledge and resources. This action frame of reference derives from, and serves to influence, the socioeconomic context, which—again—is, in part, territorially specific. Nelson and Winter (1982) are even more emphatic. They suggest that technologies develop along pathways where the choices presented are quite distinct from those posited in orthodox economics, in that every innovation introduced in the sphere of production must have a user, and as the number of users increases, it tends to restrict the introduction of alternatives—the QWERTY keyboard being the most frequently cited example. Of course, some product imitations and process innovations are introduced, because knowledge will be generalized and serve to transform other production processes, but established pathways will tend to limit their widespread introduction, frequently foreclosing effective competition.

In this regard, as Storper (1997, 20) reminds us, there are two elements involved in competition: allocational, which is the basis of comparative advantage, and technological, which is the basis for absolute advantage, as when a firm or group of firms within a region possesses superior technical know-how that cannot be challenged through lower factor prices elsewhere. Although few regions are able to emulate the success of a Silicon Valley, many are able to build upon existing strengths, whether these relate to factor costs, location, the availability of skilled labor, or the presence of a university.

The need for such restructuring is particularly urgent in old industrial regions because of the persistence of relatively high levels of unemployment.

Nord Pas de Calais in France, Tyne and Wear in the United Kingdom, and Aust-Agder in Norway provide examples of significant restructuring that has nonetheless so far failed to transform the regional economy (O'Neill 1995) in contrast to restructuring in the Swiss Jura Arc region (Maillat 1984), Baden-Württemberg, and the *cité scientifique* in Toulouse, which has. Similar examples of success are to be seen in regions dominated by machine-tools and textile manufacture.

"Where restructuring is concerned, the ability to incorporate a new network component (such as electronics) into a more traditional network (such as mechanical engineering) is essential" (Maillat and Vas-serot 1986, 171).

Even where restructuring has been limited, and whether it has been encouraged by inward investment (Nissan near Sunderland, in Tyne and Wear, and Ericsson Telecom in Aust-Agder) or through indigenous growth of SMEs (Nord Pas de Calais), the general principle of integration obtains, though the results may not have been sufficiently generalized. The encouraging fact is that in each of these examples significant change has occurred. Inward investment in Tyne and Wear has come mainly from Japan, the United States, and Germany and has introduced both product and process innovation into the regional economy, the multiplier effect of which is clearly discernible: Since car production began in Sunderland in 1986, twenty new automotive component suppliers (foreign and UK) have moved into the region, and Nissan now has component or material contracts with at least thirty-six local companies (O'Neill 1995, 21). Similarly, the decision by Sweden's Ericsson Telecom to locate in Aust-Agder in Norway served to reinforce the region's high-technology manufacturing sector and has facilitated significant downstream investment.

Inward investment elsewhere, however, has not proved as successful, mainly because manufacturing firms that had relocated tended to be branch-plant operations, vulnerable to recession. County Durham, in the United Kingdom, has experienced precisely this particular problem, and it is notable that the county's GDP index at 78 is the lowest of all the EU North Sea regions (EC = 100).

Those North Sea maritime regions whose GDP index is the highest—Groningen (at 135) in the Netherlands and Grampian (at 122) in Scotland—owe their wealth to natural gas and oil extraction; but even in these cases, where diversification should have been less problematic, there are clear examples of uneven development, and serious pockets of high unemployment remain.

In contrast, regions with no significant natural resources or raw materials, and no legacy of early industrial development, have nonetheless been able to build upon their strengths in fishing and agriculture. The Danish counties of Nordjyllands, Ringkøbing, Ribe, and Viborg are all examples of significant restructuring on the basis of existing strengths: from potatoes, beets, and grain were developed the sugar and liquor industries; from meat and fish production, the food processing and canning industries; and from animal intestines, the pharmaceutical industry. Similar examples occur in other Scandinavian regions.

This pattern of diversification from existing strengths (before these strengths turn into liabilities) also appears to be in progress in parts of Humberside, where food processing has emerged in the ports of

Grimsby and Hull to replace fishing as a significant economic activity. It was also underway in Stavanger (Norway) before the discovery of oil facilitated the rapid growth of oil-related economic activity. In both these examples, port facilities have also offered scope for significant diversification based on trade—on the import and export of commodities. That this applies to regions in the Netherlands hardly requires emphasis; the locational advantages enjoyed by both Noord and Zuid Holland are so obvious as to warrant no elaboration. Over 50 percent of Japanese firms established in the Netherlands are situated in Noord Holland, largely because Schiphol (airport) is such a favorable distribution center. Like so much of the Netherlands, it cannot seriously be described as peripheral. With a GDP index of 119 on *Eurostat*'s scale, Noord Holland ranks third among all the EU North Sea regions; and in a comparative study of 274 European regions (commissioned by the German magazine *Wirtschaftswoche*), it was ranked seventh in terms of locational advantages for business.

Other regions with no legacy of early industrialization, but whose location makes them attractive for modern manufacturing industry, are those where transport networks have brought them close to consumer and producer markets. Norfolk and Suffolk in England are examples. Throughout the 1970s and 1980s they became particularly attractive to manufacturing firms seeking to relocate from overheated southeast England, largely because improved communication networks brought them within easy reach of London and the industrial midlands. Their ports (Ipswich, Felixstowe, Lowestoft, Great Yarmouth, and King's Lynn) all provide access to European markets, most of them with container–handling facilities that, as in the case of the Humber ports further north, offer firms located in the region a competitive export advantage.

The Humber ports have developed in a not dissimilar way, but in a region that is, in part, old industrial. The ports of Hull, Grimsby, and Immingham are the most northerly in the United Kingdom to offer overnight services to and from the continent. Since 1974, investment of over £700m in a strategic road network has linked the Humber Bridge, within a four-hour drive, to a market of over 40 million people.

Improved communications elsewhere have had much the same effect. A once relatively isolated region such as Zeeland in southwest Holland (again with no legacy of heavy industrial development) is now in a very much more favorable position to diversify its regional economy and attract additional investment partly as a result of the significant road construction that accompanied coastal protection works completed in the 1980s.

The recognition of these forms of restructuring (building upon traditional strengths before they become liabilities) has led to a broadening of the network concept beyond its purely industrial definition (Maillat and Vasserot 1986, 171).

"Production systems have been increasingly moving towards the integration of manufacturing and service activities, particularly producer services" (Bailly and Maillat 1986).

Thus,

> Beyond the obvious expansion of service activities (especially in terms of numbers of jobs), it is important to realise that the future does not lie in the "tertiary," if by this is meant the range of activities which is supposed to replace industry as industry once replaced agriculture, but it lies on the contrary in reciprocal synergetic ties developed between the services and the rest of the economy. (Preel 1986)

It is therefore imperative that industrial production systems should include service activities both upstream and downstream—from research and development to the marketing operation. Or, as Perrin (1984) puts it, successful restructuring depends upon regions re-establishing coherence within territorial production systems. The paradox is that the regional environment must change, but the seeds of change need to be present. Following this line of argument, "the key aspect of localisation is the creation, within a specific geographical area, of institutions designed to promote co-operation between enterprises . . . grafting themselves onto traditional market relations" (Gaffard 1986).

On the basis of the analysis so far undertaken, it is evident that three elements appear to play a crucial and interrelated role in the process of restructuring: the network of production systems (upon which the main focus has been made), the composition of the labor market, and the industry-education interface.

THE LABOR MARKET

The composition of a region's labor market is a function of the range of enterprises located within it. A useful concept in assessing a region's potential for retaining and expanding its workforce is that of a "mobility channel" (Destefanis 1983; Held and Maillat 1984; Maillat and Vasserot 1986). This refers to "the manner in which various categories of regional employment evolve and develop, as well as to how they interact and complement each other in such a way as to enable the labour force to change jobs and transfer know-how from one job to another without having to leave the region" (Maillat and Vasserot 1986, 173).

There are vertical channels (workers join enterprises and build careers within them, or occupy several jobs in different enterprises and accumulate skills), lateral channels (where there are few opportunities to develop skills), and job entry/exit flows (where the absence of alternative employment reduces mobility to job "entries and exits"). The significance of this categorization is that "the longer the vertical mobility channels, the greater the region's power of attraction." Enterprises are thus conceived as "stations along the mobility channels," where workers travel from their first jobs to their final destinations, accumulating experience and skills on the way. Some enterprises train their own staff, others recruit from them, and some fall in between, so that a knowledge of the typology of regional firms provides an understanding of the operation of a regional labor market. The closure of a final-job establishment, for example, may result in a significant reduction in the numbers of workers being trained elsewhere, or the failure of firms to offer training may eventually induce a final-job establishment to relocate. Opportunities for mobility within a region therefore enable it to preserve and build upon the skills and experience of its workforce, and these are obviously related to education and training—undertaken both before and during employment.

THE INDUSTRY-EDUCATION INTERFACE

The various stations visited along a labor market mobility channel is a metaphor also appropriate in relation to education, when perceived as a lifelong journey from the earliest experience of infant school through and beyond further and higher education. The expectation of employers is that school leavers should be literate and numerate and that graduates have trained minds, are creative, possess analytical ability, and are competent in skills learned in vocational training.

Patrick Coldstream (1991), the director of the Council for Industry and Higher Education, has also adopted a journey metaphor in which he argues that "arts degrees make sense only if they are the start of a journey" (11). To a large extent, the same can be said of all degrees, and indeed of education in general.

This echoes Coldstream's earlier invocation:

> The most important function of (higher) education is to inspire its students with a passionate *inquisitiveness* to continue learning through life. Learning and enthusiasm for learning are bound together. (4) (emphasis in original)

The industry-education interface is therefore obviously important in terms of the quality of the regional labor force, but institutions of higher education have a wider significance. The most immediate impact of a university on its local economy is as an employer, purchaser, landlord, and cultural institution. It then becomes significant as a provider of skills, scientific and commercial information, business advice and—potentially—technology transfer. Stohr (1986) refers to a "scientific framework" as a set of relationships existing between science, industry, education, and the state, and Maillat and Vasserot (1986) take this as their starting point when they distinguish between empirical and analytical know-how:

> Empirical know-how stems from the practical relationship existing between the worker and the object or means of production. Analytical know-how, although invariably bearing a relationship to the production process, implies the additional existence of an ability to carry out a relatively thorough scientific analysis of the factors involved in that process.

"This distinction," they argue, "underlies the concept of a scientific framework constituting a source of specific skills necessary for (regional) revival" (178).

The significance of universities in facilitating business growth can be much exaggerated (see Dieperinick and Nijkamp 1984; Meyer-Krahmer 1985; and O'Neill 1995). Much depends upon the culture of the institution concerned and of the networks in which it has become involved. One form of network involves the spin-off firm, another a science/technology park, but the glamour attached to these has often focused attention away from other forms of business support through the informal networking of student placements, staff secondments, consultancies, and business advice—through European Documentation Centers where it is not technology that is being transferred but business information to SMEs. These business information centers are frequently the direct result of collaboration between universities, local firms, chambers of commerce, and local authorities; where successful, they offer an excellent introduction to SMEs of other services available from higher education (such as foreign language translation, legal advice, and so on).

Advice of this kind is provided not through market mechanisms alone (they are a necessary, but not sufficient factor), but by a network of social relationships in which a culture of enterprise and innovation has been established, and in which there is frequently a partnership between the public and private sectors, in terms of capital investment, support for SMEs, and in education and training. The more advanced the technology (particularly in the case of CIT and biochemistry), the greater the need for research and development, and for links with universities.

CONCLUSION

The main theme of this chapter has been that regionalization and business development are each related through the process of globalization—whether the definition of a region is one that extends beyond nation-states, such as the European Union, or is part of a nation-state, such as my own region of Yorkshire and the Humber. As was emphasized at the beginning, however, this is not to conclude that successful business development in a region is necessarily functionally related to its institutions, in terms of the network of associations supposedly supporting innovation, such as input-output relations, supply chains, development agencies, chambers of commerce, entrepreneurs, politicians, local government officers, academics, and so on.

As emphasized, the constellation of factors contributing to regional business development requires more comparative empirical research, but the influence of the European Commission on regional strategies is clearly evident. Each of the three planning objectives in the European Spatial Development Perspective (ESDP) listed at the beginning of this chapter forms part of the United Kingdom's own Regional Planning Guidance (RPG), and the four pillars of the European Guidelines on Employment have set the framework for the UK government's own National Employment Action Plan. This, in turn, has been the focus of my own regional development agency, Yorkshire Forward, and of analyses undertaken in the subregion by the former Humberside Training and Enterprise Council (HTEC) in its *Economic Review 2000*. Thus:

> This year, we have added a further dimension in that we have assessed our sub-regional economy against the four pillars of the National Employment Action Plan, and presented policy messages under each. This Action Plan has been drawn up by the Government in the light of EU Employment Guidelines, reflecting the convergence over the past two or three years of UK Government and EU public policy around employment. We in the sub-region also aim to connect our policies and activities. However, we have changed the order of the pillars. . . . Adaptability has been placed first, simply because it is about people and businesses adapting to change and as such directly affects the sub-region's competitiveness. (HTEC 2000, 7)

The configuration of networks at the regional and subregional levels is increasingly being driven by central government through its regional government offices and the regional development agencies. In the most recent Comprehensive Spending Review, it is proposed to increase the funding of RDAs nationally from £250m in 2000–2001 to £1.7bn by 2003–2004 (Her Majesty's Treasury, 2000). The RDAs are to do the following:

- Work more closely with the Small Business Service (SBS) to deliver Regional Venture Capital Funds.
- Provide a lead strategic role for ensuring the delivery of regional plans for the European structural funds.
- Hold representative roles on the national and local Learning and Skills Councils' (LSC) boards and to be consulted over the development of plans.
- Ensure that regional priorities are reflected in transparent decision-making.
- Have a key role in supporting local strategic partnerships to develop deprivation strategies for accessing the Neighborhood Renewal Fund.

In summary, the widespread influence of the European Commission (throughout the regions and upon the governments of the member-states)—through the European Spatial Development Perspective, in the rules prescribing the allocation of the structural funds, and in the four pillars of the European Guidelines on Employment—serves to generate precisely the comparative data needed to test the assumption that successful business development in a region may indeed be functionally related to the network of institutions purportedly designed to assist small- and medium-size enterprises. There is, therefore, much work still to do.

REFERENCES

Andersson, A. 1985. Creativity and regional development. *Papers of the Regional Science Association* 56; 5–20; cited by D. Maillat and J. Y. Vasserot, in *High technology industry and innovative environments: The European experience*, edited by P. Aydalot and D. Keeble, pp. 163–83. London and New York: Routledge, 1988.

Aydalot, P., ed. 1986. *Milieux Innovateurs en Europe*. Paris: GREMI.

Aydalot, P., and D. Keeble, eds. 1988. *High technology industry and innovative environments: The European experience*. London and New York: Routledge.

Bagnasco, A. 1977. *Tre Italie*. Bologna: Il Mulino.

Bailly, A., and D. Maillat. 1986. *Le secteur tertiaire en question*. Geneva: ERSA.

Becattini, G. 1978. The development of light industry in Tuscany: An interpretation. *Economic Notes, Monte dei Paschi di Siena* 7 (2–3): 107–23.

Castells, M., and P. Hall. 1994. *Technopoles of the world: The making of twenty-first-century industrial complexes*. London and New York: Routledge.

Coldstream, P. 1991. *Higher education, industry, and the journey of learning*. Hull: Hull University Press.

Cunat, F. 1986. *Stratégies d'adaptation d'enterprises du Nord-Pas-de-Calais*. St. Étienne: Communication á la Table-Ronde CREUSET.

Destefanis, M. 1983. *Le fonctionnement du marché de l'emploi au niveau local en France*. Cited in *Le fonctionnement du marché de l'emploi au niveau local*, edited by D. Maillat and J. Y. Vasserot. Saint-Saphorin: Georgi, 1986.

Dieperinick, H., and P. Nijkamp. 1984. Spatial dispersion of industrial innovation: A case study for the Netherlands. Communication au colloque de L'ASRDLF, Marrakech.

Foster-Carter, A. 1985. *The sociology of development*. Ormskirk: Causeway Press.

Gaffard, J. L 1986. Reconstruction de l'espace économique et trajectoires technologiques. In *Milieux innovateurs en Europe*, edited by P. Aydalot, pp. 17–27. Paris: GREMI.

Granovetter, M. 1985. Economic action and social structure: The problem of embeddedness. *American Journal of Sociology* 93 (3): 481–510.

Held, D., and D. Maillat. 1984. *Marché de l'emploi*. Lausanne: Presses Polytechniques Romandes.

Her Majesty's Treasury. 2000. www.hm-treasury.govt.uk/sr2000/index.html

Humberside Training and Enterprise Council (HTEC). 2000. *Economic Review 2000*. Hull: Humberside Training and Enterprise Council.

Leborgne, D., and A. Lipietz. 1992. Conceptual fallacies and open issues in post-Fordism. In *Pathways to industrialisation and regional development*, edited by M. Storper and A. J. Scott, pp. 332–48. London: Routledge.

MacLeod, G., and M. Goodwin. 1999. Reconstructing an urban and regional political economy. *Political Geography* 18: 697–730.

Maillat, D. 1984. Les conditions d'une stratégie de développement par le bas: Le cas de la région horlogére Suisse. *Revue d'Economie Régionale et Urbaine* 2: 257–74.

Maillat, D., A. Schoepfer, and F. Voillat, eds. 1984. *La nouvelle politique régionale: Le cas de l'arc jurassien*. Neuchâtel: EDES.

Maillat, D., and J. Y. Vasserot. 1986. Les milieux innovateurs: Le cas de l'arc jurassien Suisse. In *Milieux innovateurs en Europe*, edited by P. Aydalot, pp. 217–46. Paris: GREMI.

Markusen, A.R., C. Cambell, and S. Deitrich. 1991. *The rise of the gunbelt*. New York: Basic Books.

Markusen, A.R., P. Hall, and A. Glasmeier. 1986. *High tech America: The what, how, where and why of the sunrise industries*. Boston: Allen and Unwin.

Marshall, A. 1919. *Industry and trade*. London: Macmillan.

Meyer-Krahmer, F. 1985. Innovation behaviour and regional indigenous potential. *Regional Studies* 19 (6): 523–34.

Mosca, G. 1939. *The ruling class (Elementi de scienza politica)*. Translated by H. D. Kahn; edited and revised with an introduction by A. Livingston. New York: McGraw-Hill.

Nelson, R., and S. Winter. 1982. *An evolutionary theory of economic change*. Cambridge, Mass.: Harvard University Press.

O'Neill, N. 1995. *Economic development in North Sea regions*. Aberdeen: North Sea Commission.

Pareto, V. F. D. (with Giovanni Busino). 1974. *Scritti politici*. Torino: U.T.E.T.

Perrin, J. C. 1984. Dynamique locale, division internationale du travail et troisiéme révolution industrielle. Notes de recherches du CER, No. 50, 1984/10; quoted in *High technology industry and innovative environments: The European experience*, edited by P. Aydalot and D. Keeble. London and New York: Routledge, 1988.

———. 1993. Pour une révision de la science régionale: l'approche en termes de milieu, Centre d'Economie Régionale, University of Aix-Marsille, Aix-en-Provence, No. 148-1993/3; cited in M. Storper (1997), *The regional world*, New York and London: Guilford Press.

Peyrache, V. 1986. Mutations régionales vers les technologies nouvelles: le cas de la région de Saint-Étienne. In *Milieux innovateurs en Europe*, edited by P. Aydalot, pp. 195–215. Paris: GREMI.

Piore, M., and C. Sabel. 1984. *The second industrial divide*. New York: Basic Books.

Pottier, C. 1984. The adaptation of regional industrial structures to technical changes. Paper cited by P. Aydalot and D. Keeble from the proceedings of the RSA Congress, Milan, August 1984.

Preel, B. 1986. Pour 'servir' les enterprises que peuvent faire les collectivités locales? *Espaces Prospectifs* 4: 83–116.

Reich, R. 1992. *The work of nations: Preparing ourselves for the 21st century*. London: Simon and Schuster.

Schwartz, M., and F. Romo. 1993. *The rise and fall of Detroit: How the automobile industry destroyed its capacity to compete*. Stony Brook: Department of Sociology, SUNY.

Stohr, W. B. 1986. Territorial innovation complexes. In *Milieux innovateurs en Europe*, edited by P. Aydalot, pp. 29–54. Paris: GREMI.

Storper, M. 1995. The resurgence of regional economies, ten years later: The region as a nexus of untraded interdependencies. *European Urban and Regional Sudies* 2 (3): 191–221.

———. 1997. *The regional world*. New York and London: Guilford Press.

Thomas, J. N. 1986. Innovation et territoire: Communication á la Table-Ronde, CREUSET, St. Étienne, May. Quoted in *High technology industry and innovative environments: The European experience*, edited by P. Aydalot and D. Keeble. London and New York: Routledge, 1988.

Tömmel, I. 1998. Transformation of governance: The European Commission's strategy for creating a "Europe of the Regions." *Regional and Federal Studies* 8 (2): 52–80.

Weber, M. 1991. *The Protestant ethic and the spirit of capitalism*. London: Harper Collins.

3

Building Multilevel Governance in Britain? The Engagement of Subnational Government in EU Programs and Policies

Graham Pearce and Steve Martin

INTRODUCTION

A key feature in the current debate about governance in the European Union (EU) is the proposition that traditional forms of government, based upon distinctive and separate layers or tiers of responsibility, are too rigid and fail to take account of the interdependence and overlapping competencies of different spheres. At the subnational level, for example, there are profound problems in reconciling the complex, multifaceted problems of territory with the conventional functional, hierarchical organization of government. The implication is that both vertical and horizontal linkages in the system of governance need to be strengthened through improved communication to enhance collective learning and the effectiveness of policy making and implementation processes. "Let us start thinking of a 'Network Europe', with all levels of governance shaping, proposing, implementing and monitoring policy together" (Prodi 2000).

The EU already offers an example of this network approach because it relies upon the voluntary pooling of resources by member-states, which recognize the benefits of cooperation. Alongside this principal network are the innumerable networks of public, private, and voluntary organizations that connect with the EU policy process. Networking is considered as one of the essential conditions for greater democracy, transparency, coherency, and efficiency in decision making and implementation. Moreover, support for such networks is regarded as indispensable in the development of partnerships, which have become a defining feature of EU activity aimed at securing regional economic and social development.

Because of the breadth of its responsibilities, UK subnational government (SNG) has been expected to play a key part in facilitating this process. In addition to their domestic policy obligations, local and regional authorities are responsible for the execution and oversight of a wide range of EU directives including environmental protection, trading standards, and procurement. The outcome has been a spate of activity in which local authorities have adapted their existing policies and working practices and assisted local businesses to meet the challenges and opportunities of the internal market. Their growing reliance on Community assistance has also stimulated greater awareness of EU policies. Structural funds have not only played an important role in the economic development and regeneration program of some authorities, they also have an important symbolic value—a testimony to a local authority's competence and its commitment to Europe.

The significance of these trends has been the subject of intense debate. Responses among some of the most active European authorities have been interpreted as evidence of a shift in the locus of political control, in which power and influence have spun away from central government, upward to the EU institutions and down to subnational government. Some observers have asserted that EU regional policy and its stress on negotiation and partnership between different government tiers has helped create new policy networks and the prospect of a new triadic relationship involving local authorities, Brussels, and UK central government (Ansell, Parsons, and Darden 1997; John 1996). The outcome, it is suggested, is a new paradigm—a multilevel or multitiered polity, in which policy making evolves through networking among a plurality of policy elites from multiple levels of government and is characterized by interconnected rather than nested relationships (Börzel 2001; Ansell 2000; Marks 1997; Marks, Hooghe, and Blank 1996; Risse-Kappen 1996; Scharpf 1994; Marks 1993). A more sanguine view is that even though SNG is far more aware and responsive to EU policies than a decade ago, UK central government has continued to define the rules of engagement between locally elected government and EU institutions. In short, theories of multilevel government (MLG) may pay insufficient attention to the constraints placed upon SNG engagement in both macro EU policy making and the formation of domestic policy preferences.

This chapter begins by examining briefly the background to the debate about SNG engagement in the EU. Second, drawing upon empirical evidence, it presents an overview of how UK local authorities responded to European integration during the 1990s. Third, it focuses on the extent to which integration encouraged local authorities to participate in existing or new networks—a key feature of EU cohesion policy and theories of MLG. Finally, we reflect on the implications of current reforms to SNG; ongoing constitutional reforms in the United Kingdom and developments in the EU; and on the future relationship between subnational, national, and supranational government in the United Kingdom.

SUBNATIONAL GOVERNMENT ENGAGEMENT IN THE EUROPEAN UNION

The evolution of the European Union has been dependent upon intergovernmental action, as individual states have become increasingly unable or unwilling to perform their traditional regulatory and distributional roles and have passed responsibilities upward to supranational institutions. This is reflected in the expansion of EU competencies and the blurring of national and EU policy domains (Schmitter 1996). At the same time, in accordance with the principle of subsidiarity, there has been growing pressure from below to decentralize power from the member-state to the regional or local level. The European Commission has fostered this process, notably through the delivery of structural assistance and the emphasis placed upon regional partnerships involving a range of economic and social actors, and the creation of transnational SNG networks via Community initiatives including INTERREG and LEADER. For example, the Commission was instrumental in the formation of regional consortia in Northern Ireland and the northeast and northwest of England (Elcock 1998; Burch and Rhodes 1993; Martin and Pearce 1993). It is in the Commission's interests to pursue this approach, given the reliance it places upon SNG to deliver its policies. Support for devolution and subsidiarity may also be perceived as part of a long-term initiative by the Commission to help to bring the European Union closer to its citizens and extend its own influence in the domestic arena (Tömmel 1998).

The expanding policy competencies of the EU during the late 1980s were seen as a powerful inducement for local authorities to enhance their awareness of the emerging European polity (Roberts, Hart, and Thomas 1993; Bongers 1992; Audit Commission 1991). Moreover, the debates surrounding the Maastricht Treaty gave some comfort to those committed to a more participatory and decentralized form of governance, reflected in the notion of a "Europe of the Regions." The enlargement of the structural funds in 1988 and 1993 provided further encouragement for local authorities to examine the part European assistance might play in the development of their areas. "More than any other EU policy, structural policy reaches directly into the member states, directly engaging SNG and private actors with the Commission and Member State governments" (Marks 1996).

Structural funds were certainly crucial in stimulating local authority engagement with the Commission. Implementation of EU regional policy triggered local authority involvement in new or revitalized regional and subregional networks, which were essential if funding was to be secured and programs managed and implemented effectively. These new policy networks offered the prospect of collaboration between SNG and other agencies and advanced awareness of the need to address emerging issues in a regional context. Such alliances were not always robust, but they did contribute to the renewed interest in strategic thinking and planning at the regional level in the United Kingdom during the 1990s. The new networks greatly extended the number of domestic actors involved in the EU policy process and became important spheres of influence (Rhodes, Bache, and George 1996). The structural funds also challenged regional partners to examine new approaches to economic development, particularly through technology, community development, and sustainable development policies (Bachtler and Turok 1997). More recently, these new institutional arrangements and policy priorities have fed into the preparation of both economic development strategies and regional planning guidance in the English regions.

Structural funds and the Commission's insistence on detailed regional strategic documents and financial programs, prepared in consultation with local partners, also encouraged central government to examine its own regional capacity, which was reflected in a strengthening of its English regional offices during the mid-1990s (Mawson and Spencer 1997; Mawson 1996). More recently, the Cabinet Office's Performance and Innovation Unit (PIU) has also acknowledged the need to secure more "joined up" working at the regional level, leading to the formation of the Whitehall Regional Co-ordination Unit, public service agreements to address cross-cutting issues, and plans to strengthen the coordination role of the government offices in the English regions (PIU 2000a, 2000b).

THE LIMITS TO EUROPEANIZATION

Each of these developments may be seen as sowing the seeds of institutional innovation. However, although some commentators acknowledge the capacity of SNG to deal effectively with the implementation of EU policies, the possibility that EU regional policy might be a foil to "state-centric" approaches to political integration has often been discounted (Sharpe 1993; Anderson 1990). In essence the debate is familiar; whether the process of European integration is ultimately controlled by member-states or whether it marks the emergence of a polity in which the authority of state executives is devolved to Community institutions and SNG (Schattle 1999).

For intergovernmentalists, EU regional assistance may be regarded as primarily a side payment—an opportunity for states to advance domestic objectives and repatriate financial contributions from Brussels. They dismiss efforts to use the principle of subsidiarity to legitimize decentralization or devolution within the member-states or the possibility of direct links between SNG and the Commission. Successive reforms to the structural funds may have been intended to facilitate subsidiarity, additionality, and partnerships involving SNG and local/regional economic and social actors, but these principles have frequently been resisted by the UK national government. Indeed, EU cohesion policy objectives have steadily unraveled in favor of employment policies more likely to be coordinated by national and state authorities (Hooghe 1998).

Critics of MLG theory are also able to point to the asymmetric structure of regional and local governance across the European Union. Germany, with its highly institutionalized federal structure, could be expected to display strong evidence of MLG, but, even here, national interests have compromised direct links between the Länder and the Commission (Anderson 1996). In the United Kingdom, the limited capacity of SNG to extend its European activities is especially apparent (John 1997; Roberts and Hart 1996). Central government has been able to mobilize its extensive powers and resources to safeguard its gatekeeping role, and the prospects of any significant realignment remain remote (Bache, George, and Rhodes 1996; Moravcsik 1995). Triadic relationships may have created superficial opportunities for active subsidiarity, leading to the claim among some local authorities that by working through domestic or transnational peak organizations they have been able to influence EU policy. There are cases that demonstrate the effectiveness of SNG lobbying of the Commission—for example, the treatment of additionality in respect of the RECHAR initiative and efforts to secure assistance for declining urban areas and those affected by the restructuring of the textile and defense industries. But they have usually required at least the tacit support of the UK central government, prior to any formal approaches to the Commission.

Many UK local authorities have acknowledged the importance of structural funds, but have found it increasingly difficult to provide the matching funds necessary to draw down EU assistance. Disputes over additionality, reflected in the recent controversy over new Objective 1 funding in Wales, remain outstanding (Kay 2000; Bache 1999; Martin 1997; Pearce and Martin 1996). Moreover, local authorities have become increasingly dependent upon other public and private sector organizations to draw down EU funds, while the shift in EU structural policy away from physical infrastructure toward investment in human capital has also reduced their ability to gain direct access to EU funding. SNG actors may be involved in the implementation of EU regional policy and invited to contribute matching funding but may not see themselves as necessarily identified with these policies.

ENGAGEMENT IN EUROPE: A PROFILE

One of the outstanding difficulties faced by those seeking to develop insights into theories of MLG is the lack of empirical information. It was in response to this deficiency that Martin and Pearce undertook a survey in 1995–1996 that provided information from some 267 (55 percent of all) local authorities in England, Scotland, and Wales about their responses to closer European integration. The findings from the survey provide a comprehensive account of responses in a wide cross-section of authorities, comprising Scottish Regional Councils, English and Welsh County Councils, English, Scottish and Welsh Districts, and London Boroughs,[1] including areas both eligible and ineligible for structural fund assistance. They gave information about a range of issues, including local authority internal arrangements for dealing with European policies, involvement in networks, and constraints on their capacity (Martin and Pearce 1999).

The findings of the survey showed a far greater awareness of the implications of European integration and a much higher level and greater spread of local authority activity than was evident from earlier studies (Audit Commission 1991; Goldsmith and Sperling 1997). Three quarters of the authorities were confident about their capacity to deal with European issues, and more than two thirds considered that their council's policies were Europeanized. There were, though, marked differences both in perceptions about the impact of European integration and the level of European activity among local authorities. In general the larger, first tier, authorities were far more proactive and confident in dealing with European issues than the second tier districts and the London boroughs. Many of the former were also recipients of significant EU funding. Thus more than 70 percent of English metropolitan districts and Welsh districts and counties reported that Europe had been a significant influence on the work of the authority, compared with only 37 percent of English nonmetropolitan districts. Less than a quarter of all authorities had established a full-time European officer, and only 8 percent had dedicated European units—almost all of which were larger authorities eligible for substantial EU assistance. The size of local authority and eligibility for large-scale EU funding were not, though, the only factors; comparable local authorities differed in their responses. Thus even some smaller authorities had developed a range of European activities, engendered by the presence of enthusiastic chief officers and elected members. Nonetheless, the majority of second tier authorities were content to regard themselves as agents, drawing down funds and implementing EU policies.

Confidence in their ability to deal with European issues was lowest among many of those authorities that had adopted a more proactive approach to Europe—Scottish regions, English and Welsh counties, and English metropolitan districts—suggesting that institutional learning was matched by a more sober assessment of capacity. Two thirds of authorities recorded increasing interest in EU issues among elected members, bolstered in part by new funding opportunities, but also because of increasing awareness of the impacts of European integration, involvement in the Committee of the Regions, and other transnational links and the prospect of being left behind.

Despite the nonadditionality of EU funding and the difficulties associated with matched funding, the European Union was seen as a valuable source of discretionary funding and, for some local authorities, an opportunity to maintain their profile as agents of local economic development. Nearly 70 percent regarded Europe as primarily a funding source. However, a significant number of first tier authorities challenged this view. Some of these had developed considerable expertise in EU affairs, and their perceptions of the potential benefits of engagement in European policies had become more complex.

A key feature in the EU governance debate is the premise that actors at the supranational, national, and subnational level should interact and contribute to the overall policy process. Indeed, a crucial measure of SNG engagement in Europe is the extent to which authorities believed themselves capable of shaping EU policies. Fewer than one in four authorities were in this category, but again there were considerable variations between different types of authority. More than 60 percent of counties, Scottish regions, and Welsh districts expressed confidence in their ability to affect EU policy, but others were far less assured. In practice, such influence is likely to center on implementation—determining the local/regional content and managing Community-supported measures—although some authorities had participated in the preparation of regional plans used to negotiate Community support frameworks between the Commission and member-states.

ENGAGEMENT IN NETWORKS

Increasingly governments are seeking to balance the advantages of central control with decentralized approaches, which tap into individual and community resources and create the conditions for policy innovation. In the United Kingdom, for example, the Labour government has committed itself to partnership, empowerment, and the development of the enabling state. The relationship between actors has, therefore, increasingly been portrayed as one of cooperation and negotiation rather than one based upon hierarchy. Improving the connections between tiers of government is also a matter of growing significance for the European Union, and networking and the development of regional and subregional partnerships are increasingly perceived as vital for the formulation and implementation of territorial development strategies (Conference of Peripheral Maritime Regions [CPMR] 2001).

Networks are seen as essential in fostering learning and innovation and reflect the emphasis attached to institutional structures as the conduit through which knowledge and learning are created. The key requirement is to encourage and support the development of territorial institutions that do two things: (1) scan beyond local or regional boundaries to collect relevant knowledge and (2) create channels through which knowledge and information can flow effectively within the territory, ensuring that the key actors are aware of significant changes that pose either threats or opportunities for their activities and that they seek to cooperate as a means of competing more effectively. This implies the creation of trust between both the public and private sector organizations and the development of a shared sense of purpose (Hudson 1999).

The MLG thesis emphasizes the partnership principle, in which governments and institutions cooperate to develop and implement policy. This principle is based upon two main premises: (1) that decision-making competencies are shared by actors at different levels and (2) that subnational actors are able to operate in both national and supranational arenas, creating national and transnational associations in the process (Marks, Hooghe, and Blank 1996). The anticipated outcome is the creation of coalitions based around policy networks—a key method for developing EU regional policy. Successive reforms of the structural funds have encouraged this process. The 1988 structure fund reforms highlighted the need for close consultation between the Commission, the member-state, and competent authorities at the national, regional, or local level. The 1993 reforms extended the principle of partnership to economic and social partners—trade unions, industry associations, and voluntary organizations. The latest regulation (Council of the European Union 1999) seeks to include other relevant actors, including those working to protect the environment and to promote gender equality. The rules are intended to legitimize the participation of a certain set of social actors in the EU policy process. It might be anticipated, therefore, that one of the consequences of local authority engagement in EU policy would be their involvement in vertical networks, extending to other government tiers and the European institutions, and horizontal networks, including local and regional partners.

Links to Brussels

One third of the local authorities in our survey had judged it worthwhile to establish permanent offices or representation in Brussels, either independently or in joint ventures with others. John (1994) noted that UK local authorities had more offices in Brussels than any other member-state. However, unlike the 1980s and early 1990s, when individual authorities established their own offices in Brussels to gain competitive advantage, English local authorities are now following the experience of Wales and Scotland by increasingly pooling their resources at a regional level. There is limited evidence to indicate that access to financial resources has been the prime motive for establishing a Brussels office. Rather, the objective has been to gather information, establish direct representation in the Community, lobby the Commission and Parliament, monitor the progress of EU directives and regulations, and support regional interests within the EU political process (Jeffery 1997). Moreover, a presence in Brussels may have enabled SNG to exert additional pressure on central government via the European Union. A Brussels office also disseminates information about local economic and social conditions, which is often valued by the Commission as an alternative to information supplied by central government (Marks, Nielsen, Ray, and Salk 1996).

Despite the importance attached to a presence in Brussels, the survey showed that comparatively few authorities had regular, direct contacts with European officials, and only 9 percent recorded participation in meetings in Brussels. Less than half (46 percent) of the authorities maintained regular links with the European Commission, usually to gather information about impending changes in policy and funding opportunities. The main channels of communication with the Commission included regional associations (25 percent), members of European Parliament (MEPs) (21 percent), and central government (21 percent), usually through its regional offices in England. Only 14 percent of authorities referred to a Brussels office as a means of communication. Links with the Commission were most evident among those authorities eligible for structural funds, in particular first tier authorities, and were strongly associated with the presence of a European unit or European officers within the local authority.

Although the survey showed that the majority of local authorities had few direct contacts, some UK authorities claimed to have formed close relationships with staff in the Commission and successfully lobbied the European Union on changes to existing legislation and sources of funding, including structural funds and Community initiatives. Examples include Birmingham, Cleveland, Durham, Kent, and Strathclyde, which were able to establish strong vertical links with the Commission, leading to demonstrable changes in policy—for example, the establishment of the RECHAR, URBAN, and OUVERTURE initiatives. These initiatives were exceptional, but they illustrate the potential contribution of SNG in the context of a networked model of EU governance.

Links with Other EU Partners

European integration has encouraged a variety of bilateral and multilateral associations aimed at stimulating transnational cooperation in specific policy areas (Bennington and Harvey 1998; Weyand 1997). Engagement in such networks is perceived as an opportunity to share experience, develop cross-border initiatives with counterparts in other member-states and the accession states in Eastern and Central Europe, and lobby the Commission on matters of joint concern. These channels have attracted a good deal of public and academic interest. But less than one third of UK local authorities indicated that EU integration had encouraged them to participate in European-wide associations and networks. The most evident included participation in the Assembly of the European Regions (ARE), the Association of European Regions in Decline (RETI), and the Conference of Peripheral Maritime Regions (CPMR).

There was a clear distinction in the level of involvement in transnational networks between first and second tier authorities. Almost all the Scottish regions and 60 percent of counties and metropolitan districts recorded participation in transnational networks, an indication of their desire to promote their local economies and gain political leverage. By contrast, less than a quarter of second tier districts stated that greater awareness of European issues had encouraged them to participate in such networks.

The European Commission has autonomy over the content and timing of Community initiatives as well as the selection of participants. As such, involvement in Community initiatives may be regarded as a useful measure of an authority's involvement in EU funding, beyond those shaped exclusively by member-state executives. Our survey demonstrated that almost two thirds of local authorities had become involved in a variety of Community initiatives, many of which entailed participation in transnational networks. Of these, one third of the authorities indicated active involvement in more than five initiatives. Authorities responding to our survey had received funding from more than sixty different programs and initiatives, the most prominent being KONVER, Article 10 and RECHAR (Martin 1998).

Links to National Networks

The survey revealed that only one fifth of British local authorities claimed membership of national SNG networks concerned with European policies. But first tier authorities—83 percent of Scottish regions and 60 percent of English counties and metropolitan districts—were far more likely to belong to such networks. Their reliance on structural funds and engagement in discussions about the operation and successive reform of the priority objectives had encouraged greater collaboration between authorities, often preoccupied with similar economic and social problems.

Links with Regional and Local Partners

A key objective of the structural funds is to mobilize domestic private and public sector partners, who might not otherwise work together, to contribute to the accumulation of social capital and the creation of networks in lagging regions (European Commission 1999a; Klijn, Koppenjan, and Termeer 1995; Putnam 1993). Partnership has emerged as a key theme in the development of new approaches to policy making in both domestic and EU funding programs designed to promote economic development and regeneration. Indeed, evidence of interdependence is vital if EU funding is to be secured. UK local authorities have the opportunity to be represented on program monitoring committees, alongside other key public and private sector organizations.

Two thirds of local authorities suggested that their involvement in European programs had encouraged them to establish stronger links with a variety of regional partners, to coordinate their responses to European issues, and to manage European programs. Involvement in regional networks and alliances was almost universal among the Scottish regions, the counties and metropolitan districts, and three quarters of authorities in Objective 1, 2, and 5b regions. Over half of the authorities cited their enhanced links with Training and Enterprise Councils (and their equivalent in Scotland). Other agencies mentioned, but less consistently, included a variety of private/public sector development agencies, government regional offices (including the then Scottish and Welsh offices), chambers of commerce, universities, and colleges.

BENEFITS AND LIMITS OF ENGAGEMENT

In responding to European integration, local authorities have had to examine the potential benefits and costs. Three quarters of all local authorities and 91 percent eligible for structural funds regarded the EU as an important source of funding, specifically in assisting local economic development and regeneration. Almost all the authorities in receipt of the larger funding allocations had dedicated European units or European staff, which provided them with the capacity not only to manage funding but to acquire a broader perspective of the implications of European integration and to grasp opportunities when they arose. Most authorities acknowledged that their influence over EU policies relating to economic regeneration was limited, but half of the Scottish regions and the counties regarded their engagement as an opportunity to at least modify structural fund priorities and the delivery of EU policies at the operational level.

Apart from funding, one third of authorities considered that the experience afforded by participation in European affairs, including the opportunities for exchanging experience with other authorities and organizations in the United Kingdom and elsewhere in Europe, was valuable. Staff regarded Europe as a challenging area in which to work and acknowledged the scope it offered to promote the interests of their authority and their own careers. For those engaged in transnational networks, various motives were apparent. Some identified the opportunities they afforded members and officers to join the European cadre of regional and municipal leaders who claim to have access to the inside track of EU policy making. Other perceived benefits included the encouragement of partnership working, trading links, and increased awareness of the implications and opportunities of European integration. The Scottish regions and counties, and the Welsh districts claimed to be more aware of the wider benefits of EU membership than the majority of second tier authorities. One third of English nonmetropolitan districts were unable to identify any benefits in terms of economic development from engagement in Europe.

Authorities offered a variety of perspectives on the constraints associated with their European activities in terms of economic regeneration. By far the most pressing was being able to secure access to EU and matching funding; 65 percent of authorities identified this as being a major constraint, and more than 90 percent of metropolitan districts highlighted the issue. Despite efforts to resolve the additionality issue, there was limited evidence that this had been achieved to the satisfaction of most authorities, while dwindling capital receipts and limited basic and supplementary credit approvals had exacerbated the problem. A second major set of concerns was associated with the complex and often tortuous procedures surrounding the allocation and delivery of structural funds, one of the consequences of the need for complex negotiation between actors involved in a multilevel approach. Securing agreement at each key stage of the programming process—preparing the Single Programming Document, Community support frameworks, and operational programs—proved arduous. Disagreements arose over spending priorities and the membership of partnership committees while delayed payments caused cash flow problems, deterring the involvement of voluntary and private sector organizations. In part these problems reflected concerns about probity and administrative arrangements. But more fundamentally they indicated wariness in the Commission and the UK central government about flexibility and the possibility of externalizing or decentralizing aspects of policy making.

Other constraints cited included difficulties in working with central government, a lack of expertise and understanding of EU policies, insufficient support from elected members, and the complexities and transaction costs associated with dealing with a range of economic and social partners. The majority of authorities were generally confident of their expertise in dealing with EU issues—with the distinct exception of English and Scottish districts, three quarters of which had misgivings about their European capabilities. These districts also registered doubts about the extent of their knowledge regarding the workings of the European Union.

REVIEW

This account of attitudes and activities among UK local authorities offers some valuable insights into the capacity of SNG to respond to European integration during the 1990s. EU policies had a demonstrable impact upon the activities of many local authorities, which was re-flected in efforts to enhance their European expertise. Most authorities were confident in their ability to deal with EU legislation and finance, and there was evidence that access to structural funds and the creation of the internal market had encouraged some to strengthen their eco-nomic development activities and participate in regional, national, and EU-wide networks.

In a number of authorities, there was evidence of a strong political commitment to Europe. Some had appointed dedicated European staff and powerful European teams, set in place corporate mechanisms, involved themselves in Community initiatives, and established links with partners in other EU states. Indeed certain authorities, perhaps overestimating their competencies, expressed a desire and confidence in their ability to shape the direction of EU policies, notably through their involvement in regional associations and lobbying activities in Brussels.

Conversely, many authorities had adopted a rudimentary approach. Only half regarded Europe as having had a significant impact on their activities, while a quarter had no formal procedures for allocating responsibility for European issues. Even where formal responsibilities were identified, procedures for raising awareness of European issues and disseminating information, within the authority and to potential partners, were often elementary. Moreover, many local authorities reported that they had no regular contacts with EU officials, MEPs, or international links. For a significant proportion of authorities, European policies appeared remote from their primary task of delivering local services.

The research, therefore, confirmed the diversity of local authority responses to Europe. No single measure offers an adequate explanation of these variations. Many authorities explained their increasing involvement in EU policies largely in terms of funding gains; indeed there was strong evidence that those authorities eligible for substantial EU assistance were most likely to have developed a capacity to manage European issues. Funding, much of it nonadditional, had promoted capacity and thus assumed an importance beyond its monetary value.

Differences in capacity and attitudes to Europe among local authorities within different regions were also apparent. The Scottish regions were generally more comfortable in their relationship with central government than were many English authorities and displayed greater awareness of the wider implications of EU integration. A sense of identity and the presence of a well-resourced national representation in Brussels (Scottish EUROPA), a powerful development agency (SDA), an independent secretariat responsible for structural funds, and a single territorial department were significant in building confidence and capacity. A similar model might have been expected in Wales. However, despite apparently similar institutional arrangements, discussions during the early 1990s over EU funding, between the Welsh office and local authorities, were marked by confrontation—"open warfare" according to a county chief executive (Martin and Pearce 1994). Relations between the Welsh office and local authorities began to improve only after the establishment in 1996 of an independent secretariat, separate from the Welsh office, to serve structural fund program committees (Bache 1998).

In the English regions, a range of contrasting regional inheritances can be identified (Roberts and Lloyd 2000). Local authorities in the West Midlands and the North East have a history of collaboration (Pearce 1999; Lanigan 1997), but historic rivalries between authorities in other regions often caused difficulties in the preparation and delivery of

European strategies. The performance of apparently similar councils was also variable. Contrasts have been drawn between the entrepreneurial approach adopted by the Birmingham and Manchester city councils to Europe and the relatively lackluster performance of the Liverpool and Leeds city councils (Meegan 1994; Bentley and Shutt 1997).

Underpinning these variations are the distinct roles performed by SNG. Those authorities with extensive competencies were generally most active in European affairs. Marks (1996) observes that arrangements for EU structural programming at the member-state level are embedded in that country's system of intragovernmental relations, including the extent of autonomy at the subnational level and the prevailing culture of formal and informal partnership arrangements. Jeffery (2000) also emphasizes the importance of variations in intrastate competencies in explaining the level of SNG mobilization. Variations in responses to Europe among local authorities reflect hierarchical structures—the asymmetric distribution of resources available to local authorities, based upon their size, geographical location, and function and their status in relation to EU structural funds. Authorities are far from uniform in terms of financial or institutional capacity, and their ability to participate in EU policies reflects these variations.

Engagement in EU policies disturbed the traditional bilateral relationship between central and local government during the 1990s and encouraged some authorities to contemplate greater independence and influence in Brussels. However, much of the interest in Europe was prompted by a desire to secure EU funding and, in the absence of such rewards, it is questionable whether many authorities would have been prompted to participate so fully in EU affairs. Evidence that authorities perceived involvement in EU policy areas beyond the structural funds was limited. Moreover, although local authorities had become significant participants in the implementation of EU policies, very few expected or aspired to "set the agenda" for EU policy debates (Bache 1998). SNG engagement in Europe has been geared to practical measures—ensuring that authorities are appraised of developments in EU policy that may impact upon their own activities and the areas that they serve and involvement in the preparation and implementation of structural fund programs. Supporters of MLG may draw some comfort from the way in which many UK local authorities have developed their European competencies, which signifies the evolving interdependence and overlapping competencies of subnational and supranational activities. But forecasts of institutional transformation should be treated with caution, as central government has continued to set the rules for network and governance regimes that take place in the shadow of hierarchy.

INSTITUTIONAL AND POLICY SHIFTS

Since the election of New Labour in 1997 and its platform of constitutional reform, new political and institutional agendas have developed very rapidly, although much remains in flux. Devolution in Scotland, Northern Ireland, and Wales, the restoration of elected London-wide government, the prospect of elected assemblies in the English regions, and changes in the roles of local government may have far-reaching and unpredictable consequences for relations between subnational and central government institutions and the European Union. The debate leading to the EU white paper on European governance and the forthcoming intergovernmental conference (IGC) offers the prospect of further change. It is too early to gauge the full impact of these developments. However, it is possible to identify a number of key issues that are likely to repay careful study.

EU Policies

Key policy developments at the EU level—expansion, security and defense, and the debate about governance—may seem remote from the core business of most local authorities, but there are several aspects of EU policy that have direct implications for SNG in the United Kingdom. The latest structural fund regulations confirm the importance attached to the promotion of economic and social cohesion. Because local authorities have a leading role in developing public sector infrastructure and the integration of economic and community development, they will continue to seek to influence the content and implementation of structural measures. An important challenge for many English authorities has arisen from the reforms to structural policy that will integrate the four strands—industrial, urban, rural, and fishing—to form the building blocks of the new Objective 2 regions. The objective is to build synergy between the different types of target area and the areas surrounding them and to reinforce the links between bottom-up approaches, based upon local knowledge, and top-down strategic guidance. Individual local authorities will play a key part in implementing the new programs but, given the need to draw together urban and rural interests, they will be increasingly engaged in collaboration at the regional level. In the longer term—post 2006—the process of EU expansion may lead to a reduction in structural funds for the United Kingdom, and given the importance attached to EU assistance in stimulating their involvement, the outcome could be a diminution of local authority interest in EU issues. However, given the prospect of UK participation in the Euro and a single interest rate regime, UK regions will increasingly need to adjust their policies to ensure that their relative performance does not lag behind those of their European competitors (Vibert 1999).

The implementation of the European Employment Strategy and National Employment Plans and the redefinition of the scope of the European Social Fund (ESF) may also have consequences for local authorities, because they will be expected to work with central government to ensure that funds are targeted at the correct areas. Similarly, authorities serving rural areas will also need to take account of reforms to the Common Agricultural Policy (CAP) and the preparation by MAFF of the England Rural Development Plan (European Commission 1999b; MAFF 2000). Described as the first major step in bringing about the radical redirection of agriculture, the intention is to establish an integrated approach to rural development in a regional context. A further challenge for SNG has emerged in the form of the European Spatial Development Perspective (European Commission 1999c). Spatial development is not yet a Community competence, and the application of the ESDP framework is entirely voluntary. However, it provides the possibility of widening the EU's policy remit beyond sectoral measures, to take account of the overall situation in the European territory and development opportunities and constraints in individual regions. In the English regions it is already being regarded as a benchmark in the preparation of spatial plans, as part of a complementary group of measures, including the Sixth Environmental Action Program, designed to strengthen the EU commitment to sustainability through the development of a balanced spatial structure.

Each of these developments suggests that EU policies will continue to influence SNG, but there is growing concern that insufficient attention has been given to mechanisms to facilitate the integration of EU, national, and SNG policies. For example, whereas the CAP as a sectoral policy contributes about 90 percent of the resources allocated specifically to English rural areas, comparatively limited account has been taken of its territorial impacts (PIU 1999). The emerging European polity is complex, with no singular pattern of government; indeed, the structural measures are the only example of EU policy that displays strong connections between territorial levels and that extends to the formal participation of economic and social actors (Hooghe 1998). Structural policy has already been used as a conduit to mainstream new policy initiatives, including sustainable development and employment, and this approach might be extended to promote greater integration between EU policies. The 2000 Lisbon summit acknowledged the importance of establishing greater coherence across a range of EU policy domains (European Council 2000). But the institutional consequences of such an approach would be significant, including greater collaboration within the Commission, the dovetailing of national positions on EU policies with those of their territorial authorities, and the enhancement of SNG's capacity to implement integrated territorial policies.

Devolution

The creation of the Scottish Parliament, assemblies in Wales and Northern Ireland, the Greater London Authority, and unelected assemblies in each of the eight English regions represents a fundamental change in internal constitutional arrangements in the United Kingdom. To varying degrees, the denationalization of statehood and the territorialization of political power opens up new opportunities for more direct engagement in the rapidly developing European agenda and for advancing the standing of the proliferation of UK nations and regions in the EU. The outcome may be a fundamental shift in central-local roles and relations, with major consequences for SNG involvement in the growing range of EU policies that interface with domestic priorities at the subnational level.

Given that the larger, first tier local authorities have proved to be more adept than smaller district councils in EU policy debates and programs, the creation of new regional bodies might be expected to increase the capacity of English SNG to respond to EU policy developments. Equally, the devolution of significant powers to the Scottish Parliament and, to a lesser extent, the Wales and Northern Ireland Assemblies might be seen as signaling a shift in power and influence away from central government toward the subnational level. Regions, after all, are increasingly seen as the optimal level at which institutional networks and institutional thickness may be developed— small enough to allow for face-to-face contact upon which trust and cooperation are built, but large enough to permit economies of scale and scope (Amin and Thrift 1994). We may in effect be witnessing the filling in of the hitherto missing mesolevel in the United Kingdom, combined with the hollowing out of the central state.

The reality is, however, more complex. The asymmetric nature of devolution is in fact likely to produce contrasting patterns of multilevel governance across the United Kingdom. The Scottish Executive has been granted much greater powers than its Welsh counterpart, whereas elected English regional assemblies will have far less autonomy than the Scottish Parliament and Welsh Assembly. In England, devolution may provide the opportunity to integrate regional policies and mobilize new institutional relationships and processes. Recent research by Burch and Gomez (2002) confirms that one of the consequences of the government's measures to strengthen the regional tier has been to encourage representatives from the key bodies in each of the English regions and central government to come together to deal with European affairs. Some of these groups, for example in the southeast and the west Midlands, are beginning to look beyond the implementation of EU programs to consider their region's EU strategy more broadly (South East England Regional Planning Assembly 2001; West Midlands in

Europe 2001). Moreover, all the English regions have established offices in Brussels, usually funded by a range of regional stakeholders. Increasingly, these offices are seen not just as listening posts and information gatherers but as active lobbyists for their regions in the EU institutions and as participants in debates about European strategy in the regions. Domestically, measures to enhance regional capacity are also giving rise to increasing links between regions relating to common issues—including Europe. Decentralized politics is clearly part of the New Labour Project, but there is a tension between Labour's rhetoric of pluralism and its practice of continuing tight regulation over most local authority functions (Pearce and Mawson 2003). Elected regional government in England is not high on the list of the government's priorities, and there has been a lack of procedures for cooperation between central government departments and the decentralized institutions. Concerns have also been expressed about the roles and effectiveness of the Regional Development Agencies and Assemblies and the reliance placed upon the Government Offices in the English regions to internalize policy overlaps and contagion (Mawson and Saunders 2000; House of Commons Environment, Transport and Regional Affairs Select Committee 1999). While advocating the merits of active subsidiarity, the government has been accused of stifling regional autonomy, leading to tensions, uncertainty, and pressures for change (Bognador 1999; House of Commons Trade and Industry Select Committee 1998).

There is scope for considerable conflict between central government and the newly devolved bodies about their respective relationships with Brussels. Indeed, the publication of the *Memorandum of Understanding* between the UK government, Scottish ministers, and the Welsh Assembly dealing with the responsibilities and powers of the different institutions and their relationship with the European Union illustrates the need for coordination (HM Government 1999a; Scott 2000). Similar issues are currently being addressed in England, where regional protocols or concordats are being promoted to help clarify the roles and responsibilities of the key partners. Protocols offer the prospect of delineating clear undertakings between the parties on the basis of common, shared objectives and precise definitions of individual responsibilities. However, their effectiveness is likely to be more closely linked to the interests of the various parties in implementing joint actions than to the framework chosen.

A key outcome of the emerging arrangements is that competition between territories seems set to intensify and become more explicit. In terms of EU regional policy, the process by which funding was historically "negotiated and resolved behind closed doors by senior officials and ministers in Whitehall and Brussels, will now be subject to far greater openness and transparency. . . . The hidden geographical tradeoffs between different parts of the UK to secure the national interest will be exposed, making the resolution of these matters far more difficult from both a political and administrative point of view" (Mawson 1999). Under the new asymmetric constitutional arrangements, long-standing debates, about the relative abilities of different parts of the United Kingdom to capture inward investment and differences in the levels of subsidies received from central government, are likely to intensify and may be subject to increasing public scrutiny (Raines 2000; Midwinter 1999; Yuill, Bachtler, and Wishdale 1998).

Local Government

It is widely acknowledged that many of the issues facing local communities demand a more coordinated cross-cutting response by UK central and local government, which may require increased decentralization of administrative responsibilities and devolution. Since 1997, local authorities have been inundated with new initiatives and change programs inspired by central government's attempt to revitalize local democratic processes and improve local services. Ministers are seeking a fundamental change in the culture of local government, demanding that it provide more citizen-centered services and stronger community leadership (Department of the Environment, Transport and the Regions [DETR] 1998). Local authority leaders have been repeatedly warned of dire consequences should they fail to modernize rapidly. As the prime minister put it, "If you are unwilling or unable to work to the modern agenda then the government will have to look to other partners to take on your role" (Blair 1998). The consequence is that authorities are presently grappling with a raft of initiatives, including a demanding statutory duty to provide "best value," the development of a comprehensive process of community planning built around local strategic partnerships, and radical changes to the traditional committee systems and patterns of political leadership (Martin 2000; DETR 2000a, 2000b; HM Government 1999b).

In addition, many councils have found themselves at the forefront of a wave of new action zones, pilot initiatives, and pathfinder experiments designed to promote greater partnership between local service providers, the private and community sectors. Many of the same senior policy officers and leading politicians who were most closely involved in responding to European issues in the mid-1990s are now endeavoring to implement this plethora of new domestic initiatives and programs. Five years ago many of these key actors saw Europe as one of the few areas in which it was possible for them and their authorities to exert influence or to gain any room for maneuvering. Many now see the domestic agenda as being much more relevant and interesting and have either chosen, or simply been forced by lack of time, to refocus their efforts on these rather than EU issues.

There are in any case doubts about the continuing capacity of local authorities to participate fully in EU debates and programs. Reforms introduced during the late 1990s, leading to a redistribution of functions, alongside the creation of unitary authorities in Wales and Scotland and parts of England, are likely to have already reduced the capacity of SNG to engage in EU issues. The new, smaller unitary authorities are unlikely to match the capabilities of some of the former regions and counties. In many cases local authorities simply do not have access to the policy actors whose decisions may have a profound impact on the quality of life in their areas. Few local authorities, for example, are likely to have examined the likely implications for their areas of British participation in EMU or reform of the CAP. In England the establishment of new regional offices in Brussels, supported by local authority associations and other key regional actors, offers scope for local authorities to be better informed of EU policies. But their participation seems likely to be increasingly dependent on their capacity to engage in these regional networks, rather than on separate links with European institutions.

Labour's approach to devolved government remains unpredictable. Under the emerging devolution/decentralization process, powers are to be transferred away from the center, but it also seems likely that at least some of the new powers and resources granted to devolved institutions will be drawn up from the local level. But here again the emerging pattern is unlikely to be homogenous. The Scottish Executive has expressed its support for the principle of strong local government, and the National Assembly for Wales has a statutory duty to promote a healthy local democracy. Indeed, there are some signs that both bodies will be willing to promote frameworks for local government that diverge from those imposed on English councils by Whitehall departments. Scotland and Wales inherited a unitary system of local government, and it is not inconceivable that English local government might be similarly reorganized alongside devolution of further powers to the regions. The "Devolution" white paper (Cabinet Office and Department for Transport, Local Government and the Regions 2002) indicates that the local government structure in regions seeking to establish elected assemblies should be predominantly unitary.

CONCLUSION

SNG participation in EU affairs during the 1990s may be characterized as variable, but the significance of these trends is that they have provided a broad and solid intrastate basis for SNG mobilization in EU policy making (Jeffery 2000). One of the key outcomes has been the creation of new forms of regional and local networks that provide a firm foundation upon which the newly devolved national and regional institutions can develop their responses to European policies. These new institutions are already establishing representation in Brussels, but evidence suggests that territorial interests will continue to be articulated primarily through national government. The new institutional arrangements may also give rise to greater competition between the regions, but there is also scope for improved coordination through interregional networks to assert common territorial interests both domestically and within the Community, and for the European Commission to be more involved in territorial development.

The constitutional changes introduced in the United Kingdom since the late 1990s challenge hierarchical power structures and established systems for the coordination of government policies. At the same time, there is growing interest in the United Kingdom and in the European Union in strengthening the interconnections between the various territorial actors (Community, national, and subnational) and policy fields. The ramifications of these trends for SNG are potentially complex and contradictory. They seem set to produce an increasingly differentiated polity within the United Kingdom. Our earlier empirical work demonstrated that local government's capacity and inclination to engage with European issues was already quite variable—both between and within different territories and tiers of government. Recent reforms, in particular devolution in Scotland and Wales, have increased institutional asymmetries and will almost certainly exacerbate the contrasts found in the 1990s. In crude terms, the most likely trajectory seems to be a partial transfer of opportunities upward from local authorities to regional bodies in England and both upward from local government and downward from Whitehall to the Scottish Parliament and Welsh Assembly.

The variable capacity of British SNG and the newly devolved institutions to mobilize resources and engage in the European polity suggests that the underlying pattern will become far more complex, with variations between policy arenas and at different stages of the policy cycle. No single theory of European integration is likely to be sufficient to encapsulate and account for such variations. Nonetheless, because it acknowledges the role of vertical and horizontal connections between policies and institutions and capacity building at all levels of governance, MLG does offer a useful starting point for mapping the impacts of current domestic and EU institutional and policy developments upon future relations between SNG and the European Union.

NOTES

The survey on which this paper draws was funded by the Economic and Social Research Council, Award Number R000234671.

1. At the time of the survey, the major conurbations in England were administered by unitary authorities—London boroughs and metropolitan district councils. A two-tier structure existed across the rest of England and the whole of Scotland and Wales. In the two-tier areas of England and in Wales, local government consisted of county councils and smaller, nonmetropolitan districts. In Scotland, local government comprised regional councils and nonmetropolitan districts. English and Welsh counties, Scottish regional councils, and the unitary authorities were referred to collectively as first tier authorities. Nonmetropolitan districts were known as second tier authorities.

REFERENCES

Amin, A., and N. Thrift. 1994. Living in the global. In *Globalisation, institutions and regional development in Europe*, edited by A. Amin and N. Thrift, pp. 1–23. Buckingham: Oxford University Press.

Anderson, J. 1990. Skeptical reflections on a "Europe of the Regions": Britain, Germany and the European Regional Development Fund. *Journal of Public Policy* 10: 417–47.

———. 1996. Germany and the structural funds: Unification leads to bifurcation. In *Cohesion policy and European integration: Building multi-level governance*, edited by L. Hooghe, pp. 163–94. Oxford: Oxford University Press.

Ansell, C. 2000. The networked polity: Regional development in Western Europe. *Governance* 12 (3): 303–33.

Ansell, C., C. Parsons, and K. Darden. 1997. Dual networks in European regional development policy. *Journal of Common Market Studies* 35 (3): 347–75.

Audit Commission. 1991. *A rough guide to Europe*. London: HMSO.

Bache, I. 1998. *The politics of European Union regional policy: Multi-level governance or flexible gatekeeping?* Sheffield: Sheffield Academic Press.

———. 1999. The extended gatekeeper: Central government and the implementation of EC regional policy in the UK. *Journal of European Public Policy* 6 (1): 28–45.

Bache, I., S. George, and R. Rhodes. 1996. The European Union, cohesion policy, and subnational authorities in the United Kingdom. In *Cohesion policy and European integration: Building multi-level governance*, edited by L. Hooghe, pp. 294–319. Oxford: Oxford University Press.

Bachtler, J., and I. Turok. 1997. Conclusions: An agenda for reform. In *The coherence of EU regional policy: Contrasting perspectives on the structural funds*, edited by J. Bachtler and I. Turok, pp. 346–72. London: Jessica Kingsley.

Bennington, J., and J. Harvey. 1998. Transnational local authority networking within the European Union: Passing fashion or new paradigm? In *Policy networks in Europe*, edited by D. Marsh and R. Rhodes. Oxford: Oxford University Press.

Bentley, J., and J. Shutt. 1997. European regional policy in English regions: The West Midlands and Yorkshire and Humberside. In *The coherence of EU regional policy: Contrasting perspectives on the structural funds*, edited by J. Bachtler and I. Turok. London: Jessica Kingsley.

Blair, T. 1998. *Leading the way: A new vision for local government.* London: IPPR.

Bognador, V. 1999. *Devolution in the United Kingdom.* Oxford: Oxford University Press.

Bongers, P. 1992. *Local government in the Single European Market.* London: Longman.

Börzel, T. 2001. *Nations and regions in Europe.* Cambridge: Cambridge University Press.

Burch, M., and R. Gomez. 2002. "The English Regions and the European Union," *Regional Studies*, 436.7, pp. 767–78.

Burch, M., and R. Rhodes. 1993. *The North-West region in Europe: Development of a regional strategy.* Manchester Papers in Politics, No. 6, Department of Government, Manchester University.

Cabinet Office and Department for Transport. Local Government and the Regions. 2002. *Your Region: Your Choice: Revitalizing the English Regions,* CM5511. London: DTLR.

Conference of Peripheral Maritime Regions (CPMR). 2001. *Territorial development: Networking of territorial players.* CPMR.

Council of the European Union (1999). *Council regulation laying down general provisions on the structural funds.* OJ L 161, June 21, 1999.

Department of the Environment, Transport and the Regions (DETR). 1998. *Modernising local government: In touch with the people.* White paper. CM 4014. London: HMSO.

———. 2000a. *Preparing community strategies: Draft guidance to local authorities.* London: DETR.

———. 2000b. *Local strategic partnerships.* London: DETR.

Elcock, H. 1998. The north of England and the Europe of the Regions, or, when is a region not a region? In *The political economy of regionalism,* edited by J. Loughlin and M. Keating, 422–35. London: Frank Cass.

European Commission. 1999a. *Sixth periodic report on the social and economic situation and development in the regions of the European Community.* Luxembourg: Office of the Official Publications of the European Community.

———. 1999b. *CAP reform: A policy for the future.* Luxembourg: Office of the Official Publications of the European Community.

———. 1999c. *European spatial development perspective: Towards balanced and sustainable development of the territory of the European Union.* Luxembourg: Office of the Official Publications of the European Community.

European Council. 2000. Lisbon European Council Presidency Conclusions, March 23–24.

Goldsmith, M., and E. Sperling. 1997. Local government and the EU. In *European integration and local government,* edited by M. Goldsmith and T. Klaussen, pp. 95–120. Cheltenham: Edward Elgar.

HM Government. 1999a. *Memorandum of understanding and supplementary agreements between the United Kingdom government, Scottish ministers and the Cabinet of the National Assembly for Wales,* CM 4444. London: HMSO.

———. 1999b. *Modernising government.* CM4310. London: HMSO.

Hooghe, L. 1998. EU cohesion policy and competing models of European capitalism. *Journal of Common Market Studies* 36 (4): 457–77.

House of Commons Environment, Transport and Regional Affairs Select Committee. 1999. *Regional development agencies.* London: HMSO.

House of Commons Trade and Industry Select Committee. 1998. *Co-ordination of inward investment.* London: HMSO.

Hudson, R. 1999. The learning economy, the learning firm and the learning region: A sympathetic critique of the limits to learning. *European Urban and Regional Studies* 6 (1): 59–72.

Jeffery, C. 1997. Sub-national authorities and European domestic policy. In *The regional dimension of the European Union*, edited by C. Jeffery. London: Frank Cass.

———. 2000. Subnational mobilisation and European integration: Does it make any difference? *Journal of Common Market Studies* 38 (1): 1–23.

John, P. 1994. *The Europeanisation of British local government: New management strategies*. Luton: Local Government Management Board.

———. 1996. Centralisation, decentralisation and the European Union: The dynamics of triadic relationships. *Public Administration* 74: 293–313.

———. 1997. Europeanisation in a centralising state: Multi-level governance in the UK. In *The regional dimension of the European Union*, edited by C. Jeffery, pp. 131–46. London: Frank Cass.

Kay, A. 2000. Objective 1 in Wales: RECHAR redux? *Regional Studies* 34 (6): 581–85.

Klijn, E., J. Koppenjan, and C. Termeer. 1995. Managing networks in the public sector: A theoretical study of management strategies in policy networks. *Public Administration* 73 (3): 437–54.

Lanigan, C. 1997. The private sector and regionalism in North East England. *Regional and Federal Studies* 7 (3): 66–86.

Marks, G. 1993. Structural policy and multi-level governance in the EC. In *The state of the European Union*. Volume 2: *The Maastricht debates and beyond*, edited by A. Cafruny and G. Rosenthal, pp. 391–411. Boulder: Lynne Rienner.

———. 1996. Exploring and explaining variation in EU cohesion policy. In *Cohesion policy and European integration: Building multi-level governance*, edited by L. Hooghe, pp. 388–422. Oxford: Oxford University Press.

———. 1997. An actor-centred approach to multi-level governance. In *The regional dimension of the European Union*, edited by C. Jeffery, pp. 20–40. London: Frank Cass.

Marks, G., L. Hooghe, and K. Blank. 1996. European integration from the 1980s: State-centric v multi level governance. *Journal of Common Market Studies* 34 (3): 341–73.

Marks, G., F. Nielsen, L. Ray, and J. Salk. 1996. Competencies cracks and conflicts: Regional mobilisation in the European Union. In *Governance in the European Union*, edited by G. Marks, F. Scharpf, P. Schmitter, and W. Streeck, pp. 40–63. London: Sage.

Martin, S. J. 1997. *EU capital funding and local authorities in England and Wales*, Luton: Audit Commission.

———. 1998. Managing local economic change: EU programmes and local economic governance in the UK. *European Urban and Regional Studies* 5 (3): 237–48.

———. 2000. Implementing best value: Local public services in transition. *Public Administration* 78 (1): 209–27.

Martin, S. J., and G. R. Pearce. 1993. Regional economic development strategies: Strengthening meso-government in the UK. *Regional Studies* 27 (7): 681–85.

———. 1994. The impact of Europe on local government: Regional partnerships in local economic development. In *Contemporary political studies*, edited by P. Dunleavy and J. Stanyer, pp. 962–72. Belfast: Political Studies Association of Great Britain.

———. 1999. Differentiated multi-level governance? The response of British subnational governments to European integration, *Regional and Federal Studies* 9 (2): 32–52.

Mawson, J. 1996. The re-emergence of the regional agenda in the English regions: New patterns of urban and regional governance? *Local Economy* 10 (4): 300–26.

——. 1999. The English regions and the wider constitutional and administrative reforms. In *The new regional agenda*, edited by J. Dungey and I. Newman, pp. 85–98. London: Local Government Information Unit.

Mawson, J., and W. Saunders. 2000. *Review of the West Midlands Regional Chamber.* Birmingham: West Midlands Chamber.

Mawson, J., and K. Spencer. 1997. The government offices for the English regions: Towards regional government. *Policy and Politics* 25 (1): 71–84.

Meegan, R. 1994. A Europe of the regions: A view from Liverpool on the Atlantic Arc Periphery. *European Planning Studies* 4 (2): 59–80.

Midwinter, A. 1999. The politics of need assessment: The Treasury Select Committee and the Barnett formula. *Public Money and Management* 19 (2): 51–54.

Ministry of Agriculture, Fisheries and Food (MAFF). 2000. *England rural development program.* London: MAFF.

Moravcsik, A. 1995. Liberal intergovernmentalism and integration: A rejoinder. *Journal of Common Market Studies* 33 (4): 611–28.

Pearce, G. R. 1999. The West Midlands. In *Metropolitan planning in Britain: A comparative study*, edited by P. Roberts, K. Thomas, and G. Williams, pp. 78–96. London: Jessica Kingsley.

Pearce, G. R., and S. J. Martin. 1996. The measurement of additionality: Grasping the slippery eel. *Local Government Studies* 22 (1): 78–92.

Pearce, G. R., and Mawson, J. 2003. Delivering devolved approaches to local governance. *Policy and Politics* 31 (1): 51–68.

Performance and Innovation Unit (PIU). 1999. *Rural economies.* HMSO: London.

——. 2000a. *Reaching out: The role of central government at the regional and local level.* London: HMSO.

——. 2000b. *Wiring it up.* London: HMSO.

Prodi, R. 2000. *Reshaping Europe.* Speech to the Committee of the Regions, February 17, in Brussels.

Putnam, R. 1993. *Making democracy work: Civic traditions in modern Italy.* Princeton, N.J.: Princeton University Press.

Raines, P. 2000. Regions in competition: Inward investment and regional variation in the use of incentives. *Regional Studies* 34 (3): 291–96.

Rhodes, R., I. Bache, and S. George. 1996. Policy networks and policy makers in the European Union: A critical appraisal. In *Cohesion policy and European integration: Building multi-level governance*, edited by L. Hooghe, pp. 367–87. Oxford: Oxford University Press.

Risse-Kappen, T. 1996. Explaining the nature of the beast: International relations theory and comparative policy analysis meet the EU. *Journal of Common Market Studies* 34 (1): 53–80.

Roberts, P., and T. Hart. 1996. *Regional strategy and partnership in European programmes: Experience in four UK regions.* York: Joseph Rowntree Foundation.

Roberts, P., and M. Lloyd. 2000. Regional development agencies in England: New strategic regional planning issues? *Regional Studies* 34 (1): 75–79.

Roberts, P., T. Hart, and K. Thomas. 1993. *Europe: A handbook for local authorities.* Manchester: Center for Local Economic Strategies.

Scharpf, F. 1994. Community and autonomy: Multi-level policy-making in the European Union. *Journal of European Public Policy* 1 (2): 219–42.

Schattle, H. 1999. *European integration and intersecting models of citizenship.* Paper presented at conference, The State of the Art: Theoretical Approaches to the EU in the Post-Amsterdam Era, May, at Aston University, Birmingham.

Schmitter, P. 1996. Imagining the future of the Euro-polity with the help of new concepts. In *Governance in the European Union*, edited by G. Marks, F. Scharpf, P. Schmitter, and W. Streeck, pp. 1–14. London: Sage.

Scott, A. 2000. *The role of concordats in the new governance of Britain: Taking subsidiarity seriously?* Harvard Jean Monnet Working Paper 7/00, Harvard Law School.

Sharpe, J., ed. 1993. *The rise of meso government in Europe.* London: Sage.

South East England Regional Planning Assembly. 2001. *European Strategy for the South East, 2001-06*, available at: http://southeast-ra.gov.uk/regional-policies/europe/strategy.html.

Tömmel, I. 1998. Transformation of governance: The European Commission's strategy for creating a "Europe of the Regions." *Regional and Federal Studies* 8 (2): 52–80.

Vibert, F. 1999. British constitutional reform and the relationship with Europe. In *Constitutional futures: A history of the next ten years*, edited by R. Hazell, pp. 47–66. Oxford: Oxford University Press.

West Midlands in Europe. 2001. *West Midlands in Europe: Business Plan*, available at: http://www.westmidlandsineurope.org/wmie.html.

Weyand, S. 1997 Inter-regional associations and the European integration process. In *The regional dimension of the European Union*, edited by C. Jeffery, pp. 166–82. London: Frank Cass.

Yuill, D., J. Bachtler, and E. Wishdale. 1998. *European regional incentives 1997–98*, 17th ed. London: Bowker-Saur.

4

Devolution in the European Union: The Role of Subnational Authorities in Scotland and Catalonia

Elisa Roller and Amanda Sloat

This chapter examines the role of political elites in the emerging process of multilevel governance, comparing and contrasting the experiences of Scotland and Catalonia in the European Union (EU). It argues that domestic conceptions of governance guide the way in which Scottish and Catalan elites think about their involvement in the European Union's decision-making process, as they focus on the nation's right to become involved at the supranational level. This chapter evaluates the positions of Scotland and Catalonia within their respective systems of governance, a crucial task as "the participation of regional governments at the European level reflects their institutional capacity within their respective political systems" (Hooghe and Marks 1995, 22). It then compares the developments resulting from devolution in the United Kingdom and in Spain, focusing on elite attempts to secure greater participatory rights in EU policymaking. Finally, the chapter identifies key differences between the two case studies by analyzing domestic factors that affect the ability of elites to access the European policy arena.

DEVOLUTION IN THE UNITED KINGDOM AND SPAIN

Before considering how elites have sought greater involvement in the European legislative process, it is first necessary to place Scotland and Catalonia within the wider context of asymmetric devolution.

Scotland

Discussions about constitutional change in Scotland occurred in various forms throughout the twentieth century, motivated in part by perceptions of national identity and the development of the European Union. A Scottish Parliament was almost established in the late 1970s by the Labour government. Prior to its final reading, the 1977 Scotland Bill became subject to an amendment that necessitated a referendum of the Scottish electorate, which included the controversial 40 percent rule requiring a percentage of the total Scottish electorate to vote in favor of an assembly. Although the bill received Royal Assent, the referendum on March 1, 1979, failed to obtain the requisite support; the act was repealed less than four months later, and the Labour government was soon defeated. The opposition of Conservative governments throughout the 1980s and 1990s to devolution removed the subject from the wider political agenda. However, civic organizations in Scotland— ranging from the church and trade unions to local government and the voluntary sector—worked with Labour and Liberal Democrat politicians in the Scottish Constitutional Convention to continue the campaign for constitutional change and to design structures for the desired legislature (Conroy 1992; Kellas 1992; Lynch 1996).

The New Labour party won a landslide election in May 1997, removing all Conservative members of Parliament (MPs) from their seats in Scotland and Wales, and published the White Paper on Scotland's Parliament two months later. On September 11, 1997, the Scottish electorate voted on (1) whether a Parliament should be established, and (2) whether it should be able to vary income tax. With a 60.4 percent turnout, over 74 percent supported the first question and 63 percent the second. Donald Dewar, then–Secretary of State for Scotland, presented the Scotland Bill on December 18, and it entered the House of Commons a month later. In January 1998 the government convened the Consultative Steering Group (CSG), a civic and cross-party committee charged with collecting public views and making recommendations about the Parliament's operating methods to the Secretary of State. The CSG (1998) established four guiding principles, suggesting that the Parliament should (1) share power between the people of Scotland, the legislators, and the Executive; (2) be accountable to these groups; (3) be accessible, open, responsive, and participative; and (4) promote equal opportunities. Elections were held on May 6, 1999, and the new electoral system—which combined traditional first-part-the-post with a regional top-up list—meant that no party obtained a majority of seats. After several days of negotiations, Scottish New Labour and the Scottish Liberal Democrats formed a coalition government. The Queen officially opened the Parliament on July 1.

The 129-member legislature is responsible for legislation in devolved areas (e.g., agriculture, health, education). Scotland retains its 72 Westminster MPs, although this number is expected to decrease following the Boundary Commission review that began in February 2002 but will not conclude until December 2006. The former Scottish Office has been revised and shrunk into the Scotland Office, although the Secretary of State for Scotland remains; there is discussion of abolishing this office, amalgamating it with its Welsh and Northern Irish equivalents. Scotland's responsibility for European matters is outlined in Schedule Five of the Scotland Act, which classifies Europe under foreign affairs and stresses that relations with the European Union are reserved to the United Kingdom. It allows the Scottish Executive to play a role alongside the United Kingdom, as well as to observe and implement EU obligations in devolved areas. But it preserves the UK government's right to legislate in the event of Scotland's failure to do so, and prohibits the Executive from legislating in reserved areas or in violation of EU law.

The primary aim and main challenge of the devolution settlement was identified by then–Devolution Minister Henry McLeish in his testimony to the House of Commons' Scottish Affairs Committee:

> We foresee that the role of the new Scottish Parliament Executive will actually enhance the involvement of Scotland in European affairs without diluting, in any way, that single central [UK] voice. (1998, 105)

Given the Scotland Act's limited discussion of Scottish involvement in European affairs, most interactions between the Scottish and UK Executives are governed by concordats, which are non–legally binding agreements between the governments that primarily direct working relations between their officials. An overarching Memorandum of Understanding (Scottish Executive 1999)—a "statement of intent" that binds the administrations to good communication, cooperation, and open information exchange—is supplemented by more specific and departmental agreements. These informal arrangements suggest that the involvement of Scottish elites in EU policymaking will remain dependent on good relations between officials, further enhanced by partisan links between politicians, north and south of the border.

Spain

The creation of Spain's State of Autonomies in 1978 and the unique arrangements provided for its historic communities (such as Catalonia) were attempts to accommodate historical political and cultural cleavages within a climate of compromise and ideological change among the Spanish political leadership. By the time of General Francisco Franco's death in 1975, the general consensus among most political forces opposing the Franco regime was that the status quo would merely perpetuate the antiquated administrative and institutional structures of the Franco regime (Solozábal 1996). During the negotiations leading to the drafting of the 1978 constitution, the well-organized Catalan nationalist political leadership was able to manipulate historical events to extract concessions from the central government and other parties for significant measures of political and institutional history. Recognizing the regions' right to autonomy for either political or historical reasons, the drafters of the constitution acknowledged linguistic, cultural, and regional differences within a constitutional framework that guaranteed regional authorities a certain degree of self-government. Formal recognition of the division of powers and responsibilities at the central and regional levels were outlined, although not specified, in the text.

The constitution also stipulated the institutional arrangements for the restructuring of the state, including the establishment of institutions of self-government such as the judiciary and executive branches, that would operate within the framework of the so-called Statutes of Autonomy. These statutes, the end result of negotiations between central government and representatives of each autonomous community, are considered as a unique form of organic law. The uniqueness of every statute reaffirms the state's recognition of the varying needs and demands of the autonomous communities, listing the distribution of powers between the central government and the respective autonomous community as well as clarifying and/or extending the distribution of competencies as listed in the constitution. The Statutes of Autonomy were approved in Catalonia and the Basque Country in October 1979 following tough negotiations in which Catalan nationalists were forced to drop their demands for a regional financing system similar to that enjoyed by the Basque government.

Thus, the Spanish constitutional arrangement provides a unique model of political decentralization in which there is no identical model of autonomy for any of the regions. Each of the autonomous regions has chosen, with varying degrees of success, its own model with the inclusion or exclusion of competencies that it wishes to control. The decentralization of the Spanish state has not ceased with the drafting and eventual enactment of the 1978 constitution. The process has been one of evolution, in which the regions have negotiated and renegotiated their statutes and competencies with the central government; a series of "ongoing processes whereby central or federal governments and mobilised regional cultural communities continuously negotiate to maintain the latter's acceptance of the legitimacy of the state's claim to jurisdiction over them" (Henders 1997, 532). Thus, the Spanish system of selective or flexible devolution is characterized by a "climate of permanent political bargaining among local, regional and central governments . . . bound to remain as the most characteristic feature of the—yet unfinished—Spanish process of decentralization" (Moreno 1995, 24). Despite the uncertainty, this unique system has ensured a relatively high degree of institutional stability that some have likened to federal entities in other European states (Letamendia 1997).

Improving the access of Spain's autonomous communities to the EU policy process was an important issue following the 1996 general election. Legislation regulating this access (Law 2/1997) was approved by the *Cortes* (Spanish Parliament) less than a year later, which reinforced the existing *Conferencia para Asuntos Relacionados con las Comunidades Europeas* (Sectoral Conference Relating to EU Matters) that was institutionalized in October 1992 following its informal creation in 1988. The Sectoral Conference is not limited to EU matters, but extends to all competencies where the autonomous communities have exclusive or shared competencies. It also requires the Spanish permanent representation in Brussels to include an autonomous community delegate, who is responsible for disseminating all policy proposals and information related to devolved policy areas. However, the Catalan government felt that these measures were not sufficient in providing Spanish regions with a direct route to Europe and feared that the multilateral arrangements would undermine its own demands by diluting its representation along with Spain's other autonomous communities (Roller 1999). As a result, it has tended to rely on bilateral relations with the central government to receive information on EU matters and ensure that its views are incorporated in the Spanish government's position.

SIMILARITIES BETWEEN SCOTTISH AND CATALAN DEVOLUTION AND EUROPEAN INVOLVEMENT

Devolution developments in Scotland and Catalonia provide several interesting comparisons, particularly in terms of the ability of regional elites to pursue greater participatory rights in the European Union's decision-making process. First, both devolution processes have been characterized by their asymmetric and ongoing nature. Furthermore, the lack of constitutional clarity in the United Kingdom and Spain has caused the emerging process of multilevel governance to follow a hitherto uncharted trajectory. Second, the varying importance and increased electoral performance of nationalist movements in Scotland and Catalonia has affected elite mobilization. Third, the asymmetric nature of the devolution process has enabled regional elites to play an important role in the decentralization debates. Finally, elites have utilized various formal and informal channels to access the EU policy arena.

Asymmetric Devolution

The lack of a written constitution in the United Kingdom and the ambiguity of the Spanish constitution have forced subnational authorities in both states to follow an ill-defined course. The United Kingdom has always prided itself on a flexible, if rather opaque and ambiguous, system of government. The Scottish Parliament was established as part of a wider program of constitutional reform, whose *ad hoc* nature clearly contrasts with the thorough documentation provided in Article 23 of the German basic law (Jeffery 1997a). Additional reforms include a Welsh Assembly without legislative competence, a power-sharing executive in Northern Ireland, a directly elected mayor and assembly in London, and changing membership of the House of Lords. There are also ongoing discussions about assemblies for the English regions, which are currently managed by regional development agencies; however, some regions lack a strong identity, and others oppose the creation of an extra layer of government. The UK government's decision to make few legal stipulations about Scotland's EU involvement and to rely instead on nonbinding civil service agreements enables politicians and officials to devise informal procedures, which may either restrict Scottish participation due to limited UK cooperation or allow the Scottish Executive to push undefined boundaries.

Similarly, the inherent ambiguity of the Spanish constitution and the unfinished devolution process begun with the Statutes of Autonomy have resulted in a climate of constant political negotiation between the state and subnational forces. The different procedures envisaged by the constitution have encouraged a multispeed process, whose harmonization has been strongly resisted by Basque and Catalan nationalists. The latter have benefited from a favorable context within which constitutional and policy-making arrangements are reinterpreted to enhance its position within both the Spanish and EU decision-making processes. More specifically, the decentralization process in Spain could be characterized as "devolution through conflict" and has consistently remained one of the overarching features of Spanish politics since 1975

(Roller 1999). In the case of participation in EU matters, the reluctance of the central government to encourage the adoption of mechanisms or to support effective institutions that would serve to promote regional participation in the implementation of EU legislation has increased the level of conflict between the central and regional governments.

In particular, the nature of the 1978 Spanish constitution has had three important effects on the devolution process. First, its complex and ambiguous nature reflects great compromise on the territorial organization of the Spanish state, although its contradictory and vague terminology has frequently led to conflicting interpretations. Second, political decentralization is characterized by sovereignty being devolved and not divided. The entire process is based upon the indissoluble unity of the Spanish nation as being one of the fundamental premises of the Spanish constitution, yet it is from the same constitution that the autonomies derive the powers they are entitled to execute. Third, this decentralization is defined in the constitution as "self-government." This self-government of Spain's regions and nationalities marks a territorial redistribution of power of the state and its structural transformation, although this structure is not imposed from above by either the state or the constitution. In other words, the constitution does not establish a territorial design of the nationalities and regions but rather lays out the conditions by which the regions (with popular consent) may decide to proceed with the practice of self-government.

Role of Nationalist Movements

Scottish nationalism expressed itself in various forms throughout the twentieth century, including backing for social movements and explicitly nationalist political parties. Since the 1950s it has been accompanied by a shift in traditional partisan allegiance, most notably in Scotland through declining support for the Conservative party and increasing support for the Scottish National Party (SNP). This voting divergence not only demonstrated a greater commitment to self-determination but also highlighted an emerging sense of partisan distance from the rest of the United Kingdom:

> After 1959 it was becoming clear that Unionism—the dominant political creed—was in decline. . . . The SNP became the main challenger to Labour in the final quarter of this century by fighting on both nationalist and socialist/social democratic battlegrounds. It has drawn Labour on to its claim to be the "national" party of Scotland, while the SNP has sought to show that it is in a better position than Labour to win resources not only from Britain, but ultimately from Europe. (Brown, McCrone, and Paterson 1998, 143)

Europe became an added dimension to the devolution debates when the United Kingdom considered joining the European Economic Community (EEC) in the 1970s. The SNP initially opposed membership due to concerns in its fishing constituencies, as well as a reluctance to replace the centralization of London with that of Brussels. However, the party's position shifted rapidly throughout the 1980s: Its 1983 manifesto opposed the membership of an independent Scotland in the EEC and preferred a European trade association, but by 1987 the party supported independent Scottish membership provided interests such as oil and fishing would receive special guarantees. The next year the SNP launched its "Independence in Europe" strategy, which also served as the party's rallying cry during the 1992 general election. Responding to public anxiety about the perceived international isolation of an independent Scotland, the party argued that being situated within the larger European framework would enable Scotland to retain external security and trade options (MacCartney 1990; Marr 1992; SNP 1992, 1997). The ratification of the Maastricht Treaty bolstered the SNP's new stance, linking it to the wider campaign of self-determination among the "little nations" of Europe. Within the context of the current devolution settlement, the SNP (1998) continues to call for the Scottish Parliament's European role to be increased:

> The European dimension is incontrovertibly of great and growing importance to Scottish political, social, economic and cultural life. It is vital that the Scottish Parliament seize the opportunity to enhance and strengthen Scotland's role within Europe, irrespective of the limitations placed upon it. Scotland needs to maximise its impact in Brussels if we are to protect Scottish interests. (24)

The SNP was not unique among political parties in its changing stance on UK involvement in the European Union. For example, the Conservative party initially welcomed the economic benefits of the common market but became increasingly reluctant to surrender sovereignty to a "federal superstate." While some hardline Labour supporters originally felt devolution was inconsistent with socialist principles, the New Labour Government (1997–   ) drew parallels between domestic reform and greater support for the European project. For example, the party's 1997 manifesto emphasized subsidiarity in both EU and UK policymaking. Prime Minister Tony Blair stated at the party's 1998 conference, "It is no coincidence that debates on devolution and Europe are happening together," and then–European Minister Joyce Quin told the Northern Ireland Assembly in February 1998, "The goals of 'subsidiarity' and 'devolution' are the same." Furthermore, many of the policy areas devolved to the Scottish Parliament were already within the competence of the European Union (e.g., agriculture, environment, fisheries), which suggests that the UK government was comfortable surrendering powers within certain policy sectors to higher and lower levels of government.

Similarly, the fundamental transformation of the Spanish state led to a widespread acceptance of the state and its new constitutional arrangements among the Catalan political elite. It reinforced traditional Catalan nationalist tendencies to further objectives within the political realms of the Spanish state, as the electoral influence of nationalist parties has affected domestic politics. For most of the 1990s, both Catalan and Basque nationalists played a crucial role in central government politics, with the governing party seeking their support to retain a majority vote in the Spanish parliament. These electoral pacts have been crucial for Catalan nationalists to gain access to the domestic policy-making process, and in turn have reinforced their demands for greater participatory rights in EU decision making.

For Catalan nationalist parties, particularly the nationalist coalition *Convergència i Unió* (CiU), the process of Europeanization has been transformed into a multiple strategy incorporating an intense process of nation-building together with a pragmatic political approach aimed at reforming policy-making mechanisms at both the Spanish and European levels (Roller 1999). This strategy also includes the pursuit of the legal/constitutional recognition of the plurinational and multilinguistic composition of both the Spanish state and the European Union. Thus, the process of European integration is viewed as an opportunity for regions to participate in the process of institutional reform and to gain a greater role in the decision-making framework:

> The process of economic, cultural and social internationalisation and the practical disappearance of borders which it entails, suggests a weakening of the power of the State, which sees itself losing sovereignty over many of its traditional competencies. (Unió Democràtica de Catalunya 1996, 23)

The end result of this process, particularly its effect on the nation-state, remains to be seen as the process of European integration develops; but for Catalan nationalists, the arrangements are largely understood as providing a new framework of relations among the different levels of government (ibid.).

Elites as Dominant Actors in Devolution Process

Within the Scottish and Catalan nationalist movements just discussed, networks of associations (Moreno 1997) and elites (Llobera 1994) have played key roles in the devolution process. Networks of associations develop through cultural and social contacts, gradually reinforcing the link between individuals and their community or nation; such links constitute the crucial elements of the process of social and political mobilization within the nationalist movement. Elites are seen as the primary movers or instigators of the nationalist movement by articulating demands for greater self-government. These elites are important both at the formative stages (political activists and authors during the late nineteenth century in the case of Catalonia and throughout the twentieth century in the case of Scotland) and through political activity in the modern state (party and civil society representatives in postdevolution Catalonia and Scotland).

Scottish elites, particularly members of civic organizations, were actively involved in the campaign for and construction of the new parliament. The 1707 Treaty of Union, which dissolved the Scottish and English parliaments to create a new parliament, allowed for the continuation of Scotland's church, education system, and legal system. The retention of these institutions meant that Scotland was never fully incorporated into the United Kingdom, but retained its autonomy and flourished through a process of "negotiated compromise" (Paterson 1994). Many civic organizations—such as the trade unions, church, and local government—filled the political vacuum caused by the absence of a Scottish legislature. According to Brown, McCrone, and Paterson (1998),

> The policy networks of pluralism have bred a sense of a common Scottish interest among the influential elites. . . . Although this nationalism operates most obviously at the level of elites, it is grounded in popular preferences through the role of implementation. (117–18).

However, this arrangement began to break down during the postwar period as some people in Scotland perceived a democratic deficit in their own institutions and felt increasingly indifferent to UK institutions. Their frustration about the United Kingdom's political and economic decline was increased by the neoliberal approach of Prime Minister Margaret Thatcher; in particular, the privatization of numerous industries conflicted with the Left-Right political consensus in Scotland that supported the welfare state (McCrone 1989). In other words, many believed an "English Tory" prime minister was threatening the very institutions that represented Scottish distinctiveness. Such perceptions contributed to the mobilization of some civic actors into the Scottish Constitutional Convention and calls for democratic reform.

Scottish civil society is now adjusting to its changed role postdevolution. Some civic activists and political campaigners have been elected to the new parliament, whereas other civic organizations must shift their focus from "spokesman of" to "contributor toward." Given the predevolution importance of civil society, some commentators have asked, "Will the political institution assume primacy in speaking for Scotland? Or will Scottish civil society, which has played a prominent role in creating and shaping that Parliament, assume that it and 'the people' are paramount?" (Brown, McCrone, and Paterson 1998, 22).

Scottish politics remains characterized by the predominance of informal contacts within a small elite. Although strong interpersonal links assisted the campaign for constitutional reform, the current challenge for political leaders is ensuring that these corporatist tendencies do not exclude disenfranchised individuals from the political process.

In the Catalan case, the role of civil society was particularly important during the Franco regime. During the 1960s, the Catalan nationalist movement underwent a substantial transformation by beginning to attract supporters from all sectors of society, including the traditional non-Catalanist working classes (Conversi 1997). These developments were aided by a changing Spanish Catholic Church, which became a growing civic movement supporting a Catalan cultural and linguistic revival. Trade unions, business leaders, students, and political representatives traditionally ideologically opposed to each other also gave increasing support to nationalist demands. Thus, the involvement of civil society and the influence of Catalan intellectuals in particular were crucial in transforming the Catalan nationalist movement from an elite into a mass movement (Guibernau 2000). In the years since the establishment of the State of Autonomies, many of these intellectuals and civic leaders have become part of the Catalan political leadership, assuming a key role in the consolidation of Spain's new territorial structures. Civic organizations, many of which have been financed and nurtured by the *Generalitat*, have also evolved to play an important role in the defense and promotion of key elements of Catalan culture, language, and identity; however, these have also been highly politicized. Other organizations, such as the *Foro Babel* and *La Crida*, have provided a cross-party forum for common positions on topical political debates.

The highly developed nature of the political party system in Catalonia has meant that most social, economic, and political issues are primarily addressed within the institutional structure of the party system. In addition, the stability and continuity of the Catalan political leadership and party system have meant that political elites have remained the same over the last two decades, reinforcing close personal relationships and networks. The autonomous fervor or snowball effect that followed the ratification of the 1978 constitution led to a growing fear among Catalan elites that this process would undermine their special position within the Spanish state (Henders 1997). Nonetheless, the degree to which this fear has been felt among Catalan elites has varied widely, and the consensus in the immediate post-Franco era surrounding Catalan demands for self-government has gradually dis-integrated. Similarly, the question of greater participation in Europe has also generated growing divisions, with the principal difference lying in the extent to which Europe is employed to further nationalist objectives (Giordano and Roller 2002). Although pro-Europeanism remains a uni-fying element among Catalan elites, strategies and motivations differ quite notably among Catalan parties.

Formal versus Informal Channels of Access

Elites in Scotland and Catalonia, as well as other devolved adminis-trations throughout the European Union, have well-documented chan-nels of access into the policy-making process (see Hooghe 1995; Mazey 1995; Marks and McAdam 1996; Jeffery 1997b; Bache 1998). In particu-lar, elites can lobby their national governments in hopes of swaying their negotiating stances or can pursue more direct negotiations in Brussels. This section, which draws from observations of key actors, examines the lobbying methods of Scottish and Catalan elites. In par-ticular, it includes interviews conducted during the months before the Parliament's first elections with over 65 Scottish politicians, officials, and members of civil society (Sloat 2002). It is also based on interviews conducted with Catalan and Spanish officials and party representatives in Brussels and Barcelona over a two-year period (1997–1999) (Roller 1999).

Domestic Lobbying

According to Scottish elites, officials are the most effective pre- and postdevolution channel for relaying Scottish views to Whitehall (at least while Labour-led administrations remain in London and Edin-burgh). They believe the Scottish Executive is unlikely to sway policy outcomes, particularly as Scotland's European priorities differ from England's in emphasis on certain aspects of a policy (e.g., hill farming versus sheep farming) rather than on substantively distinct policy sectors. The devolved administration should make the process more inclusive of civic interests and is expected to highlight the existence of distinct opinions via its European Committee, Westminster lobbying, and differential implementation of directives. Many elites see the UK government as a "partner" rather than a "gatekeeper," with the excep-tion of Council of Ministers negotiations, where Scotland's role remains symbolic for the most part. Although the Scottish Executive can pursue autonomous action in Brussels, most elites believe that it will be more effective with UK backing. Recognizing the domestic repercussions of opposing the UK government, they called for the strategy to be used primarily if the UK government fails to incorporate Scottish views on important policies or to promote issues that the United Kingdom supports but does not prioritize.

In contrast, Spain's political structure has complicated efforts of regional elites to influence the negotiating stance of the central government. According to Spain's 1978 constitution, the upper chamber of the parliament, the Senate, is meant to be the "Chamber of Territorial Representation." During the 1990s, various committees were created to facilitate the Senate's transition to a true territorial chamber, which was to be designated as the autonomous communities' direct link with the European Union and the forum within which EU matters would be discussed between central and regional governments. However, reform of the Senate has been limited for various reasons. First, its existing powers are already limited, as the lower chamber can overrule any Senate amendments and vetoes of legislation. This has made regional elites reluctant to be represented by an already weak chamber. Second, opposition to Senate reform has come from widely diverging camps including Catalan (and Basque) nationalists, with repeated demands that the Senate provide special representative status for the historic communities.

As a result, regional and central government elites have been reluctant to use the Senate as a means of direct representation and dialogue in a multilateral setting. They have tended to rely instead on their political weight in the Congress of Deputies and the intervention of their respective leaders. However, the often inharmonious dialogue between the central and regional governments reflects the lack of more institutionalized means of cooperation. Despite regular meetings and conferences on various issues between the central government and the autonomous communities, relations (particularly in the case of Catalonia) have often been based on stop-and-go measures and coalition or stability pacts agreed to by the political parties in power. In other words, rather than negotiating within a set institutional framework, political parties often battle for compromises in a variety of fora.

European Lobbying

Subnational authorities also have a variety of Brussels-based channels that can complement their domestic efforts. Regional information offices are among the most widely used lobbying tools, and those established by Scotland and Catalonia are no exception. Most elites expect their respective offices to monitor EU activities, provide an early warning about forthcoming legislation, and present Scottish and Catalan views to Commission officials. But despite their democratic authority, few believe that these offices will exert greater sway on the

EU legislative process or the permanent representations of the United Kingdom and Spain. There is also confusion about the nature and extent of the offices' work, particularly given their complex construction and overlapping functions.

Predevolution Scotland was represented in Brussels by Scotland Europa, which was established in May 1992. It was originally intended to be a representative body owned by partners, but the euroskeptic Conservative government became uneasy when plans were leaked to the media; the Scottish Office backed off and Scottish Enterprise—an economic development agency publicly funded by the Scottish Office—assumed responsibility. Scotland Europa was founded as a membership organization, incorporating industry, public bodies, educational institutions, local authorities, trade unions, and the voluntary sector. It initially acted like a consultant and lobbyist by producing monthly reports, taking visitors to the institutions, and providing a Scottish presence. Because the Conservative government lacked enthusiasm for a regional office, Scotland Europa officials occasionally allowed other actors to assume that it was the same as other regional governments. Its role expanded in 1998 as the new Labour government wanted to raise Scotland's profile and improve relations with European Union. The establishment of the Scottish Executive European Office, which is colocated with Scotland Europa under the umbrella of Scotland House, provides political standing by formally representing the position of the Scottish government in Brussels; however, its success will depend on the extent to which it can achieve meaningful participation in EU policy making. Scotland Europa continues to service its members, but it has lost the ceremonial role it performed in the Parliament's absence. The Executive Office has assumed more political functions, gathering intelligence on EU issues, promoting increased interaction with EU institutions, and raising awareness among European officials about Scottish issues.

Similarly, Catalonia has set up nine trade bureaus within the European Union and established a powerful lobbying network in Brussels. The *Patronat Català Pro Europa* is a semipublic institution created 1982 by the *Generalitat* and a group of institutions in the public and private sectors including universities, local administrations, chambers of commerce, and building societies. But unlike Scotland, the Catalan *Patronat* combines both functions by serving as the Catalan government's (unofficial) representative or quasi-embassy in Brussels and acting as an informal forum for representatives of business, labor, and other interest groups to discuss EU- and Catalonia-related events. Despite the enthusiasm surrounding the creation of the *Patronat* in 1986, opinions on its performance and composition vary considerably among Catalonia's political parties: Some argue that its powers are too limited; others suggest that its scope of activity is too broad by representing government, business, labor, and civil society. There exists some confusion or ambivalence among Catalan elites about the *Patronat*'s true function and future objectives. On one hand, both *Patronat* and *Generalitat* officials painstakingly point out the information dissemination, educational, consultative, and lobbying functions of the former in both Brussels and Catalonia. On the other hand, there are continual references in documentation and discourse on the institutional and political dimension of the *Patronat* and its role in promoting Catalonia's participation in the process of European integration.

Of the European institutions, the Commission is cited most frequently in academic discussions about subnational involvement in EU policy making. Elites in both Catalonia and Scotland were pessimistic, as many failed to recognize its potential usefulness as a lobbying target. That said, those with more European experience mentioned its accessibility to subnational authorities with distinct needs, citing the benefits of communication with EU officials, the opportunity to shape the drafting of legislation at an early stage, and the ability to seek derogations from problematic aspects of directives. Finally, the Committee of the Regions is widely seen as the most approachable channel for subnational authorities, given their opportunity to participate directly in its deliberations. But the majority of Scottish and Catalan elites share academic skepticism about its utility, faulting its limited status and weak influence on policy outcomes. They also criticize its composition of local government authorities and regional ministers, and suggest that its opinions are excessive and hold little political clout.

DIFFERENCES BETWEEN SCOTLAND AND CATALONIA

The fact that the devolution process was initiated in Spain nearly two decades before its UK counterpart creates several differences, particularly in the nature of relations between government tiers and the extent of elite involvement in EU policy making. First, the degree of conflict between central and regional governments in the United Kingdom has not reached the same levels as in Spain. Although Spain's autonomy statutes had been approved for all seventeen regions by the end of February 1983, a new problem emerged regarding the degree to which services and powers would be allocated to the autonomous communities and subsequently exercised by the regional authorities. The broadness of these functions, as well as different interpretations of the true nature of central government's competencies, gave rise to a growing number of conflicts between government tiers that resulted in devolution through conflict.

Second, the apparent flexibility of interpretation in Spain has led to inordinate numbers of cases being brought to the Constitutional Court (*Tribunal Constitucional*), the body that resolves disputes arising from a differing understanding of the ranges of power allotted to either central or regional governments. The Constitutional Court has remained a crucial institutional actor in the relationship between the governments by enforcing the division of competencies and power between them. The United Kingdom lacks an equivalent constitutional court, although authorities can take cases before the Privy Council of the House of Lords on matters of competence. This situation has yet to occur within the early years of the Scottish Parliament's existence, and seems unlikely to happen with similar frequency, given extensive prelegislative checks of competence by officials, the presiding minister, and the Secretary of State.

The third crucial difference concerns the nature and extent of subnational participation in EU policy making. Research conducted before the first Scottish Parliamentary elections found that few Scottish elites believed that domestic and European channels would enable the Scottish Executive to exert more influence on EU legislative outcomes than did the old Scottish Office (Sloat 2002), although the high profile of devolution should assist Scotland's UK- and EU-lobbying efforts. Instead, elites expected constitutional change to have primarily domestic effects by changing the nature of Scottish participation through the creation of a more participatory and transparent policy-making process. Recognizing the likely continuity of policy outcomes and existing civil service procedures under Labour administrations, elites said that the greatest significance of devolution is the opportunity to devise new forms of governance. In short, they stressed domestic involvement over European influence.

In contrast, Catalan elites recognize that they already enjoy relatively high levels of influence, particularly in comparison with other regional elites. Although some type of formal representation in the European Union's decision-making process for Spain's regions was only approved in 1997, the Catalan government has continued to secure greater influence in the process by sustaining its bilateral negotiations with the central government, developing multilateral relationships (together with Spain's other regions) in the Sectoral Conferences and Senate, and resolving potential disputes through the Constitutional Court. Catalan elites initially placed a high degree of confidence in the so-called "third way" through alternative institutions such as the Committee of the Regions. This strategy has largely been abandoned in favor of a shift toward the reformulation of domestic policy-making mechanisms in securing greater participatory rights in EU matters, which has involved seeking greater involvement in the Spanish permanent representation, the Council of Ministers, and various working groups. Thus far, Catalan elites have been more successful than their Scottish counterparts in obtaining greater levels of influence (informal) rather than direct involvement (formal).

The fourth difference between Catalonia and Scotland concerns domestic political conditions. Because devolution in Scotland is a very new phenomenon, it is too early to draw significant conclusions. The UK government and the devolved administrations (with the exception of Northern Ireland) have been dominated to date by Labour or Labour-Liberal coalitions, which has resulted in the continuation of many predevolution mechanisms and relatively harmonious relations. The true test of devolution will come when different parties hold office, such as a euroskeptic Conservative government in Westminster or an SNP-led administration in Scotland. On the other hand, experienced Catalan political elites have demonstrated a high degree of political skill in negotiating favorable terms for Catalonia in securing greater access to the EU decision-making process. Political agreements with both the ruling *Partido Socialista Obrero Español* (Spanish Socialist Workers' Party or PSOE) and the *Partido Popular* (Popular Party or PP) parties in the 1990s allowed the Catalan nationalist coalition *Convergència i Unió* (CiU) to extract a series of concessions from the central government on greater involvement of subnational authorities in the EU policy process. However, following the results of the March 2000 general election in which the ruling PP obtained an absolute majority in the Spanish parliament, Catalan nationalists have been unable to attain any more concessions in this area, thereby slowing down the process considerably.

Finally, although the presence of nationalist movements in both Scotland and Catalonia has undoubtedly aided the ability of regional elites to influence the EU decision-making process, the success rates between the two vary enormously. The SNP remains a force operating primarily in Scotland, currently sending only 5 (of 72) Scottish MPs to Westminster and 2 (of 8) Scottish MEPs to the European Parliament. Some vote for SNP MPs and MEPs as a protest vote against the party in office, knowing that a strong showing will shake the main parties but is unlikely to affect the constitutional arrangements. Although the SNP may obtain greater influence over time through their efforts in the Scottish Parliament, the party's role as the self-proclaimed "official opposition" results largely from the proportional representation system used: the majority of their 35 (of 129) seats in the 1999–2003 parliament came from regional top-up lists rather than constituency-based victories, and their support is localized in certain sections of the country.

The situation differs in Catalonia, however, as domestic political considerations—most notably differences in the political opportunity structures—have until recently favored nationalists in their attempts to secure greater participatory rights in EU policy making. Together with its loss of majority in the Catalan Parliament following the October 1999 Catalan elections, CiU was left in a weaker position despite a minimal decline in support in the March 2000 general election, in which the PP was reelected by absolute majority. Internal divisions have also re-emerged within the CiU coalition on the extent to which the party should adopt a nationalist line. Following the March 2000 general election, however, CiU became Spain's third largest political force, and past experience has shown that governing parties at the central level may at times be forced to rely on its support (Roller 2001). Finally, the *Generalitat* has been ruled by CiU for nearly two decades, enabling it to consolidate and institutionalize its EU strategy.

CONCLUSION

Devolution in the United Kingdom and in Spain fits the wider trend of regionalization throughout Europe. As journalist Neal Ascherson (1994) observed,

> We can formulate a law of politics here. When European Union advances, so does regional autonomy. Conversely, when the project of union falters, Europe of the Regions also begins to slow down.

The gradual decentralization of powers in the countries analyzed in this chapter has been characterized by an absence of uniformity within political and administrative structures, providing interesting examples of subnational empowerment that has not resorted to the adoption of a federal state. This chapter highlighted some of the tensions between the historical centralizing tendencies of the UK and Spanish states and the devolution process favored by nationalist movements, explaining how the ongoing consolidation provides a framework from which current demands for greater subnational participation in the process of European integration have evolved. In both Scotland and Catalonia, the asymmetric nature of devolution, the constitutional ambiguity of the new governance arrangements, and the multiple channels employed by elites to access the EU policy process result in a complex web of networks, linkages, and relationships that have yet to be clearly defined.

From the Catalan case, it is clear that the ability of regional elites to secure greater involvement in EU policy making has reflected the uneven character of the decentralization process by remaining highly dependent on electoral outcomes and ensuing pacts of political cooperation. The youth of the Scottish Parliament makes it difficult to draw significant conclusions, particularly as many campaigners initially prioritized local autonomy and more inclusive domestic policy making. However, the European dimension—particularly Scotland's role in policy negotiations—has been and is likely to remain a key factor in discussions about further decentralization. The UK government will wish to be seen to include Scotland in negotiations, if for no other reason than to silence SNP calls for independence. The Scottish Parliament may also adopt some lobbying techniques utilized by its Catalan friends, as the link between these regions is strong and growing. During summer 2001, both Catalonia's president and presiding officer, accompanied by senior politicians, visited the Scottish Parliament. In a press release (September 18, 2001) announcing the latter's visit, Scotland's Presiding Officer Sir David Steel wrote,

> Throughout our devolution process, strong links were developed with Catalonia, particularly in terms of learning from their experience as a prominent European sub-state. . . . [During this visit we will] discuss issues of mutual interest such as the role of sub-state in Europe, cultural and linguistic diversity and participatory and electronic democracy. (Scottish Parliament 2001)

Indeed, it seems that Scots have much to learn from the quest of Catalan nationalists to achieve greater participatory rights in EU policy making.

REFERENCES

Ascherson, N. 1994. Local Government and the Myth of Sovereignty Charter 88. Sovereignty Lecture, February 25.

Bache, I. 1998. *The politics of European Union regional policy: Multi-level governance or flexible gatekeeping?* Sheffield: Sheffield Academic Press.

Blair, T. 1998. Speech to National Labor Party Conference, Blackpool, September 29.

Brown, A., D. McCrone, and L. Paterson. 1998. *Politics and society in Scotland.* 2nd ed. Basingstroke: Macmillan.

Conroy, H. 1992. Constitutional Convention's campaign. In *Scottish Government Yearbook*, pp. 74–83.

Consultative Steering Group. 1998. *Shaping Scotland's Parliament: Report of the Consultative Steering Group on Scotland's Parliament.* Edinburgh: HMSO.

Conversi, D. 1997. *The Basques, the Catalans and Spain.* London: Hurst & Company.

Giordano, B., and E. Roller. 2002. Catalonia and the "idea of Europe": Competing strategies and discourses within Catalan party politics. *European Urban and Regional Studies* 9 (2): 99–113.

Guibernau, M. 2000. Nationalism and intellectuals in nations without states: The Catalan case. *Political Studies* 48 (5): 989–1005.

Henders, S. J. 1997. Cantonisation: Historical paths to territorial autonomy for regional cultural communities. In *Nations and Nationalism*, Vol. 3, Part 4, pp. 521–40.

HM Government. 1999. *Memorandum of understanding and supplementary agreements between the United Kingdom government, Scottish ministers and the National Assembly for Wales.* SE/99/36, October. Edinburgh: HMSO.

Hooghe, L. 1995. Subnational mobilisation in the European Union. *West European Politics* 18 (3): 175–98.

Hooghe, L., and G. Marks. 1995. Channels of subnational representations in the European Union. In *What model for the Committee of the Regions? Past experiences and future perspectives*, edited by R. Dehousse and T. Christiansen, pp. 6–33. EU working paper EUF No. 95/2. Florence: European University Institute.

House of Commons Scottish Affairs Committee. 1998. *The Operation of Multi-Layer Democracy:* Second Report, Volumes 1 and 2, November 18. London: HMSO.

Jeffery, C. 1997a. Farewell the third level: The German Länder and the European policy process. In *The regional dimension of the European Union,* edited by C. Jeffery, pp. 56–75. London: Frank Cass and Co.

———. 1997b. Regional information offices in Brussels and multi-level governance in the EU: A UK-German comparison. In *The regional dimension of the European Union,* edited by C. Jeffery, pp. 183–203. London: Frank Cass and Co.

Kellas, J. 1992. The Scottish Constitutional Convention. In *Scottish Government Yearbook,* pp. 50–58.

Letamendia, F. 1997. Basque nationalism and cross-border cooperation between the southern and northern Basque countries. In *Regional and Federal Studies* 7, no. 2 (summer): 25–41.

Llobera, J. R. 1994. *The god of modernity: The development of nationalism in Western Europe.* Oxford: Berg.

Lynch, P. 1996. The Scottish Constitutional Convention 1992–95. *Scottish Affairs,* no. 15 (spring): 1–16.

MacCartney, A. 1990. Independence in Europe. In *Scottish Government Yearbook,* pp. 35–48.

Marks, G., and D. McAdam. 1996. Social movements and the changing structure of political opportunity in the European Union. *West European Politics* 19, no. 2 (April): 249–78.

Marr, A. 1992. *The battle for Scotland.* Harmondsworth: Penguin.

Mazey, S. 1995. Regional lobbying in the new Europe. In *The regions and the new Europe,* edited by M. Rhodes, pp. 78–104. Manchester: Manchester University Press.

McCrone, D. 1989. Thatcherism in a cold climate. In *A diverse assembly: The debate on a Scottish parliament,* edited by L. Paterson. Edinburgh: Edinburgh University Press.

Moreno, L. 1995. Multiple ethnoterritorial concurrence in Spain. *Nationalism and Ethnic Politics* 1 (1): 11–32.

———. 1997. *La federalización de España: Poder político y territorio.* Madrid: Siglo Veintiuno.

Paterson, L. 1994. *The autonomy of modern Scotland.* Edinburgh: Edinburgh University Press.

Quin, J. 1998. Speech to the Northern Irish Assembly, February 26.

Roller, E. 1999. Catalonia and European integration: A regionalist strategy for nationalist objectives. Unpublished Ph.D. thesis, London School of Economics.

———. 2001. The March 2000 general election in Spain. *Government and Opposition* 36 (2): 209–29.

Scottish National Party. 1992. *Independence in Europe: Make it happen now, general election manifesto.* Edinburgh: SNP.

———. 1997. *Yes we can win the best for Scotland: The SNP general election manifesto 1997.* Edinburgh: SNP.

———. 1998. *Towards the Scottish Parliament: Policy intentions for the 1999 elections.* Edinburgh: SNP.

Scottish Office. 1998. *Scotland Act.* London: HMSO.

Scottish Parliament. 2001. Catalan Parliament president to visit Scottish Parliament this week. Press release, September 18.

Sloat, A. 2002. *Scotland in Europe: A study of multi-level governance.* Bern: Peter Lang.

Solozábal, J. J. 1996. Spain: A federation in the making? In *Federalizing Europe? The costs, benefits and preconditions of federal political systems,* edited by J. J. Hesse and V. Wright, pp. 241–65. Oxford: Oxford University Press.

Unió Democràtica de Catalunya. Ponències, XX Congrés, Sitges, December 7–8, 1996.

5

The Internationalization of Scottish Politics: Who Governs Scotland?

Alex Wright

EUROPEANIZATION, MULTILEVEL GOVERNANCE, AND PARADIPLOMACY

Well before Scotland's parliament reconvened in 1999, stateless nations and regions had established informal ties with the European Union (EU). Some commentators coined the term "Europeanization" whereby a mix of actors including those from substate institutions (territorial government) were less reactive to European policies; instead they attempted to network and shape the European Union's agenda (John 1994, 739). Regional empowerment was encapsulated by the concept of multilevel governance (Hooghe 1995). This was a particularly interesting idea because it coupled the regionalization of the European Union (i.e., the formation of the Committee of the Regions, the entitlement of territorial ministers to vote in the Council of Ministers, and the principle of subsidiarity) with regionalism (i.e., regional mobilization from the grass roots up by territorial actors). Though this had its attractions, it was inherently asymmetrical because it varied from country to country due to the ability of central governments to act as gatekeepers—this led some to suggest that multilevel participation in the European Union was more appropriate (Bache 1998, 155). So, multilevel governance may have been better suited to federal states such as Germany, but it was less applicable to unitary ones like the United Kingdom, where it was of little worth to Scotland's situation (Wright 1998a).

Others have referred to paradiplomacy, which was indicative of how territorial institutions were becoming involved in international relations. As Aldecoa and Keating (1999) observed, this was by no means a new phenomenon, but its resurgence at the end of the last century was due to globalization and the emergence of continental trading regimes such as the European Union. Keating identified a number of factors at work such as the growing incapacity of states to mediate on behalf of their territories in the face of globalization coupled with the assertiveness of some territorial governments internationally. But he conceded that paradiplomacy was rather ambiguous and it did not appear to be "state transformative" (Keating 1999, 13). Others questioned the relevance of the nation-state in the era of the European Union and globalization. In so doing, they suggested that rather than paradiplomacy, the term "postdiplomatic" would be more apt. From this perspective non-central governments competed for political influence, investment, and access to markets—much of which resided in the international arena well beyond the reach of the nation-state (Aguirre 1999, 205).

What these concepts have in common is the idea that territorial governments have involved themselves increasingly in international affairs and that for the most part they cannot avoid doing so. Moreover, territories with a strong sense of national identity are liable to be more assertive internationally. Where they are less precise is the consequences for the central state-substate relations. The multilevel model suggests that the international policy of territorial actors complements that of their state. The paradiplomacy concept, although acknowledging the potential for tension and the relative weakness of states generally, does not imply that the foreign relations of substate actors has supplanted that of their central government—they have simply become additional actors in the international arena.

Scotland's situation is particularly interesting, not least because one day the Scottish National Party (SNP) might be in power and this is likely to result in a more conflictual relationship between London and Edinburgh over international affairs (Lynch 2001, 164). But as we shall see, foreign relations could well cause a rift well before then, even if pro-union parties remain in office in Scotland.

SCOTLAND AND THE EUROPEAN UNION PRIOR TO 1999: THE POTENTIAL FOR TENSION

Scotland's interests can differ considerably from the rest of the United Kingdom, and it is something of a challenge to contain them within a pan-UK position in the Council of Ministers (Wright 2000a). The bulk of the UK fishing fleet is located in Scotland. During the mid-1990s, it was evident that its priorities were quite distinct from fishermen in England when its leaders overwhelmingly preferred to remain in the Common Fisheries Policy than have fishing repatriated to the United Kingdom (Wright 1996). Oil has a major impact on the northeast's economy, with Aberdeen as Europe's leading center for exploration. Further down the coast, Edinburgh is one of the largest financial centers in Europe. Despite deindustrialization, Glasgow and its environs retain the vestiges of its engineering heritage. Environmentally Scotland is distinct by virtue of large tracts of wilderness and the fragility of its ecosystem. In the Highlands and Islands, crofting persists—there is nothing like this in the rest of the United Kingdom—the closest approximation being peasants in France. Scotland is particularly reliant on its infrastructure. Geographically it constitutes one third of the United Kingdom, but it has less than one tenth of its population, the bulk of which is situated in the Central Belt between Glasgow and Edinburgh. Road and rail links are therefore of paramount importance, and this is all the more significant as the country lies on Europe's periphery. Then there is the whiskey industry—again, nothing compares to this in the rest of the United Kingdom. It is a significant employer in rural areas where few other forms of employment are available, and it is a major export earner for Scotland, for the United Kingdom, and for the European Union.

The relationship between the European Union and Scotland provoked debate even before the United Kingdom became a member in 1973. Scottish civil servants argued in the 1960s that where appropriate they should be involved directly in policy making in the European Union rather than rely on government departments in London to represent Scotland's interests (Wright 2000a). But once the United Kingdom joined, that was not to be. After a brief lull, the issue returned to the political agenda during the 1980s and 1990s as a result of the SNP's manifesto commitment to independence in Europe. Essentially this was based on the premise that the central or state governments enjoyed the most influence in the European Union because of the Council of Ministers' role in determining policy. In effect they continued to enjoy influence collectively and individually at the European level—providing that it remained a confederal polity. In essence it rejected the *zero sum* position so beloved of Euroskeptics in the United Kingdom that when the European Union acquired more power, its member-states had less. Besides, that scenario ignored completely the consequences for the European Union's regions and stateless nations, whereby after every successive EU treaty it was they, rather than the member-states, that were relegated to ever greater political dependency. From the SNP's perspective, therefore, as more and more power was assigned upward to the European Union, Scotland was further and further removed both physically and politically from decision making (Scott 1992).

That said, in the aftermath of the Maastricht Treaty, the regionalization of the European Union did hold out the prospect of territorial government enjoying a more prominent role in the European Union's policy processes during the early 1990s. But some stood to benefit more from this than others. That applied particularly to those countries with devolved or federal systems of government where constitutional mechanisms ensured that territorial authorities exercised potentially a measure of control over how their state government conducted itself in the European Union—as was the case with the German Länder (Stolz 1994; Wright 2001). The reverse was true for Scotland prior to 1999, due in part to the highly centralized structure of the United Kingdom, with the result that its influence over EU policy was questionable (Scott, Peterson, and Millar 1994; Wright 1998b).

In the decade before devolution, much of Scotland's interests were either neglected or misrepresented by the UK government in Brussels. The oil industry failed to secure collateral funding from the UK Government with the result that it was less able to draw on EU funding for R & D due to the absence of additionality. Edinburgh failed in its bid to secure an offshoot of the European Central Bank because this was vetoed by the UK Cabinet. The whiskey industry endured successive hikes in duty in the United Kingdom, thereby weakening its case for harmonization of duty within the European Union. There was no transport strategy (Wright 1998b). The fishing industry failed to secure sufficient aid for decommissioning, with the result that overcapacity overwhelmed fish stocks to the point of collapse (Wright 1996, 2000b).

Aside from the fact that Scotland's EU interests could be quite distinct from the rest of the United Kingdom, there were essentially two interrelated deficiencies that were at the root of the problem. First, although Scotland did have its own territorial administration under the aegis of the then Scottish Office, it enjoyed little autonomy in relation to European affairs despite its attempts to develop a growing number of informal links with the European Union's institutions (Wright 1995). In effect, as far as formal processes were concerned, it was at the end of a chain extending from Brussels with London as gatekeeper. There was no assurance that it would be consulted over EU issues—though usually it was—and there was no assurance that its views would affect the United Kingdom's position in the Council of Ministers—which was questionable (Wright 1998b). But by far and away the greater defect was the absence of political leadership vis-à-vis the European Union. For the most part this did not exist, with the result that Scotland lacked its own distinctive agenda toward the European Union and European integration. Consequently Scotland was for the most part too reactive to events in Brussels, and it was one step removed from policy making in the European Union.

SCOTLAND'S RELATIONS WITH THE EUROPEAN UNION POST-1999: THE POTENTIAL FOR LEADERSHIP

There is the belief among Scots that legislative devolution will mean that Scotland would have more influence in the European Union (Brown, McCrone, Paterson, and Surridge 1999). In practice, however, will legislative devolution really make much difference to Scotland's relations with the European Union and thereby somewhat deflect the claim that Scottish independence in Europe remains the best option?

Superficially, the answer is no. Under the Scotland Act (1998), foreign affairs is "reserved" to Westminster. That is to say, legally it lies outside the competence of the Scottish Parliament and Executive. But could the Executive really afford to neglect foreign affairs—especially the European Union? That might be fine in theory, but the distinction between foreign and domestic policy is increasingly blurred (Salmon 2000; Keating 1998, 161). The European Union's policies affect a multitude of areas that have been devolved to Scotland—for example, economic development. So it would be surprising if the Executive failed to become involved, especially informally. That was acknowledged by the UK government's white paper on the Scottish Parliament (which was a precursor to the Scotland Act). The same can be said of the consultation exercise undertaken by the Consultative Steering Group (which post-dated the Scotland Act).

Both portended that Scotland would enjoy an extensive relationship with the Euopean Union, its member-states, and its territorial governments—albeit that, formally, the UK government would continue to represent Scotland in the Council of Ministers. The white paper explained,

> The Scottish Parliament and Executive will have an important role in those
> aspects of European Union business which affect devolved areas. (Scottish
> Office 1997)

In effect this was suggesting that the Parliament and Executive would
be especially involved in those EU policies that relate to devolved
matters. There could also be occasions when they might participate in
meetings of the Council of Ministers.

> The Government also propose that Ministers and officials of the Scottish
> Executive should have a role to play in relevant Council meetings and
> other negotiations with our EU partners. (Scottish Office 1997)

In practice this did not amount to anything new, as prior to devolution,
ministers from the then Scottish Office attended the Council from time
to time (Wright 1998b). It was also envisaged that the relationship
between London and Edinburgh would be close and that it would serve
the mutual self-interest of the two governments.

> Our proposals are designed to give the Scottish Parliament and Scottish
> Executive the opportunity to work constructively for the common interests
> of Scotland and the UK. The success of such a close working relationship
> and the ability to sustain it, will depend upon the way in which a Scottish
> Parliament and Executive respond to that opportunity. (Scottish Office
> 1997)

There was also the suggestion that the Executive might have its own
bureau in Brussels—this has now come to fruition with the opening of
Scotland House during 1999.

It was recognized that there was potential for conflict between the
two administrations as was the case for the new territorial arrangements elsewhere in the United Kingdom. Accordingly, a memorandum
of understanding was drawn up along with concordats in order to
formalize the intergovernmental relations between the United Kingdom and its territorial governments. An allied development was the
creation of a Joint Ministerial Committee; not only would this help to
foster good relations, it also had the potential to resolve conflicts,
though it did not have an executive function as such. That very much
set the scene for the entire arrangement. Although these various mechanisms were formal, in the sense that the UK government produced
them, they were inherently informal inasmuch as they were not legally
binding and would be subject to regular review (Wright 2000c; see also
Sloat 2000, 107). But they did serve to emphasize the hierarchical characteristics of the relationship between Westminster and the Scottish
Executive.

For its part, the Consultative Steering Group's (CSG) work was encouraging because it suggested that the Scottish Parliament would be proactive in relation to the European Union (though to be fair, there was reference to this in the white paper as well). One of its consultation documents on the European Union stated,

> The Scottish Executive and Parliament could form links with other countries and regions at a host of different levels. These might range from subject specific one-off visits (e.g. for fact finding) to co-operation programmes across a range of sectors. Links could be bilateral or multilateral. They could be taken forward in formal fora or through ad-hoc groupings (for example, in order to lobby for particular policy interests in the EU legislative process). (Scottish Office 1998, CSG)

Even though there was the rider in the document that these links should be "without prejudice to UK interests," it did imply that even in 1998 senior officials envisaged Scotland having some autonomy in relation to foreign affairs (Scottish Office 1998). When it was eventually published, the CSG report itself barely mentioned the European Union, save with regard to the function and composition of the Parliament's European Committee. This is unsurprising given that the primary role of the CSG was to offer members of the Scottish Parliament (MSP) draft procedures and working practices before the Parliament first convened. But the fact that foreign affairs had such a high profile within the Scottish civil service during the consultation exercise suggests that they at least were well aware that the issue would be significant postdevolution.

Yet once the Scottish Parliament reconvened in 1999, any sense of optimism was short-lived. In part this was because the institutional structure was complex. There was the parliament itself, the Scottish Executive, and a Scotland Office—each of which would be involved in EU matters, but it was far from clear how extensive this would be. The Secretary of State provides the political leadership at the Scotland Office, and the office holder, Helen Liddell, is a member of the UK Cabinet. There have been reports in the media that a single Cabinet minister for the United Kingdom's territories might replace this post. In the meantime the Secretary of State has two main functions. She has a watchdog role regarding the Scottish Parliament; under the Scotland Act, the Secretary of State is responsible for ensuring that the parliament not exceed its powers. She is also responsible for those matters that had been reserved to Westminster; the Scottish Secretary of State therefore sits on a number of UK Cabinet committees including those that relate to the European Union.

The Scottish Executive is responsible for those areas of policy that have been devolved to Scotland—which in effect amounts to anything that had not been reserved to Westminster. This includes fisheries, agriculture, the environment, economic development, and transport. Political leadership is provided by a group of ministers, the most senior of whom sit in the Scottish Cabinet, which is chaired by the First Minister. For its part, the Scottish Parliament has its own European committee. Despite the reserved status of external affairs, there is nothing to prevent MSPs from passing a resolution on European matters in plenary session and, if they so chose, condemning the United Kingdom's conduct in Brussels. Potentially that matters a great deal. If the parliament did pass such a resolution in relation to a given issue, in that instance how could the UK government legitimately claim to be speaking for the whole country in the Council of Ministers?

Moreover, that so many institutions have an involvement with the European Union is a recipe for confusion. For the most part the Secretary of State's profile on European matters has been nonexistent save for visits to member-states. The parliament's European committee has been meeting regularly and issuing reports on the implementation of the structural funds and the Common Fisheries Policy (CFP). But we have yet to see if it possesses the capacity for leadership—although it intends to examine the Scottish Executive's handling of foreign affairs. Until recently no Scottish minister had a remit for external relations (aside from the First and Deputy First Ministers, who had more of a ceremonial role in this instance). All of which suggested an absence of political leadership vis-à-vis external relations and by default, no EU agenda.

A DISTINCTLY SCOTTISH FOREIGN POLICY?

The issue of which minister in the Scottish Executive was responsible for Scotland's relations with the European Union remained far from clear during 1999. Alex Salmond, who was then the leader of the SNP, raised this with the First Minister during a parliamentary debate on Scotland and the European Union in November. He recounted how Robin Cook, who subsequently became Foreign Secretary, had informed the Scottish Grand Committee at Westminster that

> Labour's plans for devolution will create a Minister for European Affairs in a Scottish administration, set up a Scottish European office in Brussels accountable to a Scottish Parliament in Edinburgh, confer on Scottish Ministers the same observer status as that of the German Länder. (Official Report, House of Commons, Scottish Grand Committee, January 13, 1997; c 29)

But Mr. Salmond complained that when the Executive had been established in 1999, apparently there was no minister who had been formally assigned the European portfolio (Minutes of Proceedings, Vol. 1, No. 30, Session 1, Meeting of the Parliament, Wednesday, November 10, 1999).

At the time, the explanation rested on the premise that because European matters straddled the portfolios of several ministers, it therefore made sense for the responsibility to be shared out accordingly. Consequently no one was specifically responsible for it. Nonetheless it may well have reflected the concern that because relations with the European Union were reserved to Westminster, it was inappropriate to have created a Scottish Minister for Europe, as this would have indicated a measure of political leadership in an area of responsibility where the Scottish Parliament did not possess competence. In practice, however, the then–Finance Minister Jack McConnell played the most active role in part because of his involvement with EU funds and also because he became increasingly engaged in promoting Scotland's wider interests in Brussels. For example, McConnell was to have been at the forefront of the anniversary celebrations of Scotland House in Brussels during October 2000, though in the event they were overshadowed by Donald Dewar's death (Mr. Dewar was Scotland's initial First Minister).

In the run up to the Parliament's anniversary celebrations that autumn, McConnell was reported to be well satisfied with the dual benefits from Scotland being part of a larger state while at the same time developing its own links with the European Union postdevolution. He commented, "This is a very powerful example of devolution being a success for Scotland. I feel that European activity is one of the more successful areas where devolution has bedded down early" (*Herald* October 9, 2000). Such confidence may have been rather premature, because the European Union's impact on Scotland during 1999-2000 was relatively low key compared to the 1990s. In essence the extent to which Scotland can influence the European Union over a substantive issue has yet to be fully put to the test.

In the meantime, McConnell oversaw the development of links with international bodies such as the Congress of Local and Regional Authorities (CLRA), where he was a member of one of its working groups. This was very much what the civil servants who conducted the CSG consultation had envisaged in 1998. The CLRA was a subsidiary body of the Council of Europe (Council of Europe, http://www.coe.int), and although it lacked executive influence, it did enable politicians from territorial legislatures to meet and discuss matters of common interest. Before his death, Dewar was due to attend a conference of "the Presidents of Regions with Legislative Powers." This had been organized by the CLRA and would be held at Barcelona in November 2000. That such a figure was scheduled to attend this event demonstrates that senior Scottish politicians were quite content to participate in international fora regardless of the reserved power constraint.

When Henry McLeish became First Minister, McConnell was given a new portfolio. McConnell's formal title was to be Minister for Education, Europe and External Affairs. Although EU affairs are linked with Scottish education in all sorts of ways, this falls well short of the situation in his previous office as Finance Minister where the involvement with the European Union would have been greater. Arguably McConnell particularly wanted the European and external affairs portfolio because he recognized its political kudos and he did not hesitate to raise its profile around the time of the Nice summit in December 2000.

A week before the summit, a headline ran, "McConnell to Cast Foreign Policy Adrift from London." According to this report, he would

> Set out a new strategy for Scotland in Europe, which puts the Executive on a potential collision course with the Foreign Office in London. He is aiming to build strategic alliances with parts of the Continent to pursue Scotland's interests separately from those of the UK. Although it does not clash directly with Robin Cook, it represents the most significant extension of the Executive's role since the parliament was elected. (*The Sunday Herald*, December 3, 2000)

It also mentioned "phase two" of the Executive's "Foreign Policy" where the emphasis would be on "building links between Edinburgh and other parts of Europe." Another report also highlighted McConnell's "enthusiasm." When he spoke at a conference organized by the Scottish Center of Public Policy in Edinburgh, he implied that it was feasible to adopt a distinctively Scottish line on EU matters but still be a part of the British delegation. He said,

> One of the great benefits of devolution is that we can have a clear Scottish position in these matters and still be a part of the UK delegation that carries so much clout in Europe. It is about making sure that Scottish influence, first of all, is exercised. (*The Times*, December 15, 2000)

In sum this implies that regardless of the fact that foreign affairs are reserved to Westminster, Scotland *de facto* had a foreign policy.

According to McConnell, his primary objective was indeed to cultivate links with other regions and nations in Europe. One of his press releases explained:

> "Scotland must step up its involvement with Europe if it is to be in the premier division of legislative regions or nations within EU member

states," Jack McConnell, Minister for Education, Europe and External Affairs, said today.

"For the first time the Executive has a Scottish Minister with a specific responsibility for Europe. This demonstrates that it is a top priority for the Executive to engage constructively and thoroughly with the European Union. With the benefits of devolution, we are determined to make a step-change in our level of engagement. We have already done much to create links with other nations and regions. Now we need to move our engagement up a gear or two.". . .

"Ministers must do everything possible to raise Scotland's profile in the EU. We cannot move on alone though. We have to work in close partnership with others such as the local authorities, Parliament, our MEPs and our arts bodies. The objective of this increased activity is simple. It is to help achieve a Scotland in which both its people and businesses feel completely at ease in Europe: a Scotland influencing decisions which will ultimately affect us all and a Scotland where jobs dependent on European markets are secure." (News Release: SE3124/2000, December 4, 2000)

The tone of this release is illuminating. It implied that Scotland had not been sufficiently assertive in previous years—which presumably includes the first year of legislative devolution. It explicitly stated that Scotland should join "the premier division of legislative regions or nations." But what does that mean? It could relate simply to Scotland's economy, or it could mean that Scotland should be more influential in the European Union. That certainly seems to be the case according to the release's final few lines, where the "objective" was for a "Scotland influencing decisions which will ultimately affect us all." The conclusion to be drawn from McConnell's statement is that Scotland's government could not avoid an engagement in EU affairs primarily because it permeated so many areas of policy and also because what happened in the European Union could impact directly on Scottish interests.

This is certainly true as far as Scottish civil servants were concerned. The External Relations division, which is responsible for both EU affairs and international relations, had three priorities in relation to the European Union by early 2001:

1. To monitor and where necessary influence the UK line on the forthcoming enlargement.
2. To raise Scotland's profile within the European Union in relation to the smaller member-states, other territorial governments and the European Union's institutions.
3. To exchange ideas with other territorial governments on policy.

The division's other main concern was that because it was often responsible for transposing EU legislation into Scottish law, it should be consulted as early as possible by the European Commission, in case the latter was unaware that proposed legislation had a wider impact than intended. So, in this instance the desire to influence EU policy was concerned with functional prerequisites—the acquisition and dissemination of high-grade intelligence was therefore paramount. While Scotland House served as the Executive's eyes and ears in Brussels, its staff would also participate in the working groups of the Council of Ministers—where much of the policies were agreed upon before they were formally ratified by relevant ministers from the member-states.

This and much else was very much on Mr. McConnell's mind when he gave evidence to the European committee at the Scottish Parliament on December 12, 2000. He explained to the committee's members,

> In the EU, we see a momentum for enlargement that will take a boost from the weekend's agreements at the Nice intergovernmental conference. As enlargement takes place, the member states may retain their identity and their sovereignty in many areas and pool their strengths in other ways, but I think that we will also see an increasing demand for regional identity, regional networks and regional representation within the European framework.

The reference to increasing demand for "regional representation" demonstrated that he was well aware of territorial governments' aspiration to have greater influence over EU policy. As he subsequently observed, Scotland would not be excluded in this:

> We want to be part of that for two reasons, using the following criteria for the links that we develop and the activities that we get involved in. We cannot stand on the economic sidelines of north-west Europe and not develop the sort of trading and political links that will help the Scottish economy. That means working closely with those regions with which we have always had a close connection, such as the Scandinavian or Nordic countries, Spain, Germany, Belgium and elsewhere.

Indeed, he acknowledged that Scottish institutions had to be "ahead of the game." Although this related partly to tactics, it also was indicative of the need for a more strategic approach to the EU.

> The Executive and the committees of the Parliament should be identifying what the issues will be, not only in January, February, March, April, May and June in Sweden, but what will happen during the Belgian presidency in the second half of the year. In three or four months' time, we should start to think about what will happen in the first six months of the

following year. We should anticipate the issues that will arise and start to influence them six months ahead of the meeting of the European Council, rather than coming in at a later stage and intervening when it is too late—in European terms—to exert any influence. That is the strategy that I am trying to develop. (Scottish Parliament, European Committee, Committee Official Report, Meeting 21, December 12, 2000, Col 877)

Though much of this might be designed to convince the committee that the Scottish Executive was looking after Scotland's interests in the European Union, equally it simply affirms whether foreign affairs' reserved status amounted to much in practice.

Formally, reserved status means that ultimately only the UK government at Westminster has the authority to represent the interests of its territories. Only it can sign treaties, declare war, be a member of the United Nations, or participate in (most) intergovernmental summits. But in practice, as the authors of the paradiplomacy concept observed, diplomacy is no longer the preserve of states but a host of other actors, including substate governments. Few institutions of government beneath that of the state can afford *not* to have a foreign policy, because of the social and economic implications for their citizens.

More particularly, the capacity of states to govern their territories has declined. This is by no means a new development, but it has become more noticeable during the final decades of the twentieth century (Strange 1996). In part this is attributable to globalization, where multinational capital can have a substantive impact at the territorial level regardless of whether the state government approves. In addition, European integration has radically altered the government of Scotland (Wright 1998b). As a result of QMV in the Council of Ministers, it is perfectly possible for other member-states to agree to laws that affect Scotland directly regardless of whether the UK government is opposed to it—for example, that applied to the ban on exports of beef during the bovine spongiform encephalopathy (BSE) (mad cow) crisis. The issue of who governs Scotland is far more open-ended than it once was, which explains why some now refer to governance. All-in-all, politicians at the territorial level recognize that they have to deal with the UK government, the European Union's institutions, and its member states and where possible join or construct alliances with other actors in the international arena, whether they be other territorial governments, international fora, or multinational companies.

EXTERNAL RELATIONS: THE POTENTIAL FOR TENSION

With European integration proceeding—albeit in fits and starts—the issue of territorial empowerment may once again top the agenda.

Around the time of the Nice summit, newspaper reports suggested that some of the German Länder were calling for an EU constitution at the next Intergovernmental Conference (IGC) in 2004, which would delineate power between the various levels of government, including the substate tier (*The Times*, December 7, 2000). This may well explain McConnell's remarks to the Scottish Parliament's European committee about the growing "demand for regional representation" in the European Union.

Although an ardent unionist (with the caveat that his party is federalist), Jim Wallace, Scotland's Deputy First Minister, did emphasize the need for territorial empowerment in the European Union when he addressed the Conference of Presidents of Regions with Legislative Power at Barcelona in November 2000:

> At the same time as globalisation is having its effect, we as members of the EU, are taking forward one of our most significant projects, namely enlargement of the Union. This enlargement makes it all the more important to find ways of keeping local and regional actors positively engaged in EU policy making.

He continued,

> While we have some reservations about the details of the Conference declaration—on some of the IGC aspects, and on the Charter where we must recognise the heterogeneity of regions—we do believe that the regions with legislative powers should have a more prominent role in EU Governance.

> In Member States with a regionalised structure, decisions are taken at a level closer to regional economic and political forces, which thus have a direct means of interaction. The views of regions, and particularly those with the power to transpose EU legislation, should be tapped into to increase the effectiveness and legitimacy of EU proposals. (Wallace 2000)

Even though Wallace's words related essentially to functional issues such as policy implementation, the tenor of his speech is remarkable given the low profile of external affairs just twelve months earlier. A distinctively Scottish foreign policy has emerged within the Executive, and both the Deputy First Minister and McConnell have called for the European Union's regions (and by default stateless nations) to have more influence over its policy processes.

The change in approach to the European Union became more overt during the spring and early summer of 2001. In March the Scottish Executive and the Convention of Scottish Local Authorities (COSLA) produced a joint submission to the European Commission, in response to the Commission's (then forthcoming) white paper on the future governance of the European Union. The submission was controversial because it apparently advocated a more direct relationship between Scotland and the European Union, but how this was to be realized was rather more ambiguous. On the one hand the Executive and COSLA were calling for a greater involvement in EU decision making. For example, the second, third, and fourth principles stated

- We need to find ways of better engaging regional and local organisations in the EU decision-making process.
- It is particularly important to involve regional and local levels of government because they are democratically elected and implement much EU legislation. We think it is essential that the EU Governance debate addresses the potential for giving a greater role to Scotland and the other regions with legislative powers.
- Decisions should be taken at the lowest level (i.e. closest to the citizen) consistent with effectiveness (the subsidiarity principle). This becomes all the more important with enlargement.

The inference from this is that the authors were calling for the European Union to ensure that decision making was devolved to the lowest level of authority where appropriate, not least because it was the European Union itself that had instigated the governance debate in the first place and the paper was consequently directed at the European Commission. But the fourth principle explicitly affirmed that it should rest with the member-state to determine "the internal allocation of competencies":

- The EU institutions must respect the Member State's role in deciding the internal allocation of competences between it and sub-national authorities. (Joint Submission by Scottish Executive and COSLA to the European Commission, March 2001)

This is rather contradictory, as on the one hand the submission invokes the principle of subsidiarity and on the other it states that the member-state should decide how this should apply in practice. One conclusion, therefore, is that although this submission may have been presented formally to the European Commission, the underlying message concerning greater involvement was subliminally directed at the UK government.

However, the Executive/COSLA paper was rather overshadowed by the First Minister's involvement in the political declaration by the constitutional regions of Bavaria, Catalonia, Westphalia, Salzburg, Scotland, Flanders, and Wallonia on May 28, 2001. This is something of an ad hoc group of territorial governments all of whom have their own legislative assemblies who share the concern about their lack of influ-

ence over the European Union and its policies. The origins of this
network can be traced to September 2000, when its constituent members
hoped to have some effect on the IGC at Nice the following December.
Although Wales assisted as an observer at the September meeting, there
was no sign of Scottish involvement whatsoever, but by February 2001,
Scottish academics did participate in a colloquium of the constitutional
regions (entitled Reinforcing the Role of the Constitutional Regions in
Europe). Under the chairmanship of the Flemish minister-president, the
colloquium was intended to act as a think tank regarding institutional
reform and the role of the constitutional regions in the European
Union's policy processes.

Three months later, Mr. McLeish signed a political declaration, along
with the other constitutional regions (by this time Wales appeared to be
no longer involved). In the event, the declaration reflected the tenor of
what had been suggested at the colloquium. It identified the following
as areas of interest:

- The constitutional regions have a specific interest with regard to the
  debate on the future of the European Union. Firstly, the competencies
  of the constitutional regions are affected by the integration process.
  And secondly, the regions have an important role in implementing
  European legislation, but do not have a sufficient say in preparing
  and determining European policies and legislation. Therefore, the
  constitutional regions demand to participate directly in the prepara-
  tory work for the Intergovernmental Conference of 2004.
- The constitutional regions want a broader discussion than the
  themes listed by the Intergovernmental Conference of Nice and
  urge that 'the role and setting of the regions in the European policy-making process and the institutional framework' [emphasis added] will be
  added as a theme to be debated.
- The principle of subsidiarity has to be taken as the basis for the
  debate on the European Union's key tasks, a debate that has to
  result in an effective European Union that shall only take action if
  and insofar as the objectives of the proposed action cannot be
  sufficiently achieved on the regional and national level.
- The European Union's missions need to be carefully considered
  and, in keeping with the principle of subsidiarity, redefined by a
  clearer allocation of powers, so these can be more effectively distinguished from those of the Member States and their regions. In
  this respect the constitutional regions favour a flexible solution
  which would not hinder the European integration process.
- In order to ensure due compliance with the principle of subsidiarity and therefore guarantee full respect for the constitutional

regions' own areas of competence, the political role of these regions has to be strengthened within the European Union.

Potentially the most controversial element related to the European Court of Justice (ECJ), where the signatories demanded:

- The right for the constitutional regions, as exists for the Member States, to refer directly to the European Court of Justice when their prerogatives are harmed. Within the legislative framework, the main aim is to boost the contribution of the constitutional regions in the Council. This request is in the first directed towards the national policy level. The Member States should be required to take into account the views of their constitutional regions about matters that fall within the latter's policy areas. The European Union has to give way to the involvement of the constitutional regions in the decision-making process as has already been done through article 203 EC Treaty. (Political declaration of the constitutional regions Bavaria, Catalonia, North-Rhine Westphalia, Salzburg, Scotland, Flanders, and Wallonia)

This raises all sorts of possibilities. For instance, would it result in the UK government being brought before the ECJ by the Scottish Executive for infringing subsidiarity, in much the same way hitherto that individuals and organizations have sought redress at the European Court of Human Rights before the European Convention was incorporated into UK and Scottish legislation?

Addressing members of the European Movement in Perth on November 2, 2001, it was apparent from the First Minister's comments that the reference to the ECJ had been included in the declaration at the behest of the other signatories and that Scotland had little option but to go along with it if it was to continue as a participant. This was subsequently affirmed by Mr. McConnell during a discussion forum on Scotland and the European Union with Peter Hain, UK minister for Europe, on November 5th in Edinburgh (the author was present at both events and questioned all three ministers on the declaration). McConnell explained that although Scotland was a signatory of the declaration, he did not anticipate the Executive bringing cases on competence before the ECJ. For his part, Mr. Hain believed that the other signatories were pursuing the wrong track vis-à-vis the ECJ and that disputes over competence could best be resolved by politicians such as himself and McConnell rather than by the courts. Even so, if the declaration were to come to fruition and be incorporated in the treaties (which is unlikely at the time of writing), it would be interesting to see what would happen if completely different parties were in power in London and Edinburgh.

The European Union is not the only external affairs issue that has a high profile. As a result of the formation of the British Irish Council (BIC), Scotland is free to conduct bilateral relations with the Republic of Ireland. Some commentators claim that this can occur outside the BIC framework. According to Gerard Murray (2000), what matters most is the existence of a Scottish Executive:

> The fact that Scotland has an Executive means that the Irish government has a political engagement in Scotland. Therefore links between Scotland and the Irish Republic can be independent of the British Irish Council. (p. 131)

In 1999, Dewar visited Dublin on what was a quasi-state visit; his successor has invited Bertie Ahern, the Taosieach, to address the Scottish Parliament (albeit after an unseemly spat between the two governments over whether a formal visit by the Taosieach might incite sectarianism).

Yet external affairs remain highly controversial. After the First Minister visited Washington to celebrate "tartan day" in the United States in spring 2001, he had a brief meeting with President Bush. If that raised eyebrows in London, the subsequent announcement that an official from the Executive would be based in the United Kingdom's American embassy led to reports of a "worldwide Scottish diplomatic corps" and "Scottish envoys in the US" (*Sunday Times*, April 8, 2001, and the *Sunday Herald*, April 8, 2001). This was something of an overreaction, as for some years Scottish officials have been posted overseas under the aegis of Scottish Trade International. But the furor that surrounded this announcement is indicative of the problems that lie ahead if the Executive takes an even more overt approach to external relations than has been the case up until now.

WHO GOVERNS SCOTLAND?

Despite the reserved status of external affairs, Scotland cannot avoid having its own foreign policy. This particularly applies to its relations with the European Union. Prior to legislative devolution, the issue became ever more contentious as more and more power was assigned to Brussels. In part this was because the government of the day was unwilling and increasingly unable to promote and defend Scotland's interests in Europe. After 1997 that changed somewhat because the new Labour administration was much more sensitive to Scotland's needs than was the case hitherto and it enjoyed a more constructive working relationship with the other member-states in the European Union. Once legislative devolution had been set in train during 1999, it seemed for a short while that Scotland's approach to external relations would not alter radically, but within a year or so it was clear that the Scottish Executive was intent on developing a distinctively Scottish foreign policy. In the fullness of time it will be interesting to see the extent to which this can continue to converge with the position of the UK government. Given that Scotland's interests are distinct and given that one day, perhaps, radically different parties will be in office north and south of the border, divergence is the more likely scenario. In the meantime, increasingly it is the European Union rather than the United Kingdom that governs Scotland—regardless of its political affiliations, the Scottish Executive cannot afford to ignore this, and the same applies to globalization.

Although the potential for autonomy could be constrained by the Memorandum of Understanding, the concordats, and the Joint Ministerial Committee, the judicial legitimacy of these arrangements is questionable. Though the Scotland Act does circumscribe the potential for Scottish divergence, informally a precedent has been set. To date, there has been no objection by the UK government in London. But now Robin Cook (a Scot and allegedly pro-Europe) has been replaced by Jack Straw (an Englishman and allegedly more Euroskeptic) as the UK Foreign Secretary. News reports have suggested that the UK government might attempt to curtail Scottish expansionism into international relations (J. Robertson, *Sunday Times*, June 24, 2001). However, is it already far too late? That this situation has arisen can be attributed not necessarily to the political ambitions of ministers in the Scottish Executive, or nationalism, or benign neglect by politicians in London—although each may be partially true. Rather, it simply reflects the fact that Scotland is no longer solely governed by London but by a mix of polities, with the result that the governance of Scotland is ambiguous. Allied to which there is the seepage of state power as a result of globalization. Scottish politics has been increasingly internationalized, and the potential consequences for UK-Scottish relations will be considerable.

REFERENCES

Aguirre, I. 1999. Making sense of paradiplomacy? An intellectual inquiry about a concept in search of a definition. In *Paradiplomacy in action: The foreign relations of subnational governments*, edited by M. Keating and F. Aldecoa, pp. 185-209. London: Frank Cass.

Aldecoa, F., and M. Keating. 1999. Introduction. In *Paradiplomacy in action: The foreign relations of subnational governments*, edited by M. Keating and F. Aldecoa. London: Frank Cass.

Bache, I. 1998. *The politics of European Union regional policy. Multi-level governance or flexible gatekeeping?* Sheffield: Sheffield Academic Press.

Brown, A., D. McCrone, L. Paterson, and P. Surridge. 1999. *The Scottish electorate.* London: Macmillan.

Hooghe, L. 1995. Subnational mobilisation in the European Union. *West European Politics* 18, no. 3 (July): 175–98.

John, P. 1994. UK sub-national offices in Brussels: Diversification or regionalization? *Regional Studies* 28, no. 7 (November): pp. 739–46.

Joint Submission by Scottish Executive and COSLA to the European Commission. 2001, March. Appendix A.

Keating, M., 1998. *The new regionalism in Western Europe: Territorial restructuring and political change.* Cheltenham: Edward Elgar.

———. 1999. Regions and international affairs: Motives, opportunities and strategies. In *Paradiplomacy in action: The foreign relations of subnational governments,* edited by M. Keating and F. Aldecoa, pp. 1–15. London: Frank Cass.

Lynch, P. 2001. *Scottish government and politics* Edinburgh: Edinburgh University Press.

Murray, G. 2000. New relations between Scotland and Ireland. In *Scotland: The challenge of devolution,* edited by A. Wright, pp. 125–36. Aldershot: Ashgate.

Political declaration of the constitutional regions Bavaria, Catalonia, North-Rhine Westphalia, Salzburg, Scotland, Flanders and Wallonia. http://www.flanders.be/public/authority/search/index

Salmon, T. 2000. An oxymoron: The Scottish Parliament and foreign relations? In *Scotland: The challenge of devolution,* edited by A. Wright. pp. 150–67. Aldershot: Ashgate.

The Scotland Act. 1998.

Scott, A., J. Peterson, and D. Millar. 1994. Subsidiarity: A "Europe of the Regions" *v* the British constitution. *Journal of Common Market Studies* 32, no. 1 (March): 47–67.

Scott, P. H. 1992. *Scotland in Europe: Dialogue with a skeptical friend.* Edinburgh: Cannongate.

Scottish Office. 1997. *Scotland's Parliament.* Cm 3658.

———. 1998. Shaping Scotland's Parliament. The Consultative Steering Group on the Scottish Parliament.

Sloat, A. 2000. Scotland and Europe: Links between Edinburgh, London and Brussels. *Scottish Affairs,* no. 31 (spring): 92–110.

Stolz, K. 1994. The Committee of the Regions and Scottish self-government: A German perspective. *Scottish Affairs,* no. 9 (autumn): 13–23.

Strange, S. 1996. *The retreat of the state: The diffusion of power in the world economy.* Cambridge: Cambridge University Press.

Wallace, J. 2000. Introductory report by Mr. Jim Wallace QC MP MSP, Deputy First Minister and Minister for Justice, Scotland, CLRAE Conference of Presidents of Regions with Legislative Powers. November 23–24, 2000. Barcelona.

Wright, A. 1995. The Europeanisation of the Scottish Office. In *Region building,* edited by S. Hardy, pp. 81–85. London: Regional Studies Association.

———. Scottish fishermen and the EU: A choice between two Unions? *Scottish Affairs,* no. 14 (winter): 27–41.

———. 1998a. The Scottish Parliament and multi-level governance: Is territorial empowerment in the EU a myth or reality? Paper delivered at the University of East Anglia.

———. 1998b. Scotland and the EU: A case of subsidiarity or dependency? Doctoral thesis, University of Dundee.

———. 2000a. The Europeanisation of Scotland: A driver for autonomy. In *Europe united, the United Kingdom disunited?,* edited by M. Graves and G. Girrard, pp. 55–71. University of Brest.

———. 2000b. The 2002 review of the CFP. *Scottish Affairs*, no. 32 (summer): 59–74.
———. 2000c. Scotland and the EU: All bark and no bite? In *Scotland: The challenge of devolution*, edited by A. Wright, pp. 137–49. Aldershot: Ashgate.
———. 2001. *Scotland and the EU: Federalism or independence?* European Essay no. 18, the Federal Trust, London.

6

Wales and the European Union: Refining a Relationship

J. Barry Jones

INTRODUCTION

During the last decade of the twentieth century, the United Kingdom was subjected to contradictory pressures. On the one hand, the process of European integration toward "ever closer union" resulted in a reduction of the powers exercised exclusively by the Westminster Parliament. The United Kingdom progressively conceded its veto powers over a range of policies. Simultaneously there were pressures from the periphery for the devolution of powers from Westminster to Scotland, Northern Ireland, and Wales, which would further reduce the policy-making competence of the UK government. The United Kingdom has never been a paradigm unitary state, largely because it possesses obvious "union state" characteristics, particularly in the case of Scotland. By 1999, after the implementation of the devolution program, the United Kingdom had become a much more complicated polity with an asymmetric pattern of multilayered governance.

This chapter examines the Welsh contribution to this process and illustrates how the European integration issue became implicated in the Welsh devolutionary debate during the 1980s and 1990s. Welsh attempts to influence the European Community (EC) and later the European Union (EU), first by personal contacts and subsequently through the development of an informal policy network, reflect continuing Welsh apprehensions that its interests were not being sufficiently well articulated by the UK government. In part these concerns help to explain Wales's changing attitudes toward the United Kingdom. The dynamic of devolution released by Labour's election victory in 1997 and reinforced by the Welsh referendum in September of that year was a significant factor in the campaign to win Objective 1 status for Wales. A brief case study illustrates the political and constitutional crisis generated by this campaign. Finally, the chapter traces Wales's relations with the European Union during the postdevolution period and evaluates the new arrangements developed by the Assembly to improve those relations.

HISTORICAL BACKGROUND

In the course of the continuing debate on British accession to the then–European Community, the prevailing mood in Wales was, at best, suspicious. The Labour Party, the most dominant political force in Wales, was openly hostile. Many Welsh members of the Labour Party were opposed on ideological grounds and argued that the European Community was a "rich man's club," a capitalist creation with capitalist objectives (Welsh Council of Labour 1978). Given the enthusiasm of the Conservative government for British entry, this ideological critique was reinforced by party political interests. Nevertheless there were genuine Welsh economic apprehensions. Wales's geographic location is on the periphery of an off-shore island, and many Welsh Labour activists were fearful that Wales would become more peripheral in a European Union whose focus of economic activity was the golden triangle of the Ruhr, Germany, France, and the Benelux countries. Another concern expressed mainly, although not only, by Plaid Cymru (the Welsh Nationalist party) was that Wales did not fit the rationale and policy structures of the European Union insofar as it was a historic cultural nation rather than an economic region.

Despite the prevalence of these attitudes, the first test of public opinion on EC membership in the 1975 European Accession Referendum revealed strong support for British membership across Wales (Jones 1985, 89). Almost 65 percent of the Welsh electorate endorsed continued membership in the European Union (a higher vote than in Scotland or Northern Ireland), and Gwynedd, the Welsh county with the highest proportion of Welsh speakers, recorded a Yes vote of 70.6 percent, the second highest in Wales. Furthermore, all the Welsh counties voted in support of continued EC membership, apparently on the basis of their perceived economic interests.

In the wake of the referendum, the attitudes of the major political forces in Wales underwent a substantial change. Plaid Cymru felt obliged to change its anti-EU posture, no doubt influenced by the attitudes of Welsh-speaking farmers who recognized the probable benefits of the Common Agricultural Policy. Plaid Cymru came to regard the European Union in a different light as a more progressive, sympathetic, and supportive organization—a community of communities in which the Welsh community might thrive both economically and culturally (Plaid Cymru 1990).

The Wales Trade Union Congress (TUC), remained deeply skeptical but pragmatically decided to take advantage of the opportunities and benefits provided by the European Union, so long as Wales and the United Kingdom remained a member. The Labour Party's opposition was total, favoring withdrawal until the 1983 election when, via successive policy statements, it adopted a pro-European stance with the unqualified enthusiasm of the convert. In short, the parties in Wales learned to love the European Union.

NETWORKING THE COMMUNITY

Though there always has been a Welsh presence in the European Commission, it depended on key individuals in strategic posts. As such it was not a credible basis for the construction of an effective and continuing Welsh lobby. Arguably the most significant individual in terms of his activities in support of Welsh interests was Gwyn Morgan from the south Wales Valleys. In January 1973 he failed in his bid to be appointed the Labour Party's general secretary, resigned as assistant general secretary, and was appointed Chef de Cabinet to George Thomson, the British Commissioner for regional policies. His appointment was greeted with "great glee" in the Welsh Office (*Western Mail*, January 24, 1973). Subsequently Roy Jenkins, another expatriate Valleys Welshman, occupied the presidency from 1977 to 1981, and from 1981 to 1985 Ivor Richard, originally from West Wales, acted as Commissioner for Employment and Social Affairs. Although Welsh, and in one case Welsh speaking, they hardly represented a distinct Welsh interest other than as part of the UK interest. No doubt a sympathetic ear was granted from time to time to the odd Welsh complaint.

It is against this historical background, unpromising though it might appear, that the evolution of the complex network of consultative relationships between Wales and the EU must be judged. Within that network the role of the Welsh Office (WO) was central, but of equal and

sometimes greater significance were other UK government departments, such as the Department of Employment, Department of Industry, and the Ministry of Agriculture. In addition various government
agencies in Wales—for example, the Welsh Development Agency and
Mid Wales Development—played critical roles, as did other public
bodies such as local authority associations. Not least there was the
continual input of a wide variety of organized interest groups covering
all aspects of social, economic, and political life in Wales. On the
European Union side of the network, there was the European Commission Office in Wales, Welsh Members of the European Parliament (including its party groupings and committees), and the European
Commission (including those key directorates with an input to regional
support in all its forms). In the absence of political devolution, the
Assembly of Welsh Counties (1992) regarded itself as the only institution able to represent the whole of Wales. It established contacts with a
variety of European-wide territorial interest groups. These included the
Conference of Peripheral Maritime Regions (CPMR), the Assembly of
European Regions (AER), and the Atlantic Arc. This is by no means a
comprehensive list, but it does give an indication of the range and
complexity of the informal consultative network that evolved during
the 1980s as Welsh politicians attempted to raise the salience of Welsh
issues in Brussels.

To explain why such a network came into being, we need to look to
both political and administrative factors. The notion of a territorial
interest distinct from and possibly opposed to the UK interest was slow
to develop in Wales. The constitutional entity "England and Wales" had
put down deep roots, and the late revival of Welsh nationalism as a
political force in the 1960s made only limited progress in the business,
industrial, and trade union sectors. However, the creation of the Welsh
Office and the subsequent delegation of a wide range of administrative
functions brought an inexorable logic to which both government and
interest groups were obliged to respond (Kellas and Madgwick 1982).
A variety of organizations that did business with government, particularly but not only in those areas where functions had been devolved to
the Welsh Office, prudently established a Welsh institutional identity
within their organizations. As the Welsh Office acquired more functional responsibilities, so the tendency for Welsh interests to organize
became more pronounced. This process accelerated after 1979, when the
Select Committee on Welsh Affairs was set up, further encouraging
various sets of interests to focus their activities at the Welsh level so as
to influence the application of government policy in Wales.

Organized interests in Wales, including political parties, were equally
active in seeking to influence the European Community, an exercise
seen as complementary and—in some circumstances—as an alternative

to lobbying the British government. Throughout the 1980s the Thatcher government was unsympathetic to demands for government intervention and public investment and, consistent with its anticorporatist stance, hostile to large-scale socioeconomic groups, particularly the trade unions. Although the Welsh Office was to some degree insulated from the excesses of Thatcherite economic policies, its discretionary powers were restricted. Welsh trade unions soon realized that concessions to Wales were most likely to be extracted from London by confidential ministerial discussions and that public lobbying could, as likely as not, be counterproductive. By contrast, the institutions of the European Union were eager to be lobbied. Even though the EU benefits were small and virtually cancelled out by the nonadditionality practice, the lobbying exercise publicized and reinforced the Welsh interest and publicity gained by one Welsh pressure group encouraged others to take the Brussels road. The process did not displease the Welsh Office, whose ability to argue the Welsh case with the Treasury was enhanced by evidence of Welsh organizations actively promoting their case.

Lobbying the European Union created strange and unlikely Welsh partnerships. In 1981 the rapid decline of the Welsh steel industry, as required by the Davignon Plan, brought into existence the South Wales Standing Conference. The Conference included South Wales MPs, Welsh MEPs, local authorities, Wales TUC, Confederation of British Industry (CBI) Wales, and community organizations in the area. The intention was to focus on the industrial and social problems and come up with recommendations to help alleviate the crisis. Little was expected of Mrs. Thatcher's government, and aside from the presentation of its report and recommendations to the Welsh Office, the Standing Conference concentrated its efforts on the EU Commission. Thereafter the Welsh organizations and interest groups represented on the Standing Conference regularly lobbied Brussels both jointly and singly. After some procedural disagreements with the British TUC, the Wales TUC established its right to give its own independent evidence to European parliamentary committees. CBI Wales adopted a similar role in its dealings with Brussels, frequently acting jointly with Wales TUC in what was seen as a common Welsh interest that overrode partisan differences.

I indicated earlier that the Welsh Office occupied a central position in the informal consultative network. After the United Kingdom became a member of the European Union, the Welsh Office assumed additional responsibilities in respect to the procedures for funding applications. The European Affairs Division of the Welsh Office was set up in 1973 with a principal and one assistant and later expanded. Within the Economic and Regional Policy Division, ERPI was almost exclusively concerned with EU matters as they related to the coal and steel industries and the social aspects of their decline; ERPII was broadly concerned with tourism, the environment, and conservation matters working with and through the Welsh Tourist Board and Mid Wales Development. The European Affairs Division was reformed in 1989 to take account of the changes in the EU regional and structural funds; the larger unit within the division was concerned with applying the structural funds, consulting with and advising local authorities, promoting development programs to attract EU support, and generally trying to anticipate future trends in funding policy to ensure that Wales gained a fair share of the funding allocations. The unit, comprising three persons, was essentially a coordinating body acting as a conduit of EU information to various European sections of Whitehall departments. But of far greater importance was its role within the Welsh Office ensuring that all its sections and divisions were aware of EU policies as they affected Wales.

By 1990, EU directives impacted on virtually all divisions and departments within the Welsh Office and required intradepartmental liaison committees. In consequence an increasingly well-defined Welsh interest emerged during the Thatcher and early Major years (Jones 1995, 90). In matters relating to Europe, the Welsh Office did what any government department would do: It protected and promoted the interests of its constituency—in this case, Wales.

During the 1980s and for most of the 1990s, Wales lacked a political identity and political institutions. All power lay with the Westminster Parliament and Whitehall, and Wales's links with the European Union were strictly informal. This basic constitutional reality had significant consequences for the consultative network.

1. Welsh local authorities through their associations were inhibited from entering into agreements with European regional/local authority organizations because of their limited legal and financial powers.
2. The Welsh Office was inhibited from pushing the Welsh case because they were a British government department and were obliged to relate specific Welsh interests to more general British interests.
3. The European Commission, although eager to establish contacts with British regions (i.e., Scotland, Wales, and Northern Ireland), was constrained by the constitutional realities of the United Kingdom.

Because of these limitations, attempts were made in Wales during the early 1990s to create a more tangible framework for the consultative network. These attempts took three forms:

1. Emphasize the Welsh regional dimension by associating Welsh local authority associations with European regional organizations

such as the Conference of Peripheral Maritime Regions, the Assembly of European Regions, the Council of Regional and Local Authorities, the Atlantic Arc—in effect, a form of regionalization by association.

2. Create a center in Brussels dedicated to coordinating the lobbying activities of a variety of Welsh organizations. Welsh local authorities had been pushing for this development since the early 1980s. But the Welsh Office withstood the pressure, arguing that the Welsh interest could best be served by interdepartmental discussions between the Welsh Office and the various lead departments in Whitehall. Despite this, the Welsh Development Agency (WDA) took the initiative in April 1991 and announced that it was to set up a Center to support Welsh lobbying in Europe. The Center became a central element in the WDA's operations, particularly in supporting Welsh Development International's promotion of inward investment from the member-states of the European Union.

3. Link Wales with the regions of Baden-Württemberg, Rhône-Alpes, Lombardy, and Catalonia (the so-called four motor regions of the EU) to promote technological collaboration, research and development, and economic and cultural exchanges.

These developments reflected a growing sense of regionalism and regional competition within the European Union. Increased regional activity in Europe also changed attitudes in the British government. For example, the Welsh Office justified ending its opposition to setting up a Welsh center in Brussels with reference to the developing links with Baden-Württemberg. The WDA, a longtime supporter of the project, specifically linked the establishment of the center with the four motor regions, noting that each one had its own office in Brussels. If there was any doubt that there was a regional dynamic within the European Union, it was surely removed by the Maastricht Treaty, in which Article 198-A set up the Committee of the Regions.

PART OF THE UNION

Objective 1

As the 1976 general election came ever closer, the realization that a Labour government would be elected became increasingly certain. It was clear that devolution would head Labour's legislative program. Although the devolution project was mostly concerned with Scotland, it was accepted that Welsh devolution would be part of the package. Tony Blair's election as party leader in 1994 also confirmed that Labour's commitment to the European Union would be given a high priority. New Labour's European enthusiasm replaced the grudging acceptance of the European Union characteristic of the Major government in the early 1990s. In the new political environment, Labour ministers in the Welsh Office adopted a more proactive policy vis-à-vis the European Union.

The new government's initial objective for the Welsh Office's EU policy was to win Objective 1 status for Wales. There was a generally held view that dividing Wales into north and south regions disregarded Welsh social, economic, and cultural diversities that exist astride the east-west axis. More significantly the traditional north-south division of Wales actually disguised the economic backwardness of the south Wales Valleys and rural west Wales. In these circumstances the statistics used by Eurostat masked the imbalance of wealth between eastern and western Wales and produced data that disqualified Wales from applying for Objective 1 status. The first task of Labour's Welsh ministerial team, therefore, was to reform the Welsh Nomenclature des Unités Territoriales NUTS2 map (Cheney 2001).

There was an urgency to the project. The expansion of the European Union toward eastern European countries, whose weak economies were having to accommodate to the post-Communist world, meant that the Objective 1 program for 2000–2006 would be probably the last chance for Wales to qualify for Objective 1 funding. The sense of urgency was heightened by the government's devolution proposals and the need to show the Welsh electorate that devolution could work to Wales's benefit. That sense of urgency was reflected in the Welsh politician Neil Kinnock's interview in the *Western Mail* (January 19, 2000) in which he argued that obtaining Objective 1 status for Wales was a battle that had to be won. It was "a battle of the statisticians, bureaucrats and politicians, a battle to disrupt commonly held assumptions about Welsh demographics, a battle to beat a rapidly-ticking clock." Part of the battle—in some ways the most important part—was to convince the Office for National Statistics to accept the new east-west map and specifically that the boundaries for new Welsh NUTS2 had integrity, were coherent, and were not simply a gerrymander. The new map was the product of extensive collaboration and included not only civil servants from the Welsh Office but representatives from the Welsh European Center as well as officials from Welsh local authorities. The Welsh Secretary of State, Ron Davies, invited Jacques Santer (President of the Europe Commission) to visit west Wales and the Valleys so that he could meet with local councillors, businessmen, and trade unionists. Ron Davies and the Welsh Industry Minister, Peter Hain, subsequently went to Brussels to press Wales's case upon Monika Wolf-Mathies, the EU Commissioner for Regional Policy. By November 1998 the new map was accepted: Wales and the Valleys were shown to have a GDP of 73 percent of the EU average and were thus eligible for Objective 1 funds. Although this process was completed before the first elections to the Welsh Assembly (in May 1999), there is little doubt that devolution was an influential backdrop to the negotiations. The Labour government was determined that the Welsh Assembly would have the necessary EU funds to address Wales's problems.

A Role for the Assembly

In the wake of the September 1997 devolution referendum, the Secretary of State for Wales established a National Assembly Advisory Group (NAAG) to consider the working arrangements for the new Assembly. In its report, published in December 1998, the group called for a standing committee on European issues and, inter alia, for the National Assembly to play a role in the Wales European Center in Brussels, then sponsored mainly by the Welsh Development Agency, and Whitehall's representation in Brussels, UK Rep (NAAG 1998). Given the complexities of executive devolution and the fact that the European Union has only formal relations with member-states, it was unclear what the legal and political parameters of the National Assembly would be.

Further evidence of the importance of the European Union for the operation of Welsh devolution was provided by the establishment in June 1998 of a European Standing Group under the chairmanship of Hywel Ceri Jones, a high-profile civil servant in the European Commission until his retirement earlier that year. The report (Welsh Office 1998) vividly illustrated the high expectations of a developing relationship between Wales and the European Union. For example, it recommended that Wales should do the following:

- Take a more proactive role in shaping and developing European policies.
- Achieve a higher profile in Europe.
- Use its European connections to promote stronger growth and greater competitive capacity as well as the creation of more jobs and social solidarity throughout Wales.

In support of these high aspirations, the strategy group made a series of key recommendations. Taken together, they were designed to create a new positive culture toward the European Union, involving public and private bodies, national and local authorities within Wales, and an effective working relationship between the National Assembly and the UK government. On the narrower issue of the precise role of their proposed Standing Committee on European Policy, the group clearly envisaged the following:

- The appointment of a Cabinet Minister for Europe
- The creation of a standing committee that would specialize in European matters sufficient for it to advise the Assembly and the Cabinet on all European issues affecting Wales
- That the standing committee would meet on a quarterly basis with the Welsh Forum (a body intended to bring together various partner interests) to review progress on the promotion of Wales in Europe

Some of these designated roles for the standing committee begged serious questions about the detailed manner of its operations. Clearly it was intended that it would raise the salience of European Union issues and assist in developing Welsh policies. This was a continuing and long-term objective. Significantly, however, the short-term policy aspiration—obtaining Objective 1 status for parts of Wales and the coordinated use of EU structural funds—was to be "firmly within the Subject Committee dealing with Economic Development."

A COMMITTEE OF EUROPEAN AFFAIRS

The establishment of an overarching committee on European Affairs was one of the few statutory requirements relating to committees in the Government of Wales Act. Part of the devolution debate in Wales had focused on the frustrations in developing a progressive relationship with the European Union, attracting more funding, and resolving the problem of additionality. Both the British government and Welsh Labour politicians placed a high priority on the establishment of a European Committee.

The terms of reference of the Committee of European Affairs (CEA) are detailed in Standing Order 15 of the National Assembly for Wales. They are extensive and would appear to place an onerous burden on the CEA, which is required to keep under review the Assembly's relations with the European Union, the Assembly's liaison arrangements with UK Rep and UK government departments, and the Assembly's methods for considering documents for EU institutions. In addition, the CEA monitors the "general impact for Wales of EU Politics" and ensures "adequate liaison" with Welsh MEPs and Welsh representatives on the Committee of the Regions. These responsibilities would seem to include virtually all aspects of EU relations with Wales. The terms of reference fail to indicate either priorities or procedures; they are left for the CEA to decide. A similar discretion applies to the CEA's relationships with the National Assembly's subject committees. Whereas the terms reasonably suggest that the CEA "shall avoid duplicating the work of the subject committees," it is expected to draw particular issues to the attention of relevant subject committees. When, in the CEA's opinion, proposed European legislation affecting Wales falls within the remit of more than one subject committee, the CEA may itself report on the significance of the proposed legislation.

The terms of reference are a catchall, not so much specifying the CEA's responsibilities as facilitating its intervention in any aspect of EU relations. This would be a considerable burden on any Assembly committee, but in the case of the CEA it is virtually intolerable. Almost without exception, the CEA is composed of senior members of the National Assembly, party spokespersons, ministers, and committee chairs.

It had been expected that a powerful Minister for Europe would chair the committee, thus ensuring a high profile to European affairs. In practice it is difficult to argue that such expectations have been realized. The First Minister, initially Alun Michael and after February 2000 Rhodri Morgan, has occupied the European Committee chair. But his range of responsibilities—which include running the administration, chairing the cabinet, and usually chairing the Economic Development Committee—inevitably limits the time and energy he can devote to European Affairs. Furthermore while all the other committee chairpersons are distinct from the Executive and able to harry and criticize it, the Chair of European Affairs self-evidently is not. Some members of the National Assembly have been critical of this apparent conflict of interest. They have not been fully satisfied with the claim made by the First Minister that issues raised in the European Affairs committee can be fast tracked to the Cabinet. In these circumstances the CEA cannot reasonably be expected to perform all its functions. They must either be delegated to civil servants or disregarded.

Anticipating the pressures of discharging all its functions, the CEA decided at its first meeting that Welsh MEPs, Welsh representatives to the European Economic and Social Committee (ECOSOC) and the Committee of the Regions, European Commission Representation in Wales, and the Head of the Assembly's Office in Brussels would all receive CEA papers and be able to attend and speak at CEA meetings. This changed the nature of the CEA, further differentiating it from the other Assembly committees.

In the CEA's first year of operation, between July 1999 and June 2000, it met on five occasions, its schedule and its deliberations to some extent disrupted by political developments that resulted in one First Secretary and Chair (Alun Michael) being replaced by another, Rhodri Morgan. Nevertheless, it made significant progress in developing the Assembly's relations with the European Union (CEA 2000).

A priority for the CEA was upgrading the Assembly's representations in Brussels. The Wales European Center (WEC) was already in existence monitoring policies affecting Wales, lobbying and networking to help promote Welsh interests, and generally providing information for Welsh organizations, both public and private bodies. CEA members decided from the outset that the WEC could provide valuable support services but that the Assembly should be represented in Brussels in its own right. A Welsh Assembly office was opened in May 2000, partly occupying a building used by the Wales European Center. Two officials, appointed by the Assembly, were given diplomatic status and were able to "hot desk" at UK Rep offices. In anticipation of opening of the Assembly office, the Committee visited Brussels in March 2000 to meet with Welsh MEPs and to attend a reception arranged by the WEC. A meeting with UK Rep was followed by a meeting with Commissioner Neil Kinnock together with a number of Welsh officials working for the Commission. This was essentially a "get to know you" symbolic event, but it was important because it announced the arrival of Wales as a political actor on the Brussels scene.

The CEA also considered other avenues that might be taken to further enhance the Welsh profile with reference to the four motor regions, the Assembly of European Regions, and the Conference of Peripheral Maritime Regions but took no action at this time. The CEA also approved a program of strategic secondment from the Assembly to various EU institutions and agreed to a target of six secondments a year by 2003. In November 1999 the CEA chair (also First Minister) asked all the Assembly ministers to commission reviews of the impact of EU policies on their respective subject committees for consideration. Again one can detect a symbolic element to the task, setting the foundations for the Assembly—and its committees—to make them more aware of the EU dimension in their respective policy deliberations. There is little tangible evidence that this happened.

The impact of CEA activities on Wales and the Welsh public was slight. A Wales European Forum involving 100 delegates from the public, private, and voluntary sectors was held in Cardiff in October 1999. The following year, in May 2000, a similar event was held in Newport. Both left barely a ripple on the Welsh political scene. At the end of its first year, the CEA recognized in its first report that "EU policies were central to many of the Assemblies responsibilities" but that "there was still much to do"—a sentiment with which supporters and critics of the CEA agreed.

The Second Annual Report of the Committee on European Affairs (2001) covered four meetings over a period of ten months. The evidence therefore suggests that activity levels failed to meet those set by the CEA in its first year. There was, however, a series of "firsts" of some significance in the development of the United Kingdom's developing relationship with the European Union. In November 2000 the Assembly

Minister for Education and Lifelong Learning led the UK delegation at the Youth Council in Brussels. In the same month the Welsh Rural Affairs Minister attended the Agriculture Council. In the words of the CEA's annual report (2000–2001), "The Participation of (Welsh) Ministers in representing the UK within the European Union was a great step forward and helped raise the profile of Wales within Europe." At the end of the committee's first year of operation (June 2000) a series of criticisms had been voiced concerning the CEA's role; specifically that it had been too passive and had failed to scrutinize EU legislation. CEA's procedures were compared unfavorably with those of the Scottish Parliament (Gwilym, 2000). A Welsh Administration Paper (2000) argued for increased scrutiny of policy statements but also urged that National Assembly officials should attend departmental meetings in London to make the Welsh case prior to meetings of the Council of Ministers in Brussels in order to influence European Union policies more effectively. A similar argument was deployed by a retired diplomat, now chairman of the Welsh Center for International Affairs. He argued the case for better communication between Cardiff and Whitehall, more detailed concordats, and a role for the Welsh Secretary of State as a channel of communication between the two levels of government (Gray 2000).

These criticisms clearly concerned the committee, which desired to be more active in scrutinizing legislative proposals but was aware of the dangers of overwhelming members with the vast amount of EU documentation (CEA 2001). One possibility noted was to give the subject committees more systematic and targeted information on significant EU legislative proposals and policy and funding initiatives. The CEA's own examination of the Commission's annual work programs could thus alert the CEA to strategic priorities. Regardless of the priority allocated to this task, one cannot but suspect that the CEA's scrutiny role is compromised by a continuing manpower problem. In other areas, the CEA's intention to involve Welsh MEPs and representatives on the Economic and Social Committee (ECOSOC) and the Committee of the Regions have not been successful. MEPs, in particular, have wide responsibilities, both functional and geographic, and there have been scheduling clashes. The Wales European Forum had also fallen short of expectations, and a reform to make the body into a think tank and a place for the exchange of ideas is under consideration.

CONCLUSION

The achievements of the National Assembly for Wales in the sphere of European Union affairs are limited. The high expectations of Wales developing a positive relationship with the European Union, which played such an important part in the devolution debate during the 1980s, have not yet been realized. The most significant achievement, winning Objective 1 status for Wales, was the product of the old pre-devolution governmental institutions: the Secretary of State for Wales and the Welsh Office. The National Assembly was merely a beneficiary, and even in this area there have been criticisms that the planned program of expenditure lacks coherence and professionalism. While there have been difficulties, partisan factors have played a part in the criticisims.

One could be forgiven for concluding that Welsh devolution has moved through its initial formative period with little reference to or influence on Europe. However, it could also be that the expectations of the 1980s and early 1990s were unrealistic and failed to recognize the constitutional realities of the United Kingdom. As the *Second Annual Report* of the Committee on European Affairs notes, the real problem is concerned with developing effective relations between the Assembly and UK government departments to ensure that Welsh interests are fully taken into account at the earliest possible stage in the EU legislative process.

However, EU influences can and do penetrate deep into the Welsh economy and the Welsh political system. In the course of 1999, matched funding for Objective 1 became a political issue in the National Assembly, with opposition parties pushing for additional Treasury funds to provide the finances necessary to cover the first year of Objective 1. The Treasury proved unwilling to make a firm commitment prior to the completion of the current three-year comprehensive spending review. Alun Michael, the Welsh First Minister, was unable to persuade the Treasury, and doubts about his leadership resurfaced amid claims that he was Blair's man and part of Labour's control system. A vote of no confidence was tabled, and on February 9, 2000, the vote was taken amid much confusion and recrimination. Alun Michael lost the vote and tendered his resignation initially as First Minister and later that day as leader of the Welsh Labour Party. The issue that brought him down was a combination of EU funding, Treasury support (or lack of it), and a breakdown in relations between the Assembly and Whitehall (Jones and Balsom 2000, 265). It was a classic example of the difficulties of multilayered governance.

ACKNOWLEDGMENT

Research for this chapter is funded by the ESRC as part of its Devolution and Constitutional Change program.

REFERENCES

Assembly of Welsh Counties. 1992. *Political and economic union in Europe: The Welsh dimensions conference report, January.* Cardiff: AWC.

Cheney, A. 2001. *The Objective 1 process in Wales: The opportunity for the emergence of new Welsh politics.* Unpublished M.Phil. thesis. University of Wales.

Committee of European Affairs (CEA). 2000. *First annual report.* Cardiff: National Assembly for Wales.

———. 2001. *Second annual report.* Cardiff: National Assembly for Wales.

Gray, J. 2000. Welsh Europeanism, Whitehall and Brussels. *Agenda* (winter): 37–40.

Gwilym, L. 2000. *The ineffectiveness of the National Assembly's European Committee.* Plaid Cymru research paper.

Jones, B. 1985. Wales in the European Community. In *Regions in the European Community,* edited by M. Keating and B. Jones, pp. 89–109. Oxford: Clarendon Press.

———. 1995. Nations, regions and Europe: The UK experience. In *The European Union and the Regions,* edited by B. Jones and M. Keating, pp. 89–115. Oxford: Clarendon Press.

Jones, B., and D. Balsom. 2000. *The road to the National Assembly for Wales.* Cardiff: University of Wales Press.

Kellas, J. G., and P. J. Madgwick. 1982. Territorial ministries: The Scottish & Welsh offices. In *The territorial dimension in United Kingdom politics,* edited by P. Madgwick and R. Rose, pp. 9-34. London: Macmillan.

National Assembly Advisory Group. 1998. *Report.* Cardiff.

Plaid Cymru. 1990. *Wales in Europe: A community of communities.* Cardiff: Plaid Cymru.

Welsh Administration. 2000. The paper was tabled on November 30, 2000, and included in the minutes of the Committee on European Affairs.

Welsh Council of Labour (WCL). 1978. *The Common Market and Wales.* Cardiff: WCL.

Welsh Office. 1998. *National Assembly for Wales and the EU: European Standing Group Report.* Cardiff: WO.

7

Multilevel Governance in the European Union: The Case of Northern Ireland

Susan Hodgett and Elizabeth Meehan

INTRODUCTION

Since the Maastricht Treaty of 1993, speculation has abounded regarding changes in methods of governance within the European Union. Theorists of multilevel governance (MLG) suggest that there has been "a double shift of decision making" away from nation-states to the market and from the nation-state to the European level (Hooghe and Marks 1997, 2). The deepening of the market, it is argued, has led to a contest for power between the European Union's traditional elites, notably between the European Council and the Commissioners. Paradoxically, it seems, these changes have also allowed the involvement of nontraditional groups in the process of governance. According to theories of MLG, those who are newly drawn into the process of European governance include actors within European social movements and within interest groups.

Hooghe (1996, 95) has argued that it is on the periphery of the Union that one is likely to find the flexibility in policy-making processes to allow this process to begin. Overall, Hooghe and Marks (2001, xi) conclude that what now takes place in peripheral European regions is

"the dispersion of authoritative decision making across multiple territorial levels."

Northern Ireland is clearly a peripheral region within the European
Union. Thus, if MLG theories are correct, then we should find evidence
of changes in the way in which policy is made in Northern Ireland as a
result of shifts in power within the Union. Notably, we should find
changes in the composition of the actors involved in the policy-making
process. The argument of this chapter is that policy evolution in Northern Ireland does appear to provide some authority for such theories of
MLG. We illustrate this by analyzing shifts in the roles of institutions
(in general and in the case of Northern Ireland) and in the development
of regional and cohesion policies.

CHANGING EUROPE, CHANGING GOVERNANCE

Marks, Hooghe, and Blank (1996, 341) argue that European integration has resulted in the decline of the power of the nation-state. The
growing importance of the Commission in the policy process is clear. It
is also true that under certain conditions and in certain policy areas the
Commission is capable of autonomous action (Hooghe 1996, 92). On the
other hand, there are also changes in forms of interest representation
and active cooperation between trade unions or interest groups and the
state. Such groups also interact with Commissioners and Commission
civil servants. The latter's involvement in a diverse number of policy
networks in Europe indicates that neither the Commission nor state
executives are unitary actors with fixed preferences. Rather they are
"institutions consisting of diverse actors with divergent interests involved in variable networks" (Hooghe 1996, 92).

Central to this model of European governance is the notion that states
do not monopolize relationships between domestic and European actors and that, as Marks, Hooghe, and Blank (1996) put it, "complex
interrelationships in domestic politics do not stop at the nation-state,
but extend to the European level" (346). Thus, if power is shifting away
from the nation-state, it will be necessary to "relax the conceptual
boundaries between these historically circumscribed political forms"
(Marks, Scharpf, Schmitter, and Streeck 1996, 97). Moreover, the MLG
concept, in adopting an actor-centered approach to the decision-making process, is one that sees policy makers, including politicians, as
reliant on establishing ties and sometimes even coalitions with strategic
constituencies. This leads to the collapse of another distinction—because "neither do the rigid distinctions between interest groups and
social movements mean much in the context of the EU" (Marks, Scharpf,
Schmitter, and Streeck 1996, 97). In such a situation, MLG theorists

argue, the "boundaries" between the actors involved in making decisions of public policy become "fuzzy" and, further, the conceptual coherence of the categories themselves become problematic (Marks, Scharpf, Schmitter, and Streeck 1996, 96).

Marks, Hooghe, and Blank are correct in their view that nation-states and national governments are now constrained in their ability to control supranational organizations at the European level. While higher- order decisions are still taken by state executives, they cannot control day-to-day policy making. The process of European integration has often been technocratic. Consequently, it has been civil servants rather than politicians who conduct key negotiations and make policy (Hooghe 1996, 94–95; Marks, Hooghe, and Blank 1996b, 353; Bache and Olsson 2001).

Though the EU treaties have ensured that the powers of the Commission and its officials are limited, they remain wide enough to allow the Commission to develop its own specialisms and particular expertise. This, the Commission has done in structural policy where it has been extremely successful developing its approach and increasingly coherent policies on regional development. Recognizing the Commission's autonomous role in policy making, Marks, Hooghe, and Blank (1996) argue that this has allowed it to take note of the views of interest groups. Thus,

> Agenda-setting is . . . increasingly a shared and contested competence, with European institutions competing for control, and interest groups and subnational actors vying to influence the process. (359)

This shared agenda-setting is critical to the success of the Commission, dependent as it is "on its capacity to nurture and use diverse contacts," to "anticipate and mediate demands," and to utilize "the unique expertise it derives from its role as a think-tank of the European Union" (Marks, Hooghe, and Blank 1996, 359). The Commission's very success reinforces its need to engage with other actors and stakeholders in the process of European integration. As the bureaucracy of the Union, it constantly seeks new sources of information and support where

> [i]t has developed an extensive informal machinery of advisory committees and working groups for consultation and pre-negotiation, some of which are made up of member states nominees, but others of interest group representatives and experts who give the Commission access to independent information and legitimacy. The Commission has virtually a free hand in creating new networks, and in this way it is able to reach out to new constituencies, including a variety of subnational groups. (Marks, Hooghe, and Blank 1996, 359)

These observations about general changes in European governance lead us to ask whether there have been particular, similar changes in Northern Ireland.

CHANGING EUROPEAN GOVERNANCE AND NORTHERN IRELAND

First, it is necessary to note that Northern Ireland's specific political history has—perhaps paradoxically—provided rather fertile ground upon which new forms of governance can fall. As noted in the next section, Northern Ireland was governed from Westminster from 1972 until 1998. During this period, the lack of any devolved administration ensured that local civil servants (as noted previously in the case of the Commission) conducted much "government" that would have normally been undertaken by elected representatives. The "democratic deficits" arising from this situation led local civil servants to seek greater legitimacy in the decision-making process. Thus, there was something of a predisposition in Northern Ireland to the idea of bringing in nongovernmental actors from the private, voluntary, and community sectors (Hodgett and Johnson 2001).

This practice has been reinforced by Northern Ireland's position as an Objective 1 region in the European Union (granted despite not strictly qualifying in GDP terms as eligible). The eligibility criteria for projects, which might be supported by structural funding, demonstrate the multilayered character of the decision-making process, requiring participation through the full policy cycle by local, social, regional, and national partners, as well as the Commission itself. Moreover, the implementation of the Special Support Program for Peace and Reconciliation (Peace 1 and 2) has led to institutional innovation. Twenty-six district partnerships were set up in the areas of the corresponding district councils. In their original formation (now slightly different), one third of the members of these partnerships were drawn from the elected representatives, one third from social partners (business and labor), and one third from the civic partners—the voluntary and community sectors. An overarching Northern Ireland Partnership Board was also established (now also redesigned). The district partnerships, along with intermediary funding bodies and some statutory agencies, were charged with judging applications for funding under the Peace Programs and allocating support to them. This was intended to institutionalize the Commission's preferred bottom-up approach in the full policy cycle and to demonstrate that the Peace programs had a distinctive purpose.

Echoes of this and other European Union (EU) experience are to be found in the institutions established by the Good Friday or Belfast

Agreement. In general, it is common to note how similar are the north-south and east-west strands of the agreement to how the European Union works (Meehan 2000). Moreover, the North South Ministerial Council and British Irish Council provide new avenues through which common interests in different parts of the United Kingdom and Ireland can be pursued—notwithstanding stipulations in the documents regulating devolution in the United Kingdom (Memorandum of Understanding, concordats, and terms of reference of the Joint Ministerial Committee) that relations with the European Union and with foreign governments remain the prerogative of the United Kingdom (UK) government.

The experience of the EU-inspired district partnerships, and the philosophy underpinning them, led the Northern Ireland Women's Coalition to propose at the talks a unique constitutional innovation—the establishment of a Civic Forum. Their idea was based on a desire that the reestablishment of representative democracy should not be at the cost of losing the expertise and willingness to participate in public life of all those people (many of them women) who had kept the fabric of society together during "The Troubles" through their policy-oriented activism in civic associations (Fearon 1999). The Civic Forum was established on a similar three-stranded basis as the district partnerships and has begun to do good work on analyzing the social, inclusionary, and reconciliatory dimensions of the Program for Government.

In general, then, the Commission has been proactive in contributing to the involvement of civil society in the policy cycle. In Northern Ireland, EU officials have openly talked about using the region as a social laboratory. This bears out Hooghe's suggestion that "the periphery constitutes a rich reservoir of alternative approaches" (Hooghe 1996, 95).

NORTHERN IRELAND AS A TESTING GROUND FOR THEORIES OF MLG

Peripherality

Northern Ireland's peripherality in geographical terms is obvious. As the smaller part of an island off the continent, its landmass is some 14,623 km^2 (Ordnance Survey for Northern Ireland 1998) with a population of 1,688,600 in 1999 (Northern Ireland Statistics and Research Agency 2000). Traditionally it has suffered from out-migration of between 1,000 and 8,000 people per annum. It is also peripheral in the sense of being a "lagging region" with an unenviable political and economic history.

The Northern Ireland Economic Council (NIEC) concluded that from the 1960s the region's economy was in trouble and that this was recognized by policy makers. After the outbreak of political violence, public expenditure rose significantly from £566m in 1971 to £3,276m in 1981, mostly funding a major growth in public sector employment and provision of public services (NIEC 1996a, 73–80). NIEC research suggests that the Province was subjected to the concept of the soft budget, where public spending was not related to income (NIEC 1996a, 79). Although the soft budget option was "justified on political, economic, social and humane grounds" (NIEC 1996a, 82) and may have cushioned the effects of the political violence, it had a most undesirable effect upon the manufacturing sector. By 1987, it was clear that the government was very concerned about the risk of entrenching perpetual economic dependency on subventions from Great Britain (NIEC 1996a, 81).

Government figures show unemployment ranging from 14 percent in 1988 to 9.3 percent in 1996. Labor market statistics in 2000 cited the unemployment rate in June as 6.7 percent, significantly higher than the UK average of 5.4 percent (Department of Enterprise, Trade and Investment [DETI] 2000, 3). The Northern Ireland Statistics and Research Agency (NISRA) noted that unemployment in 1998 was the fifth highest of all UK regions (DETI 2000). Northern Ireland remains a relatively poor region of Europe and the United Kingdom, with a gross domestic product (GDP) of £15,486m in 1997 or £9,234 per head of population—approximately 80.4 percent of the UK GDP per capita (NISRA 2000, 3). The economy remains clearly skewed toward the public sector (NISRA 2000, 8).

Deconcentrated Administration

As noted earlier, Northern Ireland was governed by direct rule from Westminster from 1972 to 1998 (with the exception with two short and unsuccessful experiments with redevolution). The previous reference was made in connection with a predisposition to bringing in nongovernmental actors. On the other hand, this form of government could be argued to reinforce peripherality. The existence of a separate party system in Northern Ireland and the majoritarian convention in Westminster meant that no cabinet could ever include a member who had been elected by voters in Northern Ireland. Thus, the Secretary of State for Northern Ireland, the two Ministers of State, and two Parliamentary Under-Secretaries were representatives of constituencies in Great Britain. Their positions continued with devolution. But during the period of devolution they were no longer responsible for delivering policies that fell under devolved competencies. In the period of direct rule, all policy was the result of Orders-in-Council, decided in Westminster with the minimum of debate, and delivered by the Northern Ireland Office team. Thus, accountability to the people of Northern Ireland or their political representatives [was] essentially absent. Fiscal/financial integration and even greater budgetary dependence have been its hallmarks and with it [have] come major structural changes in the economy, illustrated by the scale of public sector employment and GDP. (NIEC 1996a, 87)

During the years of direct rule, when Ministers were preoccupied with trying to find solutions to the constitutional problems and ways to limit the intractable violence, public administration in Northern Ireland centered on the Northern Ireland Office in London; six central government departments located locally; statutory agencies, boards, quangos; and twenty-six district councils with very limited powers. The six departments tended to implement public policy on the basis of "reading over from London." Their civil servants, unaccountable to the electorate, controlled a large proportion of the budget for governing Northern Ireland (Hughes, Knox, Murray, and Greer 1998, 13). Little local regional input, save for some search for alternative channels of legitimacy (refer to earlier discussion), was possible until the setting up of the Assembly in 1998.

THE EUROPEAN UNION AND PUBLIC POLICY IN NORTHERN IRELAND

The construction of a European Regional Policy was seen as necessary to handle "the general problems of disparities in wealth through partial redistribution of wealth from the rich to the poor" (George 1991, 199). Three major European structural funds were set up to address disparities in wealth and aimed to develop and structurally adjust lagging regions. These multiannual funds were designed to promote economic development in the poorer regions of Europe and, as Hooghe (1996, 89) points out, were intended to move away from large-scale infrastructure investment to indigenous development. Nanetti (1996, 59) has suggested that what became Europe's Cohesion Policy, though explicitly economic, was implicitly both politically and socially motivated. Social Cohesion was "not simply a product of economic success but also a precondition of it" (NIEC 1996b, 187). Territorial inequities within Europe needed reducing, but this could not be done by either nation-states or the European Union itself and required the involvement of a plurality of actors and a multiplicity of resources. Nanetti comments, "At the core of the EU's cohesion policy is the concept of regional development" (Nanetti 1996, 60). However, it is not, she suggests, traditional regional development, but development that promotes cohesion or "high gains for the disadvantaged regions of the Union without halting or reversing the growth of the more developed regions"

(Nanetti 1996, 61). In Northern Ireland this was to be done in part by supporting the emerging concept of community infrastructure.

Community Infrastructure

In 1989 Northern Ireland received Objective 1 status under the first European program of structural funding, that is, the Community Support Framework (CSF), with an allocation of 702 million ECU or £522m. Birnie and Hitchens (1999, 95) state that "[a]n evaluation of the impact of the 1989–1993 Community Support Framework suggests that by 1993 Northern Ireland GDP was 3.6 per cent higher than would have been the case in the absence of EU funding (similarly 10,000 jobs had been created and sustained)." By 1993, the second five-year plan for structural funds in Northern Ireland, the 1994–1999 Single Programming Document (SPD), proclaimed: "The aim of the Structural Funds is to increase the social and economic cohesion of the European Community through the encouragement of the durable economic development in weaker regions" (Her Majesty's Stationery Office [HMSO] 1993, 11). Calculations have shown that the net economic benefit to Northern Ireland arising from EU membership was, by 1994, between £260m to £560m, that is, approximately 2 to 4 percent of regional GDP (Birnie and Hitchens 1999). For the 1994–1999 period, Birnie and Hitchens (1999, 98) note that the Department of Finance and Personnel estimated that, under Structural Funds, Northern Ireland would receive just under £1 billion, but to this needed to be added the income from the Peace and Reconciliation Program of approximately £50m to 1997. European assistance to the Province had increased by one half between 1989 and 1993 (Birnie and Hitchens 1999, 98). The question arises as to whether this influx of support had other effects of the type noted by Nanetti—for example, both political and social impacts?

The Northern Ireland 1994–1999 Structural Funds Plan document (HMSO 1993) ascribes the aim of social and economic cohesion through economic development as a response both to the Single Market and to altered world conditions. In it, many reasons are offered for Objective 1 status: the Province's geographical peripherality; the "Development Gap" between Northern Ireland and the rest of the United Kingdom/ European Union; impediments to economic and social cohesion such as inappropriate industrial structure; agriculture and rural decline; demography; unemployment; and poor education. The European Union clearly viewed Northern Ireland as peripheral to the European core.

In addition, the Commission was interested in finding constitutionally legitimate avenues through which to contribute to the amelioration of Northern Ireland's "troubles." (Prior attempts by the European Parliament to show concern had been seen in some Unionist quarters as unwarranted interference in the internal affairs of a member-state.) The 1994–1999 Structural Funds Plan (HMSO 1993, 65) outlined its "vital role" in the process of helping to "overcome structural impediments and . . . stimulating the participation of business, communities and individuals in the development effort." The Structural Funds Plan had the strategic aim of improving Northern Ireland's economic and social cohesion through economic growth, one theme of which was named Community Infrastructure.

The Community Infrastructure measure was initially unique to Northern Ireland in Europe. It was intended to address the religious and political divisions and the "human and material damage" inflicted by terrorism on the region (HMSO 1993, 73). The Structural Funds Plan notes that in Northern Ireland,

> Social as well as economic progress has been hampered. Positive action is therefore needed to overcome community alienation by promoting reconciliation between communities in Northern Ireland and by tackling sources of disadvantage, which sustain community divisions. (HMSO 1993, 73)

The funding was to build and sustain a Community Infrastructure (investment in voluntary and community activity) and thereby to contribute to economic development. Community Infrastructure programming was to be implemented under the Single Programming Document's Physical and Social Environment Program (PSEP), the aim of which was "to foster internal social cohesion" (HMSO 1993, 94). The Northern Ireland Operational Program sought to "promote economic and social cohesion both within Northern Ireland and relative to the other regions of the European Community" (HMSO 1993, 106). Its objectives were to promote competitiveness and economic growth, to increase employment, improve the physical environment, improve access to markets, reduce energy costs, and make Northern Ireland more internationally competitive.

Yet under these priorities the PSEP was clearly a piece of social engineering combining, in Community Infrastructure, the concepts of both the social and the economic. The Community Infrastructure measure represents the application of a European social model to a lagging region through regional policy. It illustrates a European desire to promote improvement in skills, welfare and trust, modernization, and democracy. It was aimed at improving Northern Ireland's social cohesion, and at the same time, empowering traditionally excluded sections of society. It was an effort to build a community infrastructure that would develop local community confidence and offer a positive alternative to the ongoing violence and despair.

Community Infrastructure: Achievement and Impact

The Community Infrastructure measure, brought in under the Structural Funds Plan of 1994–1999, was achieved through an intense three-year lobbying campaign by the voluntary sector, which targeted both the local British government administration and the relevant directorates in the European Commission (Regional Policy and Social Policy). The sector also achieved the support of the then–European Commission President, Jacques Delors, in their campaign for involvement in the policy process (Hodgett 1998).

Interestingly, contact with the Commission itself was achieved through Commission seed funding of an interest group, the European Anti-Poverty Network. The establishment of this network allowed the umbrella body for Northern Ireland's voluntary sector, the Northern Ireland Council for Voluntary Action (NICVA), to become established as the representative for the United Kingdom. This facilitated NICVA's access to Commission civil servants and eventually to Delors himself. Moreover, it seems to have caused a major redefinition of Community Infrastructure. According to sources in the voluntary sector, the measure was so named originally because the European Union understood the terms Community (in the context of the European Community) and Infrastructure (in the context of providing physical infrastructure). The terms were then repackaged and sold back to Europe as infrastructure for communities at the regional level!

NICVA's access to the Commission, combined with lobbying local civil servants at home who were involved in the negotiating with the Commission over the Structural Funds, ensured that when the Single Programming Document was being drawn up, the agenda of the voluntary sector was brought to the fore. As a result, when the final plan emerged, significant funds were included, some of which were ring-fenced for the exclusive use of the voluntary and community sectors (Hodgett 1998). These funds were available under the rubric of the Community Infrastructure measure.

The measure was innovative. Perhaps most interesting and unusual was the emphasis on involving those normally excluded from the policy process, in an attempt "to enable communities to contribute to local policy formation" (Department of Health and Social Services [DHSS] 1999, 3). Its primary purpose was to involve new groups of people in the process of working with government, using community development approaches, to engage in economic regeneration (DHSS 1999, 2). Community Infrastructure was presented as a theme that cross-cut all EU programs in Northern Ireland at the same time as a specific measure funded under the Single Programming Document (SPD). It was seen as a measure for the voluntary sector, "valuing people and working in partnership" to create new relationships in the policy process between the voluntary and statutory sectors (DHSS 1999, 2). A Department of Health and Social Services report on the measure noted:

> The purpose of the Community Infrastructure Measures was to allow experiments to be made with new ways of involving those experiencing disadvantage and/or poverty and enabling them to become actively involved in the design and management of programmes aimed at overcoming social exclusion. (1999, 2)

The measure also committed itself to Community Capacity and engaged with the concept of Social Capital (Department of Finance and Personnel 1997). Community Capacity building was interpreted in its loosest form to mean development of a community's capacity or development of an individual's capacity. Sixty-one projects were funded under the measure during the first five-year tranche of monies. Each of these was assessed using seven criteria for their contribution to

- Group support and networking
- Community resources and facilities
- Social exclusion and beneficiaries—innovation and empowerment
- Integrated area partnerships
- Independent advice giving and information
- Contribution to policy formation
- Capacity building

Such ambitious aims for inclusiveness, community-capacity building, and Social Capital may be easier to state than to achieve. However, there is both governmental and independent research that suggests that they were realized, at least in part.

The government report on the measure (DHSS 1999) found that it had been crucial to supporting community development activity and had promoted strong Community Infrastructure in many areas. It found, too, that the measure had been effective in including groups normally excluded from the policy-formation process—for example, women, children, young people, and the long-term unemployed. These groups were involved, perhaps for the first time, in identifying unmet needs in program delivery and program management. The report also found that this extended beyond simple policy rhetoric to actual service provision by the government. Evidence of increased confidence among the traditionally marginalized demonstrated the success of the priority in building human and organizational capacity. Also apparently enhanced was the capacity of community organizations to create employment, draw down new funds, and work with others in formal or informal networks. Indirectly, this increased their capacity to influence events and influence policy direction by the government. In short, increased participation in the policy process by organizations was mirrored by increased contribution by previously uninvolved individuals (DHSS 1999).

Research at Queen's University (Hodgett, McCann, and Royle 2001) shows both early difficulties with Community Infrastructure and that the measure has been effective in unexpected ways in supporting the involvement of nontraditional groups within the policy process. The problems in successfully implementing Community Infrastructure projects include difficulties in reaching across boundaries between sectors, particularly between the voluntary and statutory sectors; promoting acceptance and understanding of the language and approaches of community development; and sustainability of projects, related to short-term funding and planning. One project participant claimed there was "projectitus . . . or the Santa Claus Approach, dropping money down on people who are grateful [for it]"(Hodgett, McCann, and Royle 2001). Evidence also indicates that initially there was a lack of clarity about what was the purpose of the measure, which groups should be funded, and how selection criteria should be applied.

Yet, despite these early difficulties, there are also indications of success. For example, the Dungannon Disability Arts Project, funded under the capacity building theme (physical infrastructure), though experiencing some difficulty in contributing to policy initially, nevertheless established a very successful ongoing partnership with the Arts Council of Northern Ireland. Consequently, they have strengthened their community or social infrastructure and effected the politicization of the issue of disability within a local context. Lurgan Council for Voluntary Action was enabled to "create a voice for the community" through its work on rural community transport and with the local health trust. While funded to undertake Group Support and Networking and (physical) Capacity Building, by identifying gaps in provision of services to the local community, it has empowered other organizations to become active in campaigning. It has, thereby, developed local community capacity. Though obliged formally to apply for monies to improve the physical infrastructure of the organization, it believes that "policy development is central" to what it does on a daily basis.

Community development approaches were used by Enniskillen's Community Development Project. Funded under the community initiative to improve physical resources in the town, by 2000 it had become a training organization, employing seventeen people, with 800 adult students, and a turnover of some £300,000. It works with several community organizations and statutory bodies (Hodgett, McCann, and Royle 2001, 75–77). Also promoting these approaches is the Community

Development and Health Network (CDHN). This campaigning organization links 400 members across Northern Ireland involved in promoting health issues. The organization found Community Infrastructure invaluable in allowing people to make connections and develop their own networks for peer education, peer support, lobbying, and influencing the policy environment. As a consequence of all these experiences, there has been a move to mainstream community development approaches within many statutory bodies, so allowing them to explore new models of policy development directly involving citizens.

Other Community Infrastructure–funded projects view utilizing the measure as a first step in a process of promoting active citizenship. Related perceived effects include, for example, an increased awareness of the importance of transparency and democracy within local communities. The impact of this is linked to making the internal governance of organizations more democratic, while fully engaging in community development programs. A general increase in the profile of volunteering seems also to have resulted from the measure.

Clearly, the measure has succeeded in bringing people together "from the statutory, [and] community [sector], building up relationships between those individuals and encourag[ing] them to move beyond tokenistic support to real involvement" (Hodgett, McCann, and Royle 2001, 93). The Devenish Partnership Forum somehow encapsulates what the measure was about. Bringing together the local housing association, business representatives, the police, and the health board, it crosses the divide between the public, private, and voluntary sectors. Its long-term strategy was for regeneration and to develop the capacity of local people identifying their needs. To do this, Devenish Partnership worked with the district council and the district partnership to target and invest in areas of weak community infrastructure. Both the name of the structures established and how they worked embodied the delivery, in physical terms, of the European Union's new emphasis under structural funds on the partnership approach.

The Community Infrastructure measure (and the European Union's general approach) has received support from community activists in Northern Ireland because, as one of them told the Queen's University team, "it is the first programme that has recognized that citizens are probably the most important resources of a country and unless you start investing in those people then you can't change the problems" (Hodgett, McCann, and Royle 2001, 32).

The impact of the Community Infrastructure measure upon one women's center in a working-class area of Belfast helped the women become more politically aware. In 1993–1994, when the funding began, the terms "policy" and "policy making" were not used or understood by the women active in the center. Over the mid-1990s and going through the processes of using Community Infrastructure funds to develop their center and their people, the women acquired a new political awareness. They believe now that in getting involved in policy making, they "leapfrogged" in their own development. One interviewee commented to the Queen's University team: "It's not what we thought we were doing . . . but it is exactly what we [did]. We were strategizing and didn't realize it." The result was that people, most notably the statutory sector, began to take them seriously. The women's center developed links with the Assembly and the Women's Coalition because in their own words, they had "started to see the big picture."

This might be construed as an eloquent testimony for the measure as a whole. Although not universal, the frequency with which individuals and groups learned how to use the political system and understood how to become further involved with the process of governance has been very important. The manner in which change has been achieved is best represented by the words of one of the Community Infrastructure project leaders:

> We . . . see ourselves as a very loud voice . . . in the ear of policy makers. We are certainly taken seriously by all the policy makers locally, we are engaged at all levels of policy making. We are invited in now, whereas before we had to fight to get in. (Hodgett, McCann, and Royle 2001, 45)

Community Infrastructure has made the voluntary sector more coherent and more effective. Arguably too, it has promoted networking and effected a sector-wide value system based on good information. This, rather than the creation of physical infrastructure for community initially foreseen, has been the most significant outcome of the ideas, which make up the Community Infrastructure measure and theme (Hodgett, McCann, and Royle 2001, 41).

CONCLUSION

Laffan (1983, 389–408) has suggested that the 1988 reform of structural funds in Ireland undermined the gatekeeper role traditionally played by governments and thereby disturbed relations between central and local actors. The same can be said about both the Irish and British governments in the development of another community initiative about which we have not written here—the cross-border INTER-REG program (Laffan and Payne 2001). Today, in the task of constructing and implementing EU policy, authority must be shared and involve communication, not only among multiple tiers of government but also between government and nongovernmental actors. After the revamping of regional policy in 1988, the European Union's method of working through partnerships became commonplace, reflecting

> some form of direct contact between the Commission and non central government actors including, particularly, regional and local authorities, local action groups and local businesses. Such links break open the mould of the state, so that multi-level governance encompasses actors within as well as beyond existing states. (Marks, Hooghe, and Blank 1996b, 369)

The ebbing away of control by the nation-state has allowed what Marks has dubbed "cracks" in the system's superstructure to emerge. Marks uses the term to refer "to the existence of numerous points of access at different levels of government, which result from the extraordinarily fragmented character of decision making" (Marks, Nielsen, Ray, and Salk 1996, 171).

The contacts made thereafter develop into something more:

> Direct connections are . . . forged among political actors in diverse political arenas. Traditional and formerly exclusive channels of communication and influence are being side stepped. With its dispersed competencies, contending but interlocked institutions, shifting agendas, multilevel governance opens multiple points of access for interest, while it privileges those interests with technical expertise that match the dominant style of EU policy making. In this turbulent process of mobilization and counter-mobilization it is patently clear that states no longer serve as the exclusive nexus between domestic politics and international relations. Direct connections are being forged among political actors in diverse political arenas. (Marks, Hooghe, and Blank 1996, 372)

After nearly a decade of EU funding in Northern Ireland, it seems that cracks in the system have opened up opportunities for "outsiders" to become involved in the policy process. The Northern Ireland voluntary sector has certainly benefited from this process and has, in effect, upgraded itself to the status of a social partner in the region.

The experience of the creation of Community Infrastructure in Northern Ireland has confirmed findings of researchers elsewhere in Europe that "policy formulation is increasingly characterized by consensus seeking and communicative rationality rather than political-ideological divides" (Bache and Olsson 2001, 234). The experiment in applying distributive governance to the Province has illustrated that multilevel governance can and does, in some cases, work in practice. Northern Ireland provides an interesting example of how the theory can have relevance in the European Union of the twenty-first century. Finally, it indicates that despite some of the most dangerous and difficult policy environs in the world, participatory democracy, which includes innovative policy experiments, can have positive and ultimately beneficial results.

REFERENCES

Bache, I., and J. Olsson. 2001. Legitimacy through partnership? EU policy diffusion in Britain and Sweden. *Scandinavian Political Studies* 24 (3): 215–37.

Birnie, E., and D. Hitchens. 1999. *Northern Ireland economy: Performance, practice and policy.* Aldershot: Ashgate.

Department of Enterprise, Trade and Investment (DETI). 2000. *Northern Ireland labour market statistics.* August 16.

Department of Finance and Personnel (DFP). 1997. *Mid term review of Physical and Social Environment Programme (EU structural funds).* Belfast: DFP.

Department of Health and Social Services (DHSS). 1999. *The story of Community Infrastructure in Northern Ireland: Developing indicators for monitoring and evaluation of Community Infrastructure measures.* Belfast: DHSS.

Fearon, K. 1999. *Women's work: The story of the Northern Ireland Women's Coalition.* Belfast: The Blackstaff Press.

George, S. 1991. *Politics and policy in the European Community.* Oxford: Oxford University Press.

Her Majesty's Stationery Office (HMSO). 1993. *Northern Ireland Structural Funds Plan.* Belfast: HMSO.

Hodgett, S. 1998. *Community Infrastructure: The Northern Ireland voluntary sector and European Union regional policy.* Belfast: NICVA.

Hodgett, S., and D. Johnson. 2001. Troubles, partnerships and possibilities: A study of the Making Belfast Work Development Initiative in Northern Ireland. *Public Administration and Development* 21 (4): 321–52.

Hodgett, S., J. McCann, and S. Royle. 2001. Community development in Northern Ireland: A case study of Community Infrastructure. Unpublished research, Queen's University Belfast.

Hooghe, L., ed. 1996. *Cohesion policy and European integration: Building multi-level governance.* Oxford: Oxford University Press.

Hooghe, L., and G. Marks. 1997. *The making of a polity: The struggle over European integration.* European Integration Online Papers 1 (4). http//eiop.or.at/eiop/texte/1997-004a.htm.

———. 2001. *Multi-level governance and European integration.* Oxford: Rowman and Littlefield.

Hughes, J., C. Knox, M. Murray, and J. Greer. 1998. *Partnership governance in Northern Ireland: The path to peace.* Dublin: Oak Tree Press.

Laffan, B. 1983. Policy implementation in the European Community: The European social fund as a case study. *Journal of Common Market Studies* 21: 389–408.

Laffan, B., and D. Payne. 2001. Creating living institutions: EU cross-border co-operation after the Good Friday Agreement. A report for the Center for Cross-Border Studies at Armagh.

Marks, G., L. Hooghe, and K. Blank. 1996. European integration from the 1980s: State-centric v multi-level governance. *Journal of Common Market Studies* 34 (3): 341–77.

Marks, G., F. Nielsen, L. Ray, and J. Salk. 1996. Competencies, cracks and conflicts: Regional mobilization in the European Union. *Comparative Political Studies* 29 (2): 164–92.

Marks, G., F. Scharpf, P. Schmitter, and W. Streeck. 1996. *Governance in the European Union*. London: Sage.

Meehan, E. 2000. Europe and the Europeanization of the Irish Question. In *A farewell to arms? From 'long war' to long peace in Northern Ireland*, edited by M. Cox, A. Guelke, and F. Stephen, pp. 199–213. Manchester: Manchester University Press.

Nanetti, R. 1996. EU cohesion and territorial restructuring in the member states. In *Cohesion policy and European integration: Building multi-level governance*, edited by L. Hooghe, pp. 59–87. Oxford: Oxford University Press.

Northern Ireland Economic Council (NIEC). 1996a. *Decentralized government and economic performance in Northern Ireland*. Belfast: Northern Ireland Economic Development Office.

———. 1996b. *Successful European regions: Northern Ireland learning from others*. Belfast: Northern Ireland Economic Development Office.

Northern Ireland Statistics and Research Agency (NISRA). 2000. Annual Abstract of Statistics. www.nisra.gov.uk/featpub/annab99.htm.

Ordnance Survey for Northern Ireland. 1998. *Soil Survey for Northern Ireland*. Belfast.

8

Government or Governance in the Rotterdam Region?

Linze Schaap

INTRODUCTION

European integration is a process with great impact on member-states. It has major consequences for national governmental tasks, responsibilities, policy discretion, and steering capacities. More and more it becomes clear that national government is not the only tier of government affected by European integration processes; subnational government is influenced as well. Quinn (1999) distinguishes three impacts:

1. **Institutional impact:** The adaptation of existing institutions; the creation of new ones; the reform of institutional representation mechanisms; and the flourishing of collective institutions, bodies, and mechanisms.
2. **Impact on the channels of influence:** Channels enabling subnational government to exert influence in European-policy–making processes.
3. **Impact on policy networks:** Policy networks have emerged and the power structures of existing networks have altered as results of European policies.

This chapter focuses mainly on the institutional impact of the European integration process. In many countries the structure of subnational government is on the agenda—in some for a very long time already. Changes in the structure of subnational government, however, are not always the result of European integration. Other factors may be at stake as well. A good example is Belgium, which moved recently toward a federal system due to internal pressures. Another example is Spain, where internal pressures led to the creation and development of the autonomous communities (*Comunidades Autónomas*), although European policies have proven helpful in this effort (Newton and Donaghy 1997, 117–23). In general, in many countries, the borders of subnational authorities have changed (Sharpe 1987, 162).

In the Netherlands, since 1990 there has been an almost continuous debate on the structure of the subnational government, especially a debate on the creation of a regional tier of government. It was the perception of some policy actors that European integration constituted a pressure to integrate local government in larger regional units. Those larger units might have more and improved capabilities to act as influential actors at the European level. The Ministry of the Interior in particular used this argument in its reform plans (Ministry of the Interior 1990, 1991, 1993; Bekkers and Hendriks 1998). In this opinion, local government was to be able to act as a regional government. Other policy actors hardly mentioned European integration, but pointed at internal developments in the Dutch system of subnational government, such as decentralization and the challenge to local governments to meet complex societal issues.

This chapter is about the debate on reforming the structure of Dutch local government, not on actual reform itself. The latter never became a reality. From World War II until now, many problems in the Dutch system have been identified, which were mainly concentrated on the regional level. Many ideas and solutions were proposed, either concerning the lack of a regional governmental layer (that is, in the Netherlands, the level just above the municipalities) or concerning the provincial level, and especially concerning local government, their scale, their policy equipment, their finances, their responsibilities, and intergovernmental relations (Koppenjan 1993). The last round in this everlasting debate started around 1990, and it actually might have resulted in the establishment of a real regional tier of government, the so-called city-provinces. In the end, it did not lead to any change of structure, although some authors mistakenly thought it did (Loughlin and Peters 1997).[1]

Isn't this strange? Many problems, many ideas, many proposals, many possible solutions—so why didn't the Netherlands reform their subnational government? There might be some reasons for this. In this chapter, I attempt to shed light on the following questions:

1. For what reasons did the proposal for the creation of a city-province emerge?
2. What happened in the Rotterdam region, when the reform process actually started?
3. How can we assess the present situation: Is reform still the official goal?

These questions will be answered by analyzing a major reform attempt within the Netherlands: the formation of a so-called city-province in the Rotterdam region—or rather, the nonformation.

To fully understand this process, it may be important to have knowledge of some of the characteristics of the Dutch system of subnational government. In the next section, I therefore give a short description of the Dutch system of subnational government. After having done so, I reflect on the Dutch debate on whether or not subnational government has to be reorganized. The next sections contain the case study related to the policy-process debate concerning the establishment of a regional tier of government in the Rotterdam region. Then, I draw some general lessons and answer the research questions posed here. The chapter ends with some general theoretical prospective conclusions centered around the question whether reorganization is a useful tool in a network society (Kickert, Klijn, and Koppenjan 1997).

A SHORT CHARACTERIZATION OF THE DUTCH SUBNATIONAL GOVERNMENT SYSTEM

The Dutch state has a three-layer system all over the country: local government = municipalities (*gemeenten*), provincial government (*provincies*), and central government. Uniformity is the key word: Municipalities to a large extent have similar tasks and similar political structures. The relations between the layers are cooperative and organic. This system was created in the middle of the nineteenth century. Its founder was the great statesman Thorbecke, who, while designing the Dutch system, was inspired by the German Historic Law School (Toonen 1990, 283). It appeared to be able to cope with the immense growth of public tasks. Developed and formalized in the era of a somewhat minimal state (the night watcher's state), it remained the system until today in spite of the growth in complexity of the modern state due to the welfare system and due to the ever-increasing number of public tasks imposed by internationalization, differentiation, and crisis periods. Some would call it a success.

One of the success factors could be the nature of the intergovernmental relations; the Dutch state is a so-called "decentralized unitary state" (Toonen 1990). Characteristics of this system are the following:

- The **organic state**: The state is an evolutionary phenomenon, emerging from history, not a machine or a thought-of entity.
- Its **unitary nature,** which cannot be equaled to centralization.
- The **interdependent relations between the layers**: The relations between the layers of government are not necessarily hierarchical, or based on a clear separation of powers among the layers. They are mainly relations between interdependent entities.
- The **autonomous position of the municipalities**, and they have a general competence: no *ultra vires* principle. The "open household" of municipalities and provinces is constitutionally protected.
- **Provinces exercise supervisory powers over municipalities, whereas central government does the same over provinces.** Supervision does not mean commanding, but approval of local initiatives, or at least nonresistance.
- **The unitary character shows itself in the large uniformity of public services of the welfare state**: The level of income compensations, for example, does not depend on the city you live in or on the political color of the local council. Local government is bound to central policy guidelines; especially local income and social security policies are prohibited.
- **Co-governance is the instrument used most:** Central government make laws and plans after consultation of local governments and in particular of their representative associations and the local governments implement these central policies. This implementation, however, is not mechanistic in character.
- **The Dutch state is decentralized as well**: Municipalities are autonomous to a certain extent; and even in policy areas where their task is largely defined as implementation of central policy, they often have a large degree of policy freedom (based on discretionary competencies, local presence, knowledge, and information). Local authorities are left policy freedom to cope with local situations and the possibility of realizing political goals.

The relation between the three governmental layers is flexible. The co-governance system is particularly important (Toonen 1990). Due to co-governance, the Dutch governmental system has been able to cope with the enormous growth of its tasks and responsibilities, without structural changes and without destroying local freedom. The real amount of subnational freedom depends on discretionary competencies as well as the strategies of subnational government. The centralization resulting from the growth of the welfare state has, therefore, not destroyed the importance of subnational governments. Although their autonomy has decreased enormously, their policy freedom is still intact. Centralization does not withstand a vivid local (or provincial) democracy.

CONTINUOUS DEBATE

But there is also a different story. As stated previously, since World War II, there has been a continuous debate about this system. During the last five decades, the discussion focused on the regional level—the level between municipalities and provinces. Many authors, government advisers, public administrators, and politicians emphasized that the Dutch subnational government's structure is somewhat out of date and unable to cope with the "problems of today" (be that the 1940s, 1960s, or 1990s). There seems to be a strong urge to highlight regional problems—problems with which local and provincial authorities are believed to be unable to cope. Therefore several structural reforms were proposed in the past five decades.

None of the reform proposals was ever implemented. Is the Dutch subnational government system perhaps not just successful but resistant to change as well? Is the Dutch policy community conservative? Or are these questions inadequately formulated? Do we perhaps fail to see real changes by focusing on the lack of *structural* change? Or, again a different question: Why is it that many participants in the policy discussion on subnational government, scholars as well as public administrators and politicians, worship structure reforms as solutions? Their hypothesis is that "when we have societal problems, we have to automatically adapt our organizations," or better put, material problems are a reason to engage in a formal reorganization of the structures. Such an attitude was never challenged within the discussion. It seems that the possible side effects of a reform are not taken into consideration, or rather not completely thought out.

In the next sections, I illustrate these questions by discussing the attempts to reform the local and provincial government layers in the region with the biggest harbor in the world: Rotterdam.

THE REFORM PROCESS IN THE ROTTERDAM REGION

Since 1989, a new round of policy discussion on the structure of subnational government started in Netherlands (Koppenjan 1993). Central government, and especially the Ministry of the Interior (1990, 1991,

1993), is the great stimulator. Official policy was aimed at establishing a new governmental layer in metropolitan areas, as an intermediate structure between the present municipalities and provinces, or even as a replacement of the present provinces. Seven metropolitan areas were defined, among them Amsterdam, Rotterdam, and The Hague, each area containing the city and the surrounding municipalities. Other, less metropolitan regions were expected to be governed as usual. The choice of creating such a layer in only a few areas in the country is rather revolutionary; this was quite a turning point in Dutch administrative history. The uniformity model introduced by Thorbecke had been an unchallenged pillar of the system.

In the Rotterdam region this policy initiative was well understood and received. In some policy makers' opinion, the Rotterdam region, consisting of eighteen municipalities (eighteen local authorities), lacked a uniting governmental body. Since 1991, attempts were made to alter this situation. Especially the mayors discovered opportunities, whereas the elected local politicians did not yet see them (Cachet and Koppenjan 1996, 94).[2] They quickly started to negotiate, and in March 1991 they produced a document titled *Strategic Vision* (Overlegorgaan Rijnmondgemeenten [OOR] 1991a). This strategic vision was a list of shared regional policy problems and, to some extent, a basis for their solutions. These problems were related to several policy areas: housing, physical planning, mobility, environment, culture, public health, and tourism.

In the policy debate, there was no doubt about the necessity of a new regional governmental body as part of the solution. Instead, there was to be a regional layer of the traditional provincial government. In the policy document, two models were being discussed and rejected because they were expected to be ineffective (OOR 1991a, 62–63). A stronger structure was to be found. All participating municipalities agreed to this; they supported the strategic vision and the necessity of developing a clear regional structure. A wonderful foundation for the forthcoming reorganization process was achieved based on consensus.

The next years were used to discuss the formation of such a new regional government body. Aspects such as the structures and the responsibilities of the forthcoming government layer were discussed at length. It looked like a real innovative process: There was enthusiasm; many actors involved believed in the process of which they were part; they believed in success; they thought of many new, almost revolutionary aspects of the new regional body. Central government initially was prepared to let the local and regional actors decide, so that centralism, uniformity, and blueprint planning would definitively belong to the past.

After a few years, however, the discussion and the preparations became more complex and time-consuming. Some central policy makers became impatient, and civil servants of the Minister of the Interior, acting as guardians of the constitution, discovered that all the innovative elements in the plans formulated by the cooperating municipalities were definitely not in accordance with the constitution. The final law proposals contained very little remains of the originally proposed innovations: The regional government as proposed was called a city-province and its structure and powers resembled more and more that of an ordinary province (Derksen 1998). Ironically, the enthusiasm with which many municipal actors started, was based on the belief that they would build a new structure *without* the province. And now legislative proposals contained the idea that they were to establish a province. History has its irony.

Time pressure on local and regional actors was intensified, enthusiasm began to slip away, and differences in opinion began to become irritating and sometimes a ground for a good intermunicipal fight. Societal support coming from interest groups and citizens began to fade away. Many became aware of the fact that the reform process was a game played by few participants. Getting popular support was hardly a rule of the game. This was showed in the referendum in Rotterdam (which was not conducted in the other participating seventeen municipalities) in 1995, when over 85 percent of the voters cast their vote against the establishment of the city-province. The municipal Council of Rotterdam respected the outcome of the referendum and became an adversary of the process.

The reform process was in shambles. Some municipalities wished to stop the process, others asked central government to continue and to force Rotterdam to cooperate. Central government established a special committee in the summer 1995, with the special assignment to find a solution to the impasse. Its report contained some solutions, but all of them were unacceptable to a majority of the municipalities. It had simply overlooked the different opinions, their depths, and their nature. Augmenting time pressure generated opposite effects from those expected; in hindsight one can state that because of the constructed lack of time, many decisions that were made resulted in unintended situations. The same holds for the wish for certainty. Characteristic features of the whole process were attempts to grasp the wicked policy problems and to decide in great detail which governmental layer should get which tasks.

ANALYSIS OF THE REFORM EFFORTS: LUHMANN'S AUTOPOIESIS THEORY

To be able to look into the differences of the different groups of actors, a theoretical model based on Niklas Luhmann's theory of autopoietic social systems was developed (Luhmann 1984, 1990a, 1990b; In 't Veld c.s., 1991; Schaap, 1997).

This theory stresses the closed nature of social systems, being based on the logic of distinction (Spencer Brown 1972). In short, this logic means that in order to understand reality, distinctions are needed. An observer, one who tries to gain knowledge of the world, needs distinctions. According to those distinctions, meaning can be assigned. The same holds for social systems, which in Luhmann's understanding (1984) are communication systems. They as well create their own distinctions and, in doing so, their own boundaries: They themselves decide on what the system is and is not. Which aspects of reality mean something to the system depends on internally determined distinctions. The system, therefore, determines itself, its knowledge, its past, its future, its goals. This has fundamental impact on the possibilities for influencing the social system externally, among them political steering. Effective political intervention is hard to achieve, because of the closed nature of societal systems (Schaap 1997).

Luhmann distinguished three types of social systems:

- Society as such and its functional differentiated subsystems, such as the juridical, economic, and political subsystems
- Formal organizations, with a strong emphasis on membership as a means of inclusion and exclusion
- Face-to-face interaction

In autopoiesis theory, systems build their own identity. To analyze system identities, the central questions are the following:

1. Which social systems (communication systems) can be distinguished? Which distinctions do they apply for assigning meaning to empirical phenomena?
2. Which are their structures?
   a. *Values* underlying a system's communication
   b. *Self-steering program*
   c. *Roles* being recognized in the system's communication
3. In what way are these systems closed?

Steering closed social systems requires reflection. Governments should take into account the closure of social systems and their autopoietic identity. If they do so, their awareness of the closed nature of the social environment of government might increase. Governments may become aware of the fact that other social systems have their own perception of government and its actions. Some good advice to government, therefore, is to make an image of itself as it is possibly observed by other systems. Then governmental steering through policy measures may stand a chance to become effective. Consequently, making an analysis of the environment is a necessary condition for governance. The type of steering that might prove effective is called "context steering," that is, *inciting governance*, with the following characteristics (Schaap 1997):

- Intervention takes into account the functional differentiation of society, resulting in a nonhierarchical position of the political sub-system.
- Political intervention aims at coupling autonomous self-steering of societal systems with political wishes, using diverse steering instruments.
- Political intervention no longer aspires regulating society at large, but instead offers policy options; the effectiveness of those options increases if a choice between a limited set of options is mandatory.
- Political retreat may be dangerous and may intensify systems' closure.
- Variation of ways and means of intervention is important to prevent domination of one kind—for example, juridical instruments.

AUTOPOIETIC RECONSTRUCTION OF THE REFORM EFFORTS

The analysis of the debate in the Rotterdam region on the creation of a city-province was based on the autopoiesis theory. In the analysis, it was discovered that two autopoietic communication systems were at stake (Schaap 1997). It was necessary to adapt Luhmann's distinction of three different social systems into a distinction of four. The fourth type was the "policy communication system."

In one system, called the autonomous municipality system, every proposal was interpreted and given meaning on behalf of the distinction to be autonomous or not. Its central question was what will be the result of all this for freedom and autonomy of the municipalities?

In the other system, called the strong regional system, the basic distinction was whether there will be a strong or weak regional steering; every proposal was being interpreted along the lines of this distinction. The central question is will the new regional government have the capacity to steer it forcefully?

Along these lines both systems interpreted everything, including the basic principles of the original strategic vision. One can easily see that those interpretations, those constructions of contents, differed heavily. And so they did. The analysis resulted in the findings outlined in Table 8.1.

TABLE 8.1 Comparing Two Systems

System: Structures	Autonomous municipality system	Strong region system
Values	Municipalities should be autonomous and equal. They should build up their administrative organisation and should have a direct financial relation with the citizens (taxation capacity). Changes in proposals were perceived as unacceptable, unless they achieved in co-operation with and consent of the municipalities.	Strong regional steering was a necessity for the solution of physical and economical problems in the region. At a later stage public health, crime and drugs were added to the normative list of regional responsibilities. The regional layer should be a multi-functioned layer, with directly elected representatives.
Self-steering Program	In the first phase, mere regional co-operation was important and enough; but afterwards the participation of the Ministry of the Interior seemed to give more certainty. Trust shifted from the regional partners to the Ministry. Municipal vitality was the central issue. Because of that, the separation of responsibilities between municipalities and region had to be clear and detailed, and the regional civil service small.	The regional strength and steering capacity may, if necessary, have a negative effect on the vitality of municipalities. The region needed power and the capacities for carrying out a general steering competence. A clear and defined financial relation with citizens was perceived necessary. On behalf of procedures: certainty and control are most important.
Roles	In the first stage, the city of Rotterdam was thought to be striving for dominance. This changed over time. The Ministry of the Interior was firstly being seen as a distant partner, later as a non-constructive actor, although trusted in some specific matters. Financially, the system aimed at central governments' general grants, rather than having the city-province distribute the financial resources over to the municipalities. A clear role is wanted of the province South-Holland, one of passivity and non-participation, or even no role at all.	The city-province was projected as having large regional responsibilities. Be it via regional decision making, or via central legislation. This system did not want participation of the province of South-Holland, either. Municipalities were expected to challenge the proposals, but expected to agree in the end. Central actors might be useful in suppressing local resistance.

Because the values of both systems as well as the interpretations of reality differed completely, one of the main difficulties was to achieve mutual adjustment. Both systems, however, failed to see each others' interpretations. The regional cooperation of municipalities, a formal organization, and the linkage between both systems failed to observe the fundamental closed nature of both systems. It was therefore ineffective in its intervention strategy. The analysis points out that although agreement on the basic principles of the future city-province was reached, this agreement was immaterial because the principles were interpreted very differently.

RECENT DEVELOPMENT: NO REFORM

The city-province never became reality, despite all the efforts and debates. There are several reasons for this. There was disagreement in the Rotterdam region itself (as shown earlier) and disagreement between all the regional actors and the Ministry of the Interior. Beyond this, there were constitutional problems: The Dutch constitution recognizes only municipalities, provinces, and central government, not, however, city-provinces. Last but not least, the creation of a city-province and the splitting up of their municipality into smaller ones were strongly opposed by the citizens of Rotterdam, as it became clear in the referendum in that city in 1995.

The problems in the region, however, remained and still required effective government policies at the regional level. Although the creation of a city-province was out of the question since 1996, many actors believed that an adequate institutional setting was missing.

One of the actors who reflected on their position so far was the government of the province South-Holland. Between 1989 and 1995 it had played the role of the sad victim of the process of city-province creation. One of the main reasons the municipalities in the Rotterdam region wanted to create a regional government was their resentment against the province. The creation of a city-province would actually have led to the splitting up of the province of South-Holland. The provincial government had, reluctantly indeed, supported the reform process, despite its consequences. After the breakdown of the reform process in 1996, the provincial government slightly changed its position and began to express itself by showing to the actors of the Rotterdam region that its input might after all be useful.

During the policy-making process of the city-province creation, the provincial government had formulated a so-called "Area-oriented Program Rotterdam Region." This program was meant to be the preparation of the splitting up of the province (Ringeling, Hupe, Schaap, and de Vries 1998). When it became increasingly clear that there would be no such a thing as a city-province and that the province would continue to exist as it was, the provincial government hastily altered the goal of its special program. It was no longer aimed at preparing the splitting up of the province but at repositioning and profiling the provincial government. Until then, provinces in general were an almost unknown entity, at least unloved. This definitely was the case of the province of South-Holland. All provinces tried to gain relevance and recognition in the last decade of the twentieth century by being less invisible in the policy processes (Dam, Berueling, Neelen, and Wille 1996). This included also the province of South-Holland.

In terms of the institutional reform, the whole process stagnated in recent years. The eighteen municipalities still exist, and so does South-Holland. The municipalities still cooperate in the so-called *Stadsregio Rotterdam* (City-Region Rotterdam).[3] The City-Region is a formal cooperation of the autonomous municipalities in the Rotterdam region, assigned by the legislator. The cooperation of the municipalities within the City-Region Rotterdam and between the City-Region and the provincial government has its difficulties, but it works. It is interesting though that no actor involved in the present arrangement is satisfied. Some municipalities desperately want to leave the formal cooperation in which they are forced to stay in due to central legislation; some other municipalities rather enforce the cooperation; others still strive to establish a city-province. On the one hand, provincial government hesitantly cooperates with the City-Region (which might be seen as a competitor, even now). On the other hand, the central government does not know what to do, due to all kinds of political and historical reasons. A standstill of the reform process has been the consequence. The most recent development includes the proposal of the Ministry of the Interior to enlarge the period of the compulsory cooperation of the municipalities within the Rotterdam City-Region. Moreover, a large majority of the municipalities are demanding direct elections for the regional council.[4]

REFLECTION: GOVERNMENT OR GOVERNANCE?

The reform process in the Rotterdam region might be considered a failure. No regional government was created, no structural solution to the societal problems was developed. It is, of course, possible to come to a different and more positive conclusion. It all depends on the perspective on the issue.[5]

I like to distinguish two general approaches: the structure or government approach, and the process or governance approach.

The government approach considers public administration as one entity to be governed as a bureaucracy. It therefore emphasizes the necessity of

- Clear distinction between the levels of government
- Preferably a constitutional distinction
- Clear division of tasks between governmental levels
- Capacities and authorities being as exclusive as possible, the division being fixed
- Legalistic tradition

Problems in the way of a system of subnational government functions are mainly due to overlapping authorities, unclear distinctions of responsibilities, too much centralization, and a lack of autonomy for local governments. The solutions are more clarity of responsibilities, decentralization, and, last but certainly not least, increasing the problem-solving capacity of local government by facilitating the amalgamation of local authorities. Intermunicipal cooperation is a rejected solution, because it is supposed to obscure the separate responsibilities of each autonomous municipality. If the geographic scale of local authorities is too small compared to the scale of the societal problems at stake, then amalgamation or even the creation of a new layer of government is preferred.

The governance approach focuses on cooperation between government actors. This approach is derived from insights coming from policy networks studies (Kickert, Klijn, and Koppenjan 1997) and governance studies (Rhodes 1997).[6] If this approach is being used, the focus no longer is on creating a new layer of government but on making things work. It emphasizes the relevance of

- Checks and balances (normative statement)
- Interdependency as reality (empirical statement), therefore cooperation seen as good
- Structures ensuring flexibility and innovation
- Flexibility meaning changing performance

This approach recognizes that problems are centered around the difficulty of municipalities cooperating with each other, the possible inflexibility of the present division of tasks and the existence of veto power of some actors, and the existence of somewhat closed frames of reference. The solutions are to improve the mechanisms of facilitation of cooperation by creating overlapping authorities and making it more efficient. In this approach, it becomes clear that an efficient structure (at face value) often becomes penny-wise and pound-foolish. Intermunicipal cooperation is perceived as essential for all governmental entities, since it may prevent power concentration. Autonomy is not only impossible but unwise as well.

If the reform process in the Rotterdam region is analyzed with the government approach, then it is definitely a big failure, due to the fact that no integral regional government was achieved. Instead there is a very vague cooperation system with no clear division of responsibilities, reinforced by the process of overlapping authorities.

When the perspective changes, however, and the analysis is based on the governance approach, then reality is more than slightly altered. The overlapping authorities are a blessing in disguise, because they are the expression of checks and balances.

THE BETTER WAY: REGIONAL GOVERNANCE

Especially in the subnational government system in the Netherlands, not reforming, hence not creating a regional tier of government, is probably a sensible course of action. Dutch public administration has such a high level of complexity that a clear separation between layers of government is almost impossible. In the welfare state, the state has become omnipresent, local government playing its role in almost every policy area. Each policy area, however, has its own scale; policy problems in particular have their own geographical scale. Finding the better scale for a government layer is a useless effort. As Dahl and Tufte mentioned in 1973, "No single type or size of unit is optimal for achieving the twin goals of citizen effectiveness and system capacity. Democratic goals conflict, and no single unit or kind of unit can best serve these goals."

Administrators and scientists favoring reform as a means of solving societal problems should bear in mind that the creation of new layers of government—such as the wished-for city-provinces in the Netherlands or as the process of amalgamation of local authorities, common in most countries with the exception of France (Norton 1994)—seems to be a somewhat peculiar activity. Different solutions are at hand, if the present authorities are unable to cope with certain policy problems, such as the creation of agencies or quangos, centralization to the next higher layer of government, or functional cooperation of authorities within a certain region and around a certain issue.

In the Netherlands the latter strategy is the present one. In almost every metropolitan and rural area, countrywide, local authorities cooperate with other authorities in coping with regional problems. No municipality is able to solve its policy problems without cooperating with other local authorities; the bigger cities certainly are no exception to this rule. To a certain extent, regional authorities have emerged, although not elected directly, not having a general competence, not constitutionally established, but merely based on ordinary law.

SOME DIFFICULTIES REMAIN

Formal cooperation is, however, not without difficulties. First of all, as the case of the Rotterdam region clearly shows, cooperation does not emerge automatically. Some of the relevant participants will resent cooperating, possibly because of a supposed loss of autonomy. That fear has to be accepted as a reality. Support is relevant at all stages. Margaret Weir (2000) formulates some lessons for metropolitan cooperation, based on experiences in the United States, among others:

- Ongoing political mobilization is a necessity.
- Enemies can be turned into allies by emphasizing mutual benefits.
- Go-it-alone strategies do not work: Make regionalization efforts in different policy fields.

Another important issue from a democratic point of view is the lack of legitimacy.[7] The cooperative bodies do not have a directly elected council but only a council consisting of local representatives, nor a directly elected mayor but only a board consisting of several mayors and aldermen delegated from the individual municipalities (none elected directly). The lack of legitimacy, or even the lack of democracy, is a real problem. This was therefore brought to the fore by several government advisory boards, such as the Public Administration Council (Raad voor het openbaar bestuur [ROB], assigned to advise in matters concerning subnational government) and the Scientific Council for Government Policy (Wetenschappelijke Raad voor het Regeringsbeleid [WRR]).

One report published by the Scientific Council for Government Policy in particular shows the difficulty of gaining value-added democracy in the present subnational government (WRR 1995, 25 ff). The authors distinguish three different scales:

- **Scale of societal problems:** At which level do problems exist (local, regional, provincial, national, or somewhere in between)?
- **Scale of efficient and responsive government:** At which level can government effectively and efficiently respond to issues in such a way that popular demands are coped with?
- **Scale of popular involvement:** At which level do people feel involved in societal and governmental matters?

The problem, then, emerges when the scales show different paths of development. That clearly is the case in present society and public administration. Especially the first and the second scales are no longer the same. Problems seem to exist at a greater geographical scale than they used to; government scale has not increased at the same pace. But not all problem scales have increased; some have decreased. And to make the picture even more complex, not all problems have identical implications for government. Problems are heavily differentiated and accordingly are dealt with at the scales on which they exist. If the development of a societal problem was one of scaling up, then a scaling-up of government would probably be a sensible reaction. But because government is rather confronted with a nasty scale differentiation, scaling-up might be unwise. It will definitely be impossible to adapt the scale of government to the scale of all societal problems, because all the problems have different scales. One can easily complicate matters even more by showing that some issues require attention at the several scales; traffic policies for instance need attention at the local, regional, and European levels (Selm 1998). The conclusion is that even when we only take the scale of societal problems as a starting point in order to find the best territorial scale for governments, we already are confronted with insolvable difficulties. A further difficulty in finding the best scale for government is when we look at popular involvement and participation. In the Dutch case, participation decreases when the scale of the government increases (Herweijer 1998). One might say the larger the area, the lesser civic involvement exists.

The conclusion that one can draw from these reflections is that aiming to create the best scale for local or regional government is futile. The scale at which societal problems exist, the scale of effective government, and the scale at which people want to be involved differ heavily. No reform can change that situation. It is therefore very important to focus on the democratic legitimacy of intermunicipal cooperation. The Dutch Public Administration Council published some special advice on that issue (ROB 2000). The Council made it clear that democracy at the intermunicipal level not only depends on the kind of structures of accountability, responsibilities, and democratic control, but that it rather needs a democratic culture of the administration, a culture of openness, a willingness to be accountable and responsive. Such a culture is preferably supported by procedures against secrecy and by establishing public rights of information.

CONCLUSION: A SKETCH OF GENERAL LESSONS

One can draw the following conclusions from the Rotterdam case:

- Think twice before reforming subnational government and reflect on its necessity.

- Do not too hastily think that agreement on basic principles is a real fundamental agreement.
- Be aware of processes of interpretation, of assigning meaning. Be aware of social construction processes.
- Do not let time pressure constrain you. Augmenting time pressure sometimes generates opposite effects from those expected. In hindsight, one can state that because of the constructed lack of time, many decisions that were made in the Rotterdam region resulted in unintended situations.
- Try to cope with uncertainty. During the entire Rotterdam city-province process, attempts were made to grasp the wicked policy problems, as well as to decide in great detail which governmental layer should get what specific tasks—a very time-consuming process, with great risks of annoyance.
- Last but not least, pay attention to legitimacy. Invest in democracy at the intermunicipal level rather than in reform policy processes.

NOTES

1. They may be excused for this mistake. At some times, at least until 1995, the process really was expected to result in the creation of city-provinces.

2. Note that Dutch mayors are appointed officials, not elected politicians. The Crown (in fact, the Ministry of the Interior) appoints them.

3. This city-region is not to be mistaken for the city-province that never got beyond its *statu nascendi*.

4. Many involved fail to see that such direct elections for the regional council might be a bit confusing. What to elect? There would be no real regional government, because the city-region is formally a cooperation between autonomous municipalities (the executive of the city-region consists of a handful of mayors and aldermen of some of the participating municipalities). Despite this, there would be a council, directly elected by the voters. Some might call this confusing, or the creation of a city-province after all and at last.

5. I admit, this is not a real revolutionary statement. One only has to look at Allison (1971).

6. This also shows some similarities with Bogason's (2000) "Institutional Network Analysis Bottom-up" (109 ff).

7. Some might say that the creation of a regional tier of government is better, from the democratic point of view, because its council will be elected directly. They, however, easily forget that the reform process itself has to gain popular support as well, as those in Rotterdam who were involved in the creation of the city-province learned the hard way—by losing the votes in a referendum.

REFERENCES

Allison, G. T. 1971. *Essence of decision.* Boston: Little, Brown and Company.

Bekkers, V. J. J. M., and F. Hendriks. 1998. Gemeenten in Europees perspectief, samenwerking en concurrentie. In *Lokaal bestuur in Nederland*, edited by A. F. A. Korsten and P. W. Tops. Alphen aan den Rijn: Samsom.

Berghuis, J. M. J., M. Herweijer, and W. J. M. Pol. 1995. *Effecten van herindeling.* Deventer: Kluwer.

Bogason, P. 2000. *Public policy and local governance: Institutions in postmodern society.* Cheltenham: Edgar Elgar.

Cachet, A., and J. F. M. Koppenjan. 1996. De vorming van de stadsprovincie Rotterdam: een onmogelijke opgave? In *Het onzichtbare bestuur: Over provincies, stadsprovincies en regionale vraagstukken,* edited by M. van Dam, J. Berveling, G. Neelen, and A. Wille, pp. 91–116. Delft: Eburon.

Dahl, R. A., and E. R. Tufte. 1973. *Size and democracy.* Stanford: Stanford University Press.

Dam, M. van, J. Berveling, G. Neelen, and A. Wille, eds. 1996. *Het onzichtbare bestuur: over provincies, stadsprovincies en regionale vraagstukken.* Delft: Eburon.

Derksen, W. 1998. *Lokaal bestuur.* Den Haag: Elsevier.

Herweijer, M. 1998. Schaal en gemeente. In *Lokaal bestuur in Nederland,* edited by A. F. A. Korsten and P. W. Tops, pp. 135-57. Alphen aan den Rijn: Samsom.

Katz, B., ed. 2000. *Reflections on regionalism.* Washington, D.C.: Brookings Institution Press.

Kickert, W. J. M., E. H. Klijn, and J. F. M. Koppenjan, eds. 1997. *Managing complex networks.* London: SAGE.

Koppenjan, J. F. M. 1993. *Management van de beleidsvorming.* Den Haag: VUGA.

Loughlin, J., and B. G. Peters. 1997. State traditions, administrative reform and regionalization. In *The political economy of regionalism,* edited by M. Keating and R. J. Loughlin. London: Cass.

Luhmann, N. 1984. *Soziale systeme: Grundriß einer allgemeinen theorie.* Frankfurt am Main: Suhrkamp.

———. 1990a. *Essays on self-reference.* New York: Columbia University Press.

———. 1990b. *Political theory in the welfare state.* Berlin: De Gruyter.

Ministerie van Binnenlandse Zaken. 1990. *Bestuur en stedelijke gebieden: Bestuur op niveau* (BON 1). Den Haag: Ministerie van Binnenlandse Zaken. Tweede Kamer 1990–1991, 21062, no. 3.

———. 1991. *Bestuur op niveau, deel 2: Bestuur en stedelijke gebieden* (BON 2). Den Haag: Ministerie van Binnenlandse Zaken. Tweede Kamer 1990–1991, 21062, no. 7.

———. 1993. *Bestuur op nivo, deel 3: Vernieuwing bestuurlijke organisatie* (BON 3). Den Haag: Ministerie van Binnenlandse Zaken. Tweede Kamer 1992–1993, 21062, no. 21.

Newton, M. T., and P. J. Donaghy. 1997. *Institutions of modern Spain: A political and economic guide.* Cambridge: Cambridge University Press.

Norton, A. 1994. *International handbook of local and regional government.* Cheltenham: Edward Elgar.

Overlegorgaan Rijnmondgemeenten (OOR). 1991a. *De regio als nieuw perspectief.* Rotterdam.

Quinn, B. 1999. The effects of EU-membership on local and regional governments. Draft, paper written for the Joint European Module on Local and Regional Government, Limerick.

Raad voor het openbaar bestuur (ROB). 2000. *Bestuurlijke samenwerking en democratische controle.* Den Haag.

Rhodes, R. A. W. 1997. *Understanding governance.* Buckingham: Open University Press.

Ringeling, A. B., P. L. Hupe, L. Schaap, and G. J. D. de Vries. 1998. *Effecten van gebeidsgericht werken Rotterdamse Regio.* Rotterdam: Faculteit Sociale Wetenschappen.

Ruano, J. M. 2000. Organization, effectiveness and democracy in the local governments of the European Union. Draft, JEM paper.

Schaap, L. 1997. *Op zoek naar prikkelende overheidssturing: Over autopoiese, zelfsturing en stadsprovincie* (The search for inciting governance: On autopoiesis, self-governance and city-province). Delft: Eburon.

Selm, J. A. van. 1998. Schaal, verkeer en verkeersbeleid, *Bestuurskunde* 7: 38–47.

Sharpe, L. J. 1987. The West European state: The territorial dimension. In *Tensions in the territorial politics of Western Europe*, edited by R. A. W. Rhodes and V. Wright, pp. 148–68. London: Frank Cass.

Spencer Brown, G. 1972. *Laws of form.* New York: Juliana Press.

Toonen, Th. A. J. 1990. The unitary state as a system of co-governance: The case of the Netherlands. *Public Administration* 68 (3): 281–96.

Veld, R. J. in 't, L. Schaap, C. J. A. M. Termeer, and M. J. W. van Twist. 1991. *Autopoiesis and configuration theory: New approaches to societal steering.* Dordrecht: Kluwer Academic Publishers.

Weir, M. 2000. Coalition building for regionalism. In *Reflections on regionalism*, edited by B. Katz, pp. 127–54. Washington, D.C.: Brookings Institution Press.

Wetenschappelijke Raad voor het Regeringsbeleid (WRR). 1995. *Orde in het binnenlands bestuur.* Rapporten aan de regering no. 49. Den Haag: SDU.

9

Flanders: Do It Yourself and Do It Better? Regional Parliaments as Sites for Democratic Renewal and Gendered Representation

Karen Celis and Alison Woodward

REGIONS AS SITES FOR DEMOCRATIC RENEWAL?

The creation and empowerment of regional bodies in Europe may offer the potential of more room for diverse voices in terms of gender and ethnicity and an answer at the meso level to the problems of democratic deficit. We are witnessing a "dynamic restructuring process" (Benz and Eberlein 1998), in which both political institutions and socioeconomic boundaries at the regional level are playing larger roles. Within these constellations, the juggling of new political participants can be responsible for different approaches and content. New players and new contexts lead to different political practice in terms of both content and form. In this chapter, we consider the example of the Flemish parliament and see parallels with the case of Scotland. These cases offer initial confirmation that the players at least wish that this will be the case. However, changes in the players, in terms of gender, do not seem to be self-evident. Whereas Scotland succeeds in radically increasing women's representation, the results from Flanders are less encouraging. Nonetheless, the results from the first regional Flemish parliament indicate that women politicians behave in ways closer to the norms of the new political culture aimed at by these regional parliaments, and that across Europe, gender inroads may change the complexion of regional parliaments.

The transformation of governance in Europe from unitary and centralized states to more and more levels of jurisdiction has been gradual and included backs and forths. In the 1970s, most countries initiated consolidation of their municipalities into more centralized units, with big cities almost universally initiating metropolitan forms of governance, and smaller cities consolidated. At the same time jurisdiction was being transformed through the process of on the one hand European integration and on the other hand, or perhaps part and parcel of it, an increasing creation of regional organs with greater or lesser authority, including organs at the middle level such as new forms of provinces (Sharpe 1993, cited in Hooghe and Marks 2001) and new mini-states.

Hooghe and Marks's most recent book (2001) traces these developments, noting the lack of systematic empirical research on the transformation of levels of governance in Europe in a comparative framework. Nonetheless, there is a small-multidisciplinary industry describing the transformation of democratic decision making in Europe. The developments suggest that the authority of the central nation-state has been thinned out. On the one hand, authority has been transferred from the state to the supranational level, and on the other hand, new and powerful regional bodies have acquired jurisdiction over many matters. Further, the wave of privatization beginning with the Reagan-Thatcher period has contributed to some shrinkage of the girth of state responsibilities, so that other matters are now under the responsibility of public-private institutions or completely privatized.

Again according to Hooghe and Marks's reading of this literature, these developments are, normatively speaking, seen as a "good thing."[1] In an ever more globalizing world, national jurisdictions are insufficient for dealing with cross-border issues, while local issues require increasingly tailor-made solutions for democratic legitimacy. Multi-level governance (Hooghe 1996; Deschouwer and Jans 1999; Keating 1998; Kohler-Koch and Eising 2000; Kohler-Koch 1999; Olsen 1995) is part of dynamic restructuring process in Europe in which both political institutions and socioeconomic boundaries at the regional level are playing larger roles. Though the harmonization process of transfer of authority to the supranational level is intimately linked with the problems of democratic deficit, and transfer of authority to the local authorities, the focus here is particularly on how the new institutions in European politics have led to a reevaluation of the roles of local and regional levels. Regional parliaments are strategically placed to take advantage of developments in European multilevel governance and act as a source of political innovation. Further, as seen in Chapter 1 of this volume, they are a widespread phenomenon.

With the changing roles of national, regional, and local decision-makers, windows of opportunity have been created for new forms of political behavior and for voices seldom heard at the national level. Regional institutions are particularly interesting as they forge into vacuums created by the structuring forces of the European integration process. Across Europe, national and regional institutions have been changing. One might begin with the formation of the postwar German state and its Länder as a federation, and continue with ever accelerating speed through the regionalization of Spain in autonomous communities (Conversi 1997). The process intensified to include the reinforced role of the French regional assemblies (Down 1997), the federalization of Belgium (Fitzmaurice 1996; Dewachter, Depauw, and Thomas 1997), and the devolution process in the United Kingdom (Bogdanor 1999; Bradbury and Mawson 1997). Even the long-standing federal structure of Germany is changing with the challenges of integration of the new Länder, and European delegation of respnsibility to regions for policy delivery.

Several factors have driven recent change in the role of the regions. First, citizen demand for more responsive and representative government and disillusion with traditional forms of democratic representation (Dogan 2000) led to pressure for more transparent and accessible and local representation (De Winter and Swyngedouw 1999; Kohler-Koch 1999; Abromeit 1998; Council of Europe 1999; Schmitt and Thomassen 1999). Tensions, whether cultural and linguistic or economic at root, found an increasing voice as pacification agreements suffered from sclerosis. Regional actors began to question the myth and value of the unitary state (Keating 1998) as their political skills and resources became more sophisticated and as the benefits of unity and solidarity with weaker parts of the country became more doubtful. This pressure for representation and autonomy is especially interesting in any discussion of the regions that felt misunderstood in the national setting such as Scotland and Flanders.

Further, increasing European political integration has led to the high-status questions of defense, justice, or the economy being discussed increasingly by the national executive in international settings (bypassing the national parliamentary platform). Meanwhile significant responsibilities for social welfare have been moved to the regional level and stimulated by the European Union, creating new opportunities for regional action and democracy.

New regional parliaments are strategically placed to take advantage of these developments and have the potential to be a source of political innovation. They offer fields for new players in terms of gender, age, and minority party interests. The changing political context offers new opportunities for different political practice in terms of both content and form.

NEW PARLIAMENTS DISTANCING THEMSELVES FROM NATIONAL TRADITIONS

Though there has been considerable comparison of national parliaments, their function, and their members (Blonde 1973, 1990; Döring 1995; Mezey 1979; Norton 1996; Suleiman 1986; etc.), and also comparison between MPs and MEPs (Katz and Wessels 1999; Schmitt and Thomassen 1999; Norton 1996), little has been done on regional parliaments in a comparative framework (exceptions being Down 1997 and Loughlin, Aja, Bullmann, and Hendricks 1999). Regional parties have had substantial interest (De Winter and Türsan 1998), but regional parliaments are still a novelty.

The expanding interest in multilevel governance in Europe (Hooghe 1996; Marks, Scharpf, Schmitter, Streeck 1996; Deschouwer and Jans 1999) make clear that a better understanding of regional decision bodies and the ways they differ from their national counterparts is essential to explaining European democratic processes. Regional parliaments today, given the factors of the changing European context, the demand for a different political culture, and their frequently higher proportion of women and other political newcomers, have the potential of providing a vanguard for political renewal. Especially interesting in this context are certainly the new parliaments created in the 1990s in the United Kingdom and Belgium.

In both Flanders and Scotland, there was a dream of a new style of politics. Terry Nicholls Clark and colleagues (Clark and Hoffman-Martinot 1998) writing about the reforms in municipal culture, use the blanket term "new political culture" to refer to the sorts of political reforms which in many ways seem to mirror the societal trends identified by Ron Inglehart (1997) in his studies of postmaterialism. Transparency, efficiency, and openness to alternative voices and values are some of the characteristics of this desired postmaterialist/new political culture.

Some of the driving features of the devolved parliament in Scotland and that in Flanders were similar, and can be summarized in the phrase "What we do ourselves, we do better." Certainly in the Flemish case, the first independently elected parliament, which took office for a four-year term in 1995, was born in a period with extreme disillusion with national-level politics, which had been marked by scandals with party financing, contract awards (the so-called Augusta helicopter scandal was coupled with indictments of the Belgian head of NATO, sui-

cides and jailing of Socialist party heads) and the perceived failure of
the justice system (Marc Dutroux and the White Marches of 1996). There
was extreme citizen disillusionment with the normal order of politics
and the wish for something new. Elite launched blueprints for political
reform such as *Het Sinjaal,* and national and regional government
commissions investigated reform in the codes of honor of political
practice. In Belgium, the bundle of reform measures and attendant
debate was labeled the "new political culture" by the journalistic world
with little reference to any of the international discussion or earlier
critiques of the Belgian way of doing things (Stouthuysen 1997; Woodward 1998).

This debate found fertile ground for alliances between Flemish nationalists, who had always pleaded for a simpler unilingual political
forum and those looking for an opportunity launch a new kind of
parliamentary politics. The process of transformation to a federal state
that had rocked Belgian politics since the 1970s would reach one of its
culmination points with the full regionalization of authority (including
democratic decision making) over a number of policy areas. Ultimately
six regional assemblies were created who represented respectively the
French-, German-, and Flemish-speaking communities and the territories of Wallonia, Brussels, and Flanders. In the case of Flanders, territory
and language community overlapped sufficiently to lead to the creation
of the mightiest of the regional parliamentary bodies with wide-ranging
authority over virtually all issues except justice, national budget, and
defense. With the potential for a very powerful parliament, the
challenge to demonstrate that Flanders "could do it better" was intense.

The ambitions for the new parliament were high. The president of the
Flemish Parliament launched a proposal for a "new political culture"
(which was initially a journalistic concept) in 1995. He called it "Refinement of Democracy." The central goal was to reestablish confidence in
democracy by bridging the gap between "the outspoken civilians" and
politicians. The Flemish Parliament would make the policy process and
legislation more transparent and take measures to prevent political
scandals. Concretely several structural changes were suggested to create a parliament that contrasted with the national parliament. These
included making commission meetings public; regulations to increase
the contacts and control between the parliament and the executive (for
example, election of the president of the parliament and the reformation
of the parliamentary questions to increase control over the executive);
the introduction of theme debates as a measure to increase in the role
of the Flemish Parliament as a forum for societal debate; improving
relations between the parliament and citizens (reducing the role of
parliamentarians as personal intermediaries for citizens); and including
a code of ethics, the so-called deontological code.

This history has meant that the Flemish Parliament is not just a regional backwater but has substantial budgetary and legislative discretion. Its authority concerns all matters directly connected to citizens living in the territory of Flanders. As such it represents more than one half of the population of Belgium (circa 6 million) and decides on the larger questions of education, health, culture/media, and other person-connected public services including roads, city planning, and the environment. It has competencies in trade and employment and engages in friendly competition with the national level in its attempts to profile itself on these issues. European programs such as the European Structural Fund form a handy lever for the Flemish government to obtain extra revenues and develop its own profile in cooperation with other regions in Europe. Finally, because of the federal structure, the Flemish Parliament is expected to approve the large majority of international treaties concluded with Belgium and thus has competencies in foreign affairs as well.

As there is a substantial and vocal group in the Flemish elite that voices desire for an independent Flemish state, and given the competencies that the regions of Belgium are responsible for, it is perhaps not astonishing that their relation with Europe is frequently very direct, to the extent that in a number of Council meetings, Belgium is represented by the Minister from the regional level (Kerremans 2000). This is rather different to the way the Scottish debate proceeded. The autonomy desired by Scottish elites was not so much to be able to deal in an international forum, as to be a better mirror of domestic issues.

In Scotland, according to Sloat (2001a and 2001b), the years preceding the reestablishment of the Scottish Parliament in 1999 were also eventful, as political and civic elite actively discussed the new style of politics that should be practiced in the parliament. In her interviews with actors from the national administration, Scottish civic life, and both national and regional political parties, Sloat sketches how the dreams of the architects of Scottish devolution are translated by builders from the civil services and carried out by the first tenants, a new generation of politicians with their own ideas about what the new home should hold.

Sloat also traces a history of desire for new forms of governance in Scotland, identifying a consensus around policy making that prioritized a holistic approach, democratic accountability, and transparency. These are the same key words found in Flanders. She cites the CSG's 1998 proposal recommending that Parliament "share power, be accountable, be accessible, open responsive and participative." Finally, she notes something not to be found in the Flemish account; recognition of "equal opportunities" (Sloat 2001a, 13). Even if she discovers in interviews that the various categories of actors have different understandings of governance, the parallel ambitions for the quality of regional governance are striking. As far as relations with Europe go, she reports that elites did not necessarily perceive Whitehall as a competitor, as is often the case in Flanders, nor as a gatekeeper, but most often as an important partner. This is because of the substantial resources that the central UK government has in Brussels. Whereas Flanders has structurally created a "Brussels bypass" through the wide- ranging competencies in the government, Scotland seems to be more cautious in pursuing "Westminster bypasses" as they may backfire and lead to Whitehall opposition on other issues important to Scotland.

PLACES FOR NEW PLAYERS? HOW PERMEABLE IS THE REGIONAL FORUM?

Structurally and institutionally, the Scottish and Flemish and other new regional parliaments enter onto a playing field where the new issues of Europe offer an unexpected action terrain. Further, their newness opens an additional level of politics so that temporarily at least there is a chance for demographic renewal. Generally, it has been held that lower levels of political representation are more open to minorities than higher. Thus state-level politics in the United States and city and provincial governments can be expected to have more women than small and powerful national legislative bodies. The rule of thumb has been that the higher the stakes, the fewer the women. This rule certainly still holds true in the world of the economy.

In European politics, the last thirty years have shown a variable record on the representation of women at the mesolevel. In the majority of EU member-countries with regional parliaments, women make up more than 25 percent of the members (8/11). Yet in only half of the countries is the representation of women higher at the regional than at the national level (Women in Decision-Making 2001; Rule 1993). Regional bodies thus present an uneven record in terms of women's representation. This does not seem to be clearly related to their power and authority, method of election, or political color. Politics is important, however, as anecdotal and case studies seem to indicate that women's representation in regions may be related to local party organizational factors and level of women's activism in particular parties. Table 9.1 indicates the comparative situation of regional and national parliamentary representation in Europe. The countries are grouped according to a rough estimate of the level of constitutional federalism. The relative power of the regional assemblies in comparison to the national assemblies is roughly estimated in terms of budget control and breadth of responsibilities. Table 9.1 further provides the percentage of seats held by women in regional and national assemblies.

TABLE 9.1   Are Women More Likely to be Present at Lower Levels of Government? Presence of Women in Parliaments by Level of Constitutional Federalism

	Number of Regions	Number of Members in regional assemblies	Women as % of regional assembly members	Women as % of national parliaments	Power: Level of constitutional federalism	Power of national versus regional assembly
AUSTRIA	9	448	26.1	24.7	High	More
BELGIUM	5	393	21.6	25.6	High	Less
GERMANY	16	1970	30.7	29.6	High	More
SPAIN	17	359	30.4	27.1	High	Less
FRANCE	22	1693	25.8	8.7	Mid	More
ITALY	20	933	8.4	10.2	Mid	Less
UK	3	71	27.3	17.1	Mid	More
DENMARK	14	374	30.2	37.1	Low	Less
NETHERLANDS	10	761	27.3	33.3	Low	Less
PORTUGAL	2	111	11.7	19.6	Low	Less
SWEDEN	23	810	47.2	45	Low	More
FINLAND	-	-		37	None	
GREECE	-	-		10.3	None	
IRELAND	-	-		14.6	None	
LUXEMBOURG	-	-		16.7	None	

Source: Own compilation of data from European database: *Women in Decision Making,* February 2001, http://www.db-decision.de/ Fact sheets. See classification of governments according to degree of regionalization in Chapter 1.

A generalization that lower levels of power lead to a higher percentage of women in legislatures is not clearly supported by this table. There are equally many regional parliaments above and below the national parliament figure. Any detailed exploration of the data at the subnational level indicates that gender balance is a highly variable item. Representation in German Länder varies from 17 percent in Baden-Württemberg to 40 percent in Bremen. That many other factors are at work in producing this distribution, including the level of organization of the women's movement and the power of socialist parties, seems to be indicated. This is also the case in regions discussed as the detailed data on the various regional assemblies indicates.

In Scotland, the women's movement was highly aware of the problem of representation (Brown 1998; Consultative Steering Group 1999). During the constitutional convention as well as in lobbying efforts within political parties and through action coalitions in the women's movement and civic movements, dramatic efforts and suggestions were made to guarantee a higher representation of women in politics. The activities of women around devolution, especially within the Labor party, but also more generally in the Constitutional Conventions led in

TABLE 9.2 Women's Representation at the Regional Level in the United Kingdom and Belgium (2001) (percents)

UK ASSEMBLIES	17.1	BELGIAN ASSEMBLIES	23.2
Northern Ireland	13.0	Brussels Region	34.7
Scotland	37.3	Flanders Region & Community	20.2
Wales	41.7	French Community	18
		Wallonian Region	12
		German Community	32

Source: European database, Women in Decision Making, February 2001, http://www.db-decision.de/ Fact sheets.

two of the three new United Kingdom parliaments to a dramatically improved representation of women as compared to the situation in London. The UK, with its first-past-the-post system of voting, has always hung at the bottom of league tables in political representation of women. One of the important strategies was transformation of the electoral system and processes of nomination within the party.

The Flemish women's movement was less clever in taking advantage of these new opportunities. There are certainly numerous explanations for the relative lack of concentrated effort to radically perform a gender transformation of the parliament. Most important perhaps is the gradual history of the creation of the body out of the side of its mother. For a long period, Flemish issues were handled by the Flemish members of the national parliament. The clean break that was present in the UK cases was much less dramatic in Belgium. The issue of women's representation had also long been a thorn for feminist politicians and femocrats in Belgium. As in the United Kingdom, Belgium, too, has hung low on the totem pole of representation (7th place in 2000) in Europe. It made virtually no progress, while neighboring countries with similar political culture and voting structures rocketed forward. In contrast to Scotland, however, there were a number of women in the national government, including a Minister for Equal Opportunity. After years of frustration, many activists pinned their hopes on hard measures such as the law requiring quotas on electoral lists (Carton 1995, 1998). The women's movement itself may have not understood the full implications of the creation of the new parliament. The reforms that led to the direct election of the parliament were not at all straightforward, and even commentators were not sure of what the relative power of the national versus the regional assemblies would ultimately be. Whatever the explanation, the fact remains that there was little strategic action to commandeer seats in the new parliament beyond the traditional "Vote for a woman" sensibilization campaigning.

SPECIFIC IMPLICATIONS OF THESE
DEVELOPMENTS—THE EVERYDAY LIFE OF
THESE NEWLY IMPORTANT PARLIAMENTS
AND THEIR VARIATIONS

These developments of demographically new representatives and different anticipations of what democratic governance is all about can make us wonder if regional parliamentary opportunity leads to political renewal, T. Nicholls Clark and Hoffman-Martinot's new political culture? As we have seen, both the Flemish and the Scottish parliament officially pronounce that there should be a focus on team approaches, transparency, and efficient performance. In the Flemish case, many of the carriers of these ambitions have been parliamentary newcomers, including women, minorities, and youth (sometimes in minority parties such as the Greens).

The new parliaments in the United Kingdom and the developing parliaments in Belgium have been the subject of some research. Both Scottish and Flemish studies demonstrate that politicians come to regional institutions with different career ambitions and understandings about how to reach political decisions, the tasks of politics and parliaments, and the methods to achieve political successes, as compared to their national counterparts (Belgians profiled by De Winter [1992]). Decision making that occurs in consensus is looked on with favor, especially by women and newcomers. This is promoted through an emphasis on content work in commissions. Work on gender in organizations indicates that the accents that were placed by female politicians are typical of what occurs when gender-mixed groups solve problems, and they are also accents emphasized by demands of the women's movement (Leijenaar 1993, 1989; Randall 1991; Randall and Waylen 1998; Ferree and Martin 1995).

DO THE NEW WINDOWS AND NEWCOMERS
MAKE A DIFFERENCE? EVIDENCE FROM
FLANDERS

For this chapter, evidence from Flanders can help us begin to explore the extent to which the regional setting offers new opportunities for different political practice in European parliaments. The ambition is to compare the experiences in Flanders with other parliaments both within Belgium and in older and newer parliaments in Europe. In our study of the Flemish Parliament, it is clear that there are new political accents and institutional practices that reflect another conception of democracy closer to that accented by alternative social movements.

Though the case in Scotland seems to have brought many newcomers into politics, the first Flemish Parliament actually had fewer newcomers than the same election's federal chamber of representatives. Thus the newcomer effect is a relatively minor variable present in the Flemish case.

First we present some background information on the parliament. Demographically the first elected parliament is young, with one third of its members between thirty-six and forty-five years old; and 40 percent between forty-six and fifty-five years old. Ironically after the election, the Federal Chamber also became younger. Further, in the 1995–1999 legislature, there were actually fewer political newcomers in the Flemish Parliament than in the Federal Chamber (40 percent in Flanders, 45 percent in the National Chamber, as the restructuring led to a new form of Senate with a higher age profile). The first Flemish Parliament was a highly educated (two thirds university trained) and masculine (82 percent) one.

The Flemish MPs are convinced that the Flemish Parliament is a unique institution that distinguishes itself from the national parliament. With the exception of one member of Flemish Parliament (MFP), all the interviewees considered the Flemish Parliament as a unique parliament. The MFPs formulated several arguments during the interviews to prove the different character of the Flemish Parliament. According to the interviewees, the two main reasons for the uniqueness of the Flemish Parliament were that the Parliament has its own building and its new mission.

While the other new regional parliaments had to make-do with borrowed buildings, the simple fact of having its own building was seen as an important feature of its autonomy. The design of the building has also been a subject of discussion in the Scottish case. Initially, in 1995 and the first months of 1996, the Flemish Parliament was housed in the building of the Federal Parliament. The Flemish Parliament building was considered to be symbolic of a different style, one that would be of a new order. Many deputies stressed that the architecture of the building symbolizes the ideology of the Flemish Parliament as being a transparent political institution that "has nothing to hide." The Flemish Parliament is a very modern building, and its most striking feature is the glass roof over the chamber. However, this aspect is not visible from the street, as in fact it hides behind a traditional façade in the quarters of the Belgian legislative buildings. Thus its façade does not reflect this vaunted transparency.

According to the interviewees, being a new parliament in the sense of being a young parliament generated a specific dynamism and a new spirit. This different culture in the Flemish Parliament showed itself according to the interviewed deputies—in different elements. There is a rather informal and open atmosphere. Structurally there have been a number of changes, such as the public nature of the committee meetings and the use of hearings. When they compared their situation with the Federal Parliament, the FP was seen as a better work climate and situation. This was more specifically defined as more efficient, faster, less aggressive, more directed toward consensus, with a less clear partition between the majority and the opposition, and a more objective way of interacting instead of a confrontational mode. Many identified the presence of the will to create a new political culture and practice and to act in accordance with it. They claimed that the Federal Parliament would have difficulty in achieving this. We examine this aspect of new political culture (NPC) further.

CREATING A NEW INSTITUTIONAL PRAXIS: NEW POLITICAL CULTURE AND ETHICS

A number of the reforms in this body also seemed calculated to meet the demands of a more responsive and transparent political culture. The culture in this parliament is less adversarial than in the national forum. In order to force a cultural change, the Flemish Parliament introduced several regulations regarding the structure of the parliament. It also introduced regulations regarding the deontology of the MFPs. This deontological code or code of ethics was a central element in the new political culture debate. The code of ethics was put into force in 1998 and imposed rules concerning "case work" or surgeries. The existence of "case work" or "services to citizens" is a typical characteristic of Belgian political practice. Politicians have "office hours" during which citizens can go to them to obtain information or help (for example, for filling in their tax declaration form). This practice has sometimes led to illegal favors or preferential treatment. This is strongly linked with old political culture.

The code of ethics put restraints on this by making a clear distinction between legal and illegal case work. For example, helping with a tax declaration is still legal, but interference to influence court decisions is illegal. Although this ethical code was minimal according to some politicians, there was resistance to implementing it in the Flemish Parliament. It was never accepted in the Federal Parliament in spite of several attempts.

The discussion of the relation between the citizen and the politician at the regional level puts some of the most important issues of the present discussion of democracy and democratic deficit into central place. European institutions have been criticized for being beyond democratic control and far from the citizen, but the national parliaments in both the United Kingdom (where MPs do not even live in their districts) and in Belgium have also suffered from similar criticism. Yet at the same time, the Belgian manner of doing politics with case work was seen as a source of unseemly influence and corruption. The muddiness of the debate about future European democracy comes to a head here. In the Flemish data, there was widespread disunity among MFPs about the role of direct citizen consultation in democracy.

Interestingly, the female MFPs (who are admittedly a small minority) consistently took the higher ground in terms of political practice, showing a higher commitment to knowing their dossiers, more hours per week spent in parliament and commission meetings than their male colleagues, and a higher level of parliamentary activity in general (Celis 2001). Yet on the issue of case work, they were strongly divided. Many think that women politicians feel most able to realize their ambitions at local levels, as many of the areas of competence overlap with women's interests in welfare, health, and education (Lovenduski and Norris 1996; Darcy, Welch, and Clark 1987; Bergqvist et al. 1999), but the Flemish experience seems to suggest that it is not so much that women are bearers of new political culture as that there is a generation shift to a new kind of politician whose talents are differently mobilized at the regional level.

Time budget

The time budget of the Flemish MPs could be an indicator for the presence of NPC—for example, if more time was dedicated to the study of political issues and committee meetings and less time to clientelism (see Table 9.3.).

For members of the Flemish Parliament, an average working week consisted of 56.1 hours per week. Federal MPs work more: in 1983, an average of 71.6 hours per week (De Winter 1992) and in 1995, 65.5 hours per week (Woodward and Lyon 2000). This rather large difference in week average is due to the difference in time spent outside parliament. Concerning the time spent inside parliament, we find that the Flemish members devote less time to plenary meetings and more time to committee meetings. This difference is further increased among the female MFPs.

Is it possible to conclude from this time budget that Flemish MPs behave more according to the NPC ideas? In many ways, yes. Comparatively speaking, a larger part of the Flemish parliamentarians' time was devoted to work inside the parliament. The MFPs spent most of their time on committee meetings, the federal parliamentarians on participating in local events. Inside the parliament, Flemish MPs devote more time to committee meetings and less to plenary meetings. Accord-

TABLE 9.3   Time Budget of the Members of the Flemish Parliament (1995-1999) and of the Members of the Federal Parliament (1983)

	Average hours per week devoted to activity by the members of the Flemish Parliament (1995-1999) N=103, Women=15	Average hours per week devoted to activity by the members of the Federal Parliament (1983)
Attending plenary meetings	5.2 h/week (5.9)	8.3 h/week
Attending committee meetings	11.1 (12)	6.9
Attending party meetings within parliament	2.8 (3.4)	2.5
Study and preparation of dossiers	9.8 (11.3)	9.4
TOTAL INTRA-PARLIAMENTARY ACTIVITIES	28.9 (32.6)	27.1
Attending party meetings outside parliament	4.9 (6.1)	7.3
Local mandate	7.8 (5.4)	7.5
Case work (helping individual citizens, surgery hours, "clientelism")	3.0 (2.7)	5.2
Meetings with representatives of lobbies and pressure groups	2.5 (4.0)	4.6
Participation in local socio-cultural events, debates, speeches	4.6 (4.0)	11
Practising a non-political profession	4.4 (3.0)	8.9
TOTAL EXTRA-PARLIAMENTARY ACTIVITIES	27.2 (25.2)	44.5
TOTAL INTRA+EXTRA:	56.1 (57.8)	71.6

Source: Celis with Woodward 2000 and DeWinter 1992, own comparison.

ing to the interviewees, the plenary sessions are rather superfluous moments mainly used to gain publicity. Instead, the committee meetings are the most important sessions, where the discussions concerning content take place. Spending more time on committee meetings means spending more time on the content of parliamentary activity and can thus be considered as being more NPC-like. However, Flemish MPs did not spend more time on study and preparation of dossiers. Concerning extraparliamentary time management, we see that Flemish parliamentarians devote less time to party meetings, case work, local events, local mandates, and nonpolitical professions. This can be interpreted as signs of NPC in the sense that Flemish MPs see their job as a full-time occupation that requires their full attention. Flemish parliamentarians spend less time on case work and handle fewer cases of individuals.

Members of the Flemish Parliament handled an average of 415.7 cases a year; federal parliamentarians handled more than 2,000 (2,134). In the light of seeking traces of NPC in the Flemish Parliament, this can be called significant. Our hypothesis here is that acting according to NPC ideas would imply having a representational style that is more directed toward the citizen and is a reflection of the desire of regional parliamentarians to practice a different kind of politics than the national parliamentary tradition.

Table 9.4 explores the extent to which these parliamentarians see themselves more as a delegate and less as a trustee. De Winter (1992) found that national parliamentarians tended to see themselves as "trustees" (63 percent as opposed to 26 percent feeling themselves to be delegates). Of the eighty-nine Flemish parliamentarians in the survey who answered the same question, more than half considered themselves as "delegates" who as much as possible try to find out about the interests of the groups they represent.

One third based their opinion on their own judgment, and about 15 percent conform to the opinion of their political party in looking after the interests of the group(s) they represent. These last two groups (49.4 percent) can be considered as trustees because they take an independent position toward the groups they represent. Of course these findings are based on "self-evaluation," meaning that the distinction between wish and reality is rather thin. Nonetheless, we can conclude that the actual or desired degree of independence to the civilians diminished strikingly in the Flemish Parliament compared to the federal parliament. Again, the small group of women distinguish themselves by being even more delegate-natured, as 66.7 percent of the women identify as "delegates" as opposed to 47.3 percent of the men.

New political culture in Flanders has referred to structural changes (such as the deontological code) and to a new concept of good political practice. NPC exists not only in the heads of the parliamentarians. We can actually find traces of this NPC in parliamentary activities—for

TABLE 9.4   Representational Style of Flemish MPs (1995-1999): Alternative Answers to "In Order to Look after the Interests of the Group I Represent..."

...I always try to find out about their desires and interests."	Count %	45 50.6
... I base my opinion on my own judgement and insights."	Count %	30 33.7
...I conform to the opinion of my parliamentary fraction and my political party."	Count %	14 15.7

Source: Celis 2001

example, with regard to bills introduced by a majority party together with a minority party, the time budget of the Flemish MPs, and in their representational style. Thus the Flemish case demonstrates that devolution at least in some ways can act as a sort of temporary breaking point in political institutional culture. Happily, the Flemish MPs are content in their jobs, and 83 percent think that they realize valuable things, while 71 percent consider their job as a challenge, so this new way of working is also satisfying. In this way the devolution process in Europe may ultimately indeed create new parliaments rather than shiny and smaller copies of the national bodies.

CONCLUSION

The members of the first directly elected Flemish Parliament are convinced that the Flemish Parliament is a unique institution and to some extent a better parliament than the Federal Parliament. The new political culture is one of the distinguishing characteristics. Clark and Hoffman-Martinot's (1998) conviction that NPC may first appear at the urban and regional level is probably a grounded one. National parliaments with long traditions may be less amenable to new types of political practice. Democratic developments in Europe since 1989 have opened many windows for rethinking what is meant by democracy and representation. The multilevel governance literature identifies new areas of authority and overlap that create opportunities for democratic renewal. The argument here is that recently established regional parliaments have ambitions, as clearly evidenced in the devolution processes in both the United Kingdom and Belgium, and further may be able to achieve a more direct connection with the citizen than is the case with older national bodies. New sociological groups are in part carriers of these ideas. In this chapter we focus particularly on the potential of women and use data from the new parliament in Flanders to demonstrate that even when women are in a minority position, they profile themselves in ways that reflect the goals of transparency and openness striven for in both the Scottish and Flemish parliaments. The fact that many of the new parliaments in Europe have a high percentage of new players will make for interesting research on the process of democratic participation in multilevel Europe in the future.

NOTES

The information in this paper on the Flemish parliament stems from the study *Het Vlaams Parlement: Nieuwe Politieke Cultuur en het Potentieel voor een Valorisering van het Maatschapelijk Kapitaal van Vrouwen in de Politieke Besluitvorming* carried out by the Center for Women's Studies of the Vrije Universiteit Brussel.

This study of the first directly elected legislature in Flanders (1995–1999) investigated the extent to which its members see the body as representing a new political culture. Qualitative interviews with 47 out of 124 parliamentarians as well as a total survey of the sitting parliamentarians (75 percent response rate or 93 of 124 MFPs) provide the findings. Full documentation is available in Celis with Woodward (2000) or in the final report (Celis 2001).

1. Authors who consider the welfare state, labor markets, and social issues—such as Scharpf (1999) or Leibfried and Pierson (1995)—take a considerably more cautious view, and note that many changes are beyond democratic control and inevitably take forms that will fundamentally change the welfare state and its provisions.

REFERENCES

Abromeit, H. 1998. *Democracy in Europe: Legitimising politics in a non-state policy.* New York: Berghan Books.

Bergqvist, C., A. Borchorst, et al., eds. 1999. *Equal democracies? Gender and politics in the Nordic countries.* Oslo: Scandinavian University Press.

Blondel, J. 1973. *Comparative legislatures.* Englewood Cliffs, N.J.: Prentice-Hall.

———. 1990. *Comparative government: An introduction.* Hemel Hempsted: Philip Allan.

Bogdanor, V. 1999. *Devolution in the United Kingdom.* Oxford: Oxford University Press.

Bradbury, J., and J. Mawson. 1997. *British regionalism and devolution.* London: Jessica Kingsley.

Brown, A. 1998. A deepening democracy: Women and the Scottish Parliament. *Regional and Federal Studies* 8(1): 103–19.

Carton, A. 1995. Paritaire democratie: een definitieve stap vooruit. In *Jaarboek van de vrouw 1994*, pp. 71–89. Brussel: Nederlandstalige Vrouwenraad.

———. 1998. Over de actie 'Stem Vrouw' en de plaats van de vrouw in de politiek. In *De (on)redelijke kiezer. Onderzoek naar de politieke opvattingen van Vlamingen. Verkiezingen van mei 1995*, edited by M. Swyngedouw, J. Billiet, A. Carton, and R. Beerten, pp. 27–49. Leuven (Louvain): Acco.

Celis, K. 2001. *Het Vlaams Parlement: Nieuwe politieke cultuur en het potentieel voor een valorisering van het maatschappelijk kapitaal van vrouwen in de politieke besluitvorming.* Brussels: Ministerie van de Vlaamse Gemeenschap/ Gelijke Kansen Wetenschappelijke monografie 5.

Celis, K., with A. Woodward. 2000. *Het Vlaams Parlement: Nieuwe politieke cultuur en het potentieel voor een valorisering van het maatschappelijk kapitaal van vrouwen in de politieke besluitvorming.* Brussels: Center for Women's Studies, Vrije Universiteit Brussel.

Clark, T. N., and Hoffman-Martinot. 1998. *The new political culture.* Boulder: Westview.

Council of Europe, Science and Technology of Democracy. 1999. *Federal and regional states in the perspective of European integration.* Bologna.

Conversi, D. 1997. *The Basques, the Catalans and Spain.* London: John Hurst and Company.

Consultative Steering Group. 1999. Report to the Secretary of State for Scotland.

Darcy, R., S. Welch, and J. Clark. 1987. *Women, elections and representation.* New York: Longman.

Deschouwer, K., and T. M Jans. 1999. *Politics beyond the state: The capacity of decision-making in the new institutional organization of modern politics.* Brussels: Department of Politics, Vrije Universitiet Brussel.

Dewachter, W., S. Depauw, and I. Thomas. 1997. *Afscheid van het laatste dubbelparlement.* Leuven: Acco.

De Winter, L. 1992. *The Belgian Legislator.* Unpublished doctoral thesis. Florence: European University Institute Firenze.

De Winter, L., and M. Swyngedouw. 1999. The scope of EU government. In *Political representation and legitimacy in the European Union,* edited by H. Schmitt and J. Thomassen. Oxford: Oxford University Press.

De Winter, L., and H. Türsan, eds. 1998. *Regionalist parties in Western Europe.* London: Routledge.

Dogan, M. 2000. Deficit of confidence within European democracies. In *The role of the social sciences in the making of the European Union: A critical survey,* edited by M. Haller, pp. 241–61. Berlin: Springer Verlag.

Döring, H., ed. 1995. *Parliaments and majority rule in Western Europe.* Frankfurt: Campus; New York: St. Martin's Press.

Down, W. M. 1997. *Coalition government, subnational style: Multiparty politics in Europe's regional parliaments.* Columbus: Ohio State University Press.

Ferree, M. M., and P. Y. Martin. 1995. *Feminist organizations: Harvest of the new woman's movement.* Philadelphia: Temple University Press.

Fitzmaurice, J. 1996. *The politics of Belgium: A unique federalism.* London: Hurst and Company.

Hooghe, L., ed. 1996. *Cohesion policy and European integration: Building multi-level governance.* Oxford: Oxford University Press.

Hooghe, L., and G. Marks. 2001. *Multi-level governance and European integration.* Lanham, Md.: Rowman and Littlefield.

Inglehart, R. 1997. *Modernization and postmodernization: Cultural, economic and cultural change in 43 societies.* Princeton, N.J.: Princeton University Press.

Katz, R., and B. Wessels, eds. 1999. *The European Parliament, national parliaments and European integration.* Oxford: Oxford University Press.

Keating, M. 1998. *The new regionalism in Western Europe: Territorial restructuring and political change.* Aldershot: Edward Elgar.

Kerremans, B. 2000. Determining a European policy in a multi-level setting: The case of specialised co-ordination in Belgium. *Journal of Regional and Federal Studies* 10 (1): 36–61.

Kohler-Koch, B. 1999. *A Europe in search of legitimate governance.* Oslo, ARENA. Working Paper 99/27(27).

Kohler-Koch, B., and R. Eising, ed. 2000. *The transformation of governance in the European Union.* London: Routledge.

Leibfried, S., and P. Pierson. 1995. Semisovereign welfare states: Social policy in a multitiered Europe. In *European social policy: Between fragmentation and integration,* edited by S. Leibfried and P. Pierson. Washington, D.C.: The Brookings Institute.

Leijennar, M. 1983. *Vrouwen en politieke macht: trendrapport over vrouwenstudies en emancipatieonderzoek op het gebied van vrouwen en politieke macht.* Den Haag: Voorlopige Begeleidingsgroep voor emancipatie-onderzoek.

———. *De geschade heerlijkheid: Politiek gedrag van vrouwen en mannen in Nederland, 1918–1988.* s'Gravenhage: SDU.

———. 1993. *Vrouwen en politieke macht.* Den Haag: Voorlopiege Begeleidingsgroep voor emancipatie-onderzoek.

Loughlin, J., E. Aja, U. Bullman, and F. Hendriks. 1999. *Regional and local democracy in the European Union*. Luxembourg: Office for Official Publications of the European Community.

Lovenduski, J., and P. Norris, eds. 1996. *Women and politics*. Oxford: Oxford University Press.

Marks, G., F. Scharpf, P. Schmitter, and W. Streeck. 1996. *Governance in the European Union*. London: Sage.

Mezey, M. 1979. *Comparative legislatures*. Durham, N.C.: Duke University Press.

Norton, P., ed. 1996. *National parliaments and the European Union*. London: Frank Cass.

Olsen, J. P. 1995. *European challenges to the nation state*. Oslo, ARENA, University of Oslo, Norway.

Randall, V. 1991. *Women and politics: An international perspective*. Basingstroke: Macmillan.

Randall, V., and G. Waylen. 1998. *Gender, politics and the state*. London: Routledge.

Rule, W. 1993. Why are more women state legislators? In *Women in politics: Outsiders or insiders? A collection of readings*, edited by L. L. Duke Englewood Cliffs, N.J.: Prentice-Hall.

Schmitt, H., and J. Thomassen, eds. 1999. *Political representation and legitimacy in the European Union*. Oxford: Oxford University Press.

Sharpe, L. J. 1993. *The rise of the meso government in Europe*. London: Sage.

Sloat, A. 2001a. Multi-level governance: An actor-centered approach. Paper read at Multi-Level Governance Interdisciplinary Perspectives, June 2001, at University of Sheffield, PERC.

———. 2001b. *Scotland in Europe: A study of multi-level governance*. Bern: Peter Lang.

Stouthuysen, P. 1997. Is nieuw noodzakelijk ook beter? Aantekeningen bij vier publicaties over de nieuwe politieke cultuur. *Samenleving en Politiek* 10: 13–20.

Suleiman, E. 1986. *Parliaments and parliamentarians in democratic politics*. New York: Holmes and Meier.

Women in Decision-Making. 2001. http://www.db-decision.de

Woodward, A. 1998. Sterft de NPC door gebrek aan vrouwen? *Vrouwenraad*, no. 3, pp. 20–27.

Woodward, A., and D. Lyon. 2000. Is leadership time gendered time? Time as a threshold in women's access to power. In *Gendering the elite: A cross-national study on gender and power*, edited by M. Vianello and G. Moore, pp. 91–103. London: Macmillan.

10

Gent-Terneuzen: The Rise of a Euroregion?

Wouter-Jan Oosten

INTRODUCTION

There are a variety of forces at work in the regions of Europe. Is it possible to assess where these forces will lead to within the international and European context? In the Gent-Terneuzen region one can at first sight identify merely geographical aspects. Such geographical aspects are two industrial cities in Flanders (Belgium) and the Netherlands respectively, a canal, and the river Scheldt. However, a closer look reveals that on both sides of the border, public and private actors have found new ways in spatial planning and environmental care (ROM)—specifically, to tackle pollution in the canal zone. Against the background of further cross-border relations regarding business and knowledge transfer, this ROM-governance practice might strengthen the region within the European context.

The central question of this chapter is, What are the opportunities for the rise of the Gent-Terneuzen region within the European context against the background of the integration of the two centers and their immediate surroundings? And what is or might be the role for the different layers of government therein: the province of Zeeland in the

Netherlands, and in Belgium the province of East Flanders and the state of Flanders?

This chapter focuses mainly on three aspects of cross-border cooperation: the growing network of relationship between the chambers of commerce, the institutionalization of higher education cooperation within the International Scheldt Faculty, and the cooperation concerning spatial planning and the environment in the canal zone. All these programs are mainly bottom-up and rather strictly confined to the Dutch-Flemish situation. The European context might be regarded as a motive, or at least an argument, for undertaking such efforts toward cross-border policy integration and joint action. But at present, the practical meaning of the European Union is restricted to possible gains in structural funds. The international cooperation within the Gent-Terneuzen region consists of action by local actors in answer to policy formulation and making from Flanders and the Netherlands respectively. The cause of this limited European perspective for the region is that the European dimension of the Gent-Terneuzen region probably still is too narrow. The maritime-industrial cluster featuring three large companies—Dow Chemical in Terneuzen, and Sidmar and Volvo in Gent—is not sufficient to place the region on the map of Europe. There will only be a European perspective if the European dimension of the region can be widened geograhically and functionally. And this might become the case in the future. This chapter first contextualizes the Gent-Terneuzen region. Afterwards, cross-border policy formulation is discussed at length. A third section deals with the impact of European integration on the initiatives of the Euroregion Scheldemond. Last but not least, conclusions are drawn from this case study of cross-border cooperation.

CONTEXTUALIZING THE GENT-TERNEUZEN REGION

The inland city of Gent in the Belgian province of East Flanders and the coastal city of Terneuzen in the Dutch province of Zeeland are the centers of a socioeconomic and a historic binodal region (Houtum 1999). A canal fit for seagoing ships has linked these two industrial centers since 1827. "Region" is defined here as city-region, and not as a super-region like in the case of the French *régions* or German *Länder* (Newman 2000). For this reason, and also because of its autonomy regarding international trade policy, Flanders is referred to as a state and not a region.

Dutch and Flemish joint regional policy on spatial planning and the environment targets the Gent-Terneuzen canal zone. Recent developments, however, may have centrifugal effects on the cooperating businesses and local governments in this region. Two such developments should be mentioned in this context. First, the Westerscheldetunnel, a—technically rather daring—new tunnel under the river Scheldt, will soon end the isolated geographical position of the Terneuzen area within the Dutch province of Zeeland (Gelder 2000; Sande 2000). Will this link turn the face of Terneuzen away from Gent toward its Dutch surroundings? Or will the tunnel strengthen the axis Rotterdam-Gent and further integrate the region at large? The port authority for the two Dutch ports of Terneuzen and Vlissingen, Zeeland Seaports, states that the tunnel will strengthen the already strong ties between Terneuzen and Vlissingen. A second development that might have centrifugal effects on the actors in the region is that across the Dutch-Belgian border, Flemish planning is forcing the city of Gent to work closer with the surrounding Flemish municipalities. Will Gent have less power of autonomy if those developments become a reality?

GEOGRAPHY, GOVERNMENT, AND POLICY

History of the Region

Motives for cross-border cooperation may be derived from history, so this study starts with some history. The partners of the Euroregion Maas-Rhine, for instance, in particular both the Dutch and Flemish provinces of Limburg, have similar economic, religious, and cultural backgrounds (Spoormans, Reichenbach, and Korsten 1999, 17). To explain the cross-border relations in that Euroregion, three partial factors can be mentioned. First, Flemish and Dutch Limburg both have a history of foreign rule, so these two provinces have more in common than being marginal zones within the respective national territories as are all border zones. Second, the region's population is more Catholic than Protestant in comparison with large parts of the Netherlands or Germany. Third, the local economies of the Flemish, German, and Dutch border zones were all dependent upon the mining industry. The structural economic changes after World War II put an end to the coal mine production in the region, leading to the unemployment of a large part of its working population.

What similarities or factors can help understand cross-border cooperation in the Gent-Terneuzen region? In the Middle Ages, the county of Flanders and the duchy of Brabant were the first economic, governmental, and cultural heart of the Low Countries. At the end of the sixteenth century, the then seventeen provinces of the Low Countries rose against their lord's tendency to centralize government. The southern provinces quickly returned to Spanish hands, but the north continued its fight against first Emperor Charles V and then his son Philip II.

Flanders and Brabant declined as a result of this Eighty Years War during the sixteenth and seventeenth centuries, and the province of Holland expanded. Holland was the economic and political center of the now independent Dutch Republic. As part of the Spanish, Austrian, and French empires successively, the southern provinces did not regain their economic position. After the formation of an enlarged Kingdom of the Netherlands in 1815, and after the independence of Belgium in 1830, economic development in the southern part of the Low Countries began again to take off. The Gent city center indeed shows this history: It has a medieval core and nineteenth-century additions.

Historically, the Dutch province of Zeeland comprises islands south of the province of Holland. Flanders is situated south of these islands. The land strip across the river Scheldt was held by several parties over the course of the centuries; one of these was the Dutch Republic, and later on it became an integral part of the Kingdom of the Netherlands (Israel 1995). The Nassau counts and Orange princes who held the stadholderate captured Hulst in 1591, Sas van Gent in 1644, and, after losing it, Hulst in 1645 again.[1] During most of the era of the Dutch Republic, this land strip was indeed part of the territory of the States General and therefore called States Flanders; the southern provinces of the low countries were held by the Spanish and Austrian Hapsburg rulers. As a consequence, the conflict between the Republic and the Hapsburg monarchy at its southern border led to the closure of the river Scheldt in 1585 by the Dutch Republic at the cost of the Flemish city of Antwerp. The river Scheldt remained closed for commercial traffic until 1863. As a further side effect of this conflict, the decline of Antwerp made possible the rise of Amsterdam. The Zeeuws-Vlaanderen area was kept isolated by the border between States Flanders—now Zeeuws-Vlaanderen—and Flanders in the south, and by the river Scheldt between the land strip and the province of Zeeland in the north. Only after World War II did any significant development take place. Terneuzen became an industrialized city, and its canal zone was extended to the city of Gent. Zeeuws-Vlaanderen no longer has railroads for passenger trains, although the Dutch rail network is still quite dense. Only with the completion of the Westerscheldetunnel will the land strip be directly linked to the Dutch network of main roads, so ending the long isolation of Zeeuws-Vlaanderen.

Spatial Planning and Environment (ROM) in the Netherlands

The Dutch planning system closely follows the administrative structure of the country, a decentralized unitary state. Each layer of government has its own position that is constitutionally guaranteed and sustained by a strong consensual tradition. The Ministry of Transport, Public Works, and Water Management is responsible for the main transport infrastructure, including its implementation. The Ministry of Housing, Spatial Planning, and the Environment formulates the national planning strategies with input from the other departments and other public and private actors. These strategies are to be approved by parliament, the States General. In answer to national policy, local needs, and ambitions, the twelve provinces formulate planning strategies concerning spatial planning, water management, conservation of nature, and the environment. The municipalities, however, are the government layer with the authority to allocate land use with binding force. National and provincial documents, then, have only an indicative status, informing other authorities of policy intentions. Allocating land use with binding force is something a municipality does with its zoning plan; besides that, most municipalities produce several nonbinding planning documents. In recent years, national government has itself started to produce planning documents with a status making them binding for other layers of government and for citizens. The municipal zoning plan, prescribing the functional use of land, is still the most prominent but no longer the only binding planning document. The concepts of *Rechtsstaat* (rule of law) and democracy inspire legal possibilities for redress and citizen participation at all stages. In response to drafts of national, provincial, and municipal planning documents, one can petition the authority concerned with one's own views or interest. Planning documents can still be altered after parliament or council, having taken notice of the popular views received, has decided upon the executive's draft: One can send petitions to the Council of State. In response to granted or refused land-use permits, which are the local executive's decisions based upon the municipal zoning plan, one first petitions the council and after that the local court of law before going to the Council of State. Most local governments organize all sorts of public information meetings and design workshops in the course of drafting their planning documents. Communicative planning is now so much accepted that even development corporations start to involve the urban population before they redevelop a site.

Dutch spatial policy is guided by national planning documents. Peter Hall (1995) characterized the Dutch government as follows:

> [G]overnment has taken some kind of a worldwide lead in trying to integrate land use and transport planning, within an environmental strategy, at a national level. (77)

We perhaps could say that the Dutch want too much. In 1988 the Fourth Report on Spatial Planning (*Vierde nota over de ruimtelijke orden-*

ing, Ministerie van Volkshuivesting) mentioned the integration of environmental and spatial policy on a regional level.[2] The First National Environmental Policy Plan (Nationaal milieubeleidsplan 1) in 1989 and an action plan for regional environmental policy (Actieplan gebiedsgericht milieubeleid) in 1990 specify this integrated policy approach. Within a ROM-project, there would be three phases: each more specifying the separate and joint efforts, and each concluding with a signed agreement (an agenda-setting agreement, an agreement on an action program, and an implementation agreement).[3] The organizational structure of the projects was not prescribed by the Ministry of Housing, Spatial Planning, and the Environment. The execution of the policy finally agreed upon would be undertaken by the involved actors, such as the province, municipalities, water board, and businesses within the area. The integrated regional approach was from the start appreciated for its accent on coordination, policy execution, intergovernmental cooperation, and public-private partnership. Questions still existed with regard to the democratic nature of decision making and the financial footing of the regional projects. The overall approach counted on the support of public-private partnerships and European funds for financing the projects. The ROM policy was evaluated several times and continued until this day.

One of the ten so-called ROM areas is the canal zone stretching from Terneuzen to the Dutch-Belgian border (ROM-gebied Kanaalzone Zeeuws-Vlaanderen). The city of Terneuzen and the towns of Sas van Gent and Axel are situated in this area; the area is inhabited by almost 60,000 people. Predating the national ROM policy the province of Zeeland formulated a regional initiative in 1985, adding environmental concerns to the economic development of the canal zone. The provincial initiative followed the 1984 national policy document *More Than the Sum of Its Parts* (*Meer dan de som der delen*), which aimed at coherence in environmental policy.

The main problem of the area concerned the friction between housing, industry, and recreation. The canal zone ROM project would feature the use of existing instruments to improve the noise, smell, and safety situation. The project, both as a provincial initiative and as a ROM project, did not have an easy start: The actors initially showed some distrust, they stressed their distinctive interests, and changes were made in the organizational structure in attempts to improve cooperation. Business representatives and an environmental action group were involved, but the process cannot be considered participatory from the perspective of (individual) citizens. The final action plan was produced after five years and accepted by most of the public and private actors. The business representatives, however, did not agree to finance the policy implementation in addition to the existing taxes, and the environmental pressure group Zeeuwse Milieufederatie did not sign the final agreement. Given the circumstances in the area and the history of interaction between the actors, the ROM project still can be seen as a modest success for it did facilitate consultation and coordinated action. The now existing working relations between public and private actors are to be appreciated, considering that at the time when the ROM policy was first proposed, business and government thought of each other as adversaries and not potential partners and that projects and coherence were almost unknown in policy making. Industries and environmental pressure groups whose representatives used to meet only in court now actually spoke with each other.

Spatial Planning in Flanders

Subsidiarity is a leading principle in both the Netherlands and Flanders. Like the Dutch planning system, Flemish spatial planning features the instruments of strategic plans from the state, provinces, and municipalities. Unlike its northern counterpart, the system not only allows municipalities to allocate land use with binding force, but higher levels of government as well.

Flemish spatial policy is in rapid development. The Flemish spatial policy document *Ruimtelijk Structuurplan Vlaanderen* dating from 1996–1997 is the first of its kind. The state of Flanders initiated its planning efforts following devolution in Belgium, but also because of a growing awareness of problems caused by unwise land use. This first plan identifies the Gent-Terneuzen region as one of the areas to be developed in international cooperation. Furthermore, it distinguishes between urban and rural areas and calls for the bottom-up recognition of the boundaries within which municipalities will cooperate with regard to housing, industrial zones, and conservation or development of nature. Flemish planning demands that the large cities and their surrounding municipalities join to care for the urban fabric. Yet Belgium has little tradition of cooperation among municipalities or of regional policy. For instance, the urban renewal program of the city of Gent does not take the regional context into consideration, not even in the analysis of the urban economic structure (Sociaal Impulsfonds 1999). The agreement between the state of Flanders, the city of Gent, and the Gent public welfare center (Openbaar Centrum voor Maatschappelijk Welzijn van Gent), according to which this renewal program was designed and was financed by the Flemish Social Impulse Fund, states only that their policy plan will be brought into line with Flemish and European programs, without mentioning any specific Flemish or European policy (Beleidsovereenkomst 1999, 2).[4] The extension of the ROM approach in the canal zone across the border introduced a kind of governance that was new to Flemish authorities and private organizations.

EUROPEAN DIMENSION

Maritime-Industrial Cluster

In the wider Gent-Terneuzen area, cooperation exists between the Dutch and the Flemish, also with an eye for the hinterland Europe. There is a Euroregion Scheldemond in which the provinces of Zeeland, East Flanders, and West Flanders participate. Additionally, there is an International Scheldt Faculty and quite strong cooperation between the chambers of commerce. Yet, all this does not indicate an integrated European orientation across sectors, nor a significant regional awareness that mitigates or minimizes the meaning of the border.

In 1989 the provinces of Zeeland, West Flanders, and East Flanders initiated their cross-border cooperation, which soon attracted financial support from the European Union. The Euroregion Scheldemond nowadays comprises a secretariat, its INTERREG program, and the Scheldemond Council. The secretariat, located in Gent, facilitates the design and coordination of several projects and provides public information concerning the Euroregion. The secretariat itself also offers a small project that aims at supporting civil associations in the respective border zones. The small number of staff members at the secretariat does not allow more proactive or intensive direct relations with citizens. The Euroregion can successfully develop sociocultural projects. Its activities with regard to fiscal and socioeconomic affairs, however, are held in check by national regulations. The national fiscal and socioeconomic systems do not allow the provinces and municipalities much autonomous action.

Private companies and municipalities are very interested in the possibility of European funds for investment projects in the region. At the close of INTERREG II and the start of INTERREG III, the provincial executives did evaluate the effects of projects and aim at some improvement. The support and involvement of local politicians were stimulated by the creation of the Scheldemond Council within the Euroregion— mayors and eldermen took seats in this body.

The International Scheldt Faculty has developed from an initiative to organize summer courses in Zeeland. Academics now working in universities, business, and government, mostly beyond the Zeeland confines, took this initiative for adult education in their province of origin. The International Scheldt Faculty was founded in 1990 by a Dutch polytechnic, the Hogeschool Zeeland. The polytechnic and the Gent University wish to involve schools, businesses, and politicians in their research and education programs. It remains a loose structure that aims at the advancement of knowledge. The coordination of research by the International Scheldt Faculty includes the application for grants from the European COMETT, LEONARDO, and SOCRATES programs. Drewe (1999), in his evaluation of the International Scheldt Faculty, mentions that the maritime-industrial sector receives considerable attention from this higher-education institution. In this way the International Scheldt Faculty is supportive of the development of the maritime-industrial cluster. According to Drewe, the structure of the Faculty should have been incorporated and better integrated within the Euroregion Scheldemond. The overall quality of the region largely depends on the state of the physical environment and level of education of the population. Because of this, initiatives such as the ROM policy and the International Scheldt Faculty should be at the core of the Gent-Terneuzen development. The Faculty management experienced that Euregion functionaries did conceive the International Scheldt Faculty as a competitor of the Euroregion Scheldemond. Steps have now been taken to develop some cooperation between the two entities.

Within the Dutch-Flemish coastal region, international cooperation is most likely to occur in relation to infrastructure building. In Gent particularly, one realizes that the city's port and labor market are quite dependent upon canal access in Terneuzen. The report *Dynamic Center within the Delta* (Allaert et al. 2000), which was written for the city of Terneuzen, mentions the prospect of a maritime and industrial cluster that comprises Vlissingen, Terneuzen, Gent, and Antwerp. It advises to extend the existing rail link with Flanders and open up the possibility for passenger rail transport. In the future, Terneuzen might be part of the main rail network stretching from the coast into Germany. The improvement of the railroad in the canal zone is also a proposal brought to the fore in the Dutch ROM project. Infrastructure is mentioned at the national level as well. In the course of the 1990s, the importance of water management was increasingly recognized by both the Dutch spatial community and the political elites. The recent *Fifth Report on Spatial Planning* (*Vijfde nota over de ruimtelijke ordening*, Ministerie van Volkshuisvesting) highlights water interests, for environmental and safety reasons. The orchestrated action that is needed from water boards, municipalities, provinces, national government, and private companies may be realized with cooperation like that defined in the ROM policy document (Slobbe 2001). Water interests might be an extra reason for the Dutch national government to stimulate the Gent-Terneuzen region with its river and canal. The growing cooperation between Dutch ports in Zeeland and in Rotterdam, however, might turn Terneuzen away from Gent.

Broadening the Approach

In 1952, the Benelux gave an opening for adjusted spatial policy in its member-states (Siraa 1989, 184–85). As from the 1970s within the legal framework of the Benelux, the Netherlands, Belgium, and Luxembourg are mutually obliged to adjust their spatial planning for the border areas. The Euroregion Scheldemond in the early 1990s functioned as a multiprovincial platform without full participation of other organizations, such as municipalities in particular (Kessen 1992, 213–15). The recent ROM approach on both sides of the border in the Gent-Terneuzen canal zone probably involves public authorities, businesses, and even action groups in more intensive international cooperation than any other structure or program has done until now. Because this is essentially an action program concerning spatial planning and the environment, one may wonder whether the intense cooperation, and the supposed increase of regional and European awareness, will last. The cooperative approach of the ROM policy is confirmed by more general strategies at the levels of national government and the European Union, and this could mean that effective governance practices will continue to be chosen in the future.

The Expert Group on the Urban Environment (1996) report titled *European Sustainable Cities*, from the European Commission's Directorate General XI, formulates a holistic view of urban problems and an integrated approach to their solution. It mentions five ecosystem management tools: collaboration and partnership, policy integration, market mechanisms, information management, and measuring and monitoring. The report insists on community consultation and participation in a network approach, on a discursive and consensual approach at the local level. In this way environmental policy, urban renewal, and spatial planning are drawn into a public administration of governance known as network steering (Kersbergen and Waarden 2001), which seeks to involve all relevant public and private actors in policy processes from an early stage, individual citizens included. This public administration hopes to transcend a symbolic call on society that takes place once policy makers have formulated their plans.

Cross-Border or Transnational Structures

A border does not need to be a boundary or a barrier (compare Paasi 1996). The patterns of economic and cultural activities, of demographic developments, and certainly of geomorphology may ignore the division of national territories. The growth of the welfare state in Western Europe and modernization in general have intensified national patterns, including policy networks. The European INTERREG program, which made money available for the Euroregion Scheldemond, aimed at extending policy networks across borders in neighboring areas. Crossing borders does not necessarily involve a transnational orientation. If cross-border social patterns include a sociopsychological dimension, and a (regional) awareness within a European framework, a transnational orientation may emerge. It is within such a context that a European cross-border region can rise.

With regard to transport, the environment, and spatial planning, cross-border governance in the Gent-Terneuzen region is likely to be extended. In case of activities with (possible) cross-border effects, a European member-state is bound by law to inform and consult with the neighboring country with respect to environmental impacts, and to give foreign citizens access to environmental impact assessment procedures. The approach of the ROM policy transcends such minimal measures. In addition to layers of government, a range of private organizations and citizens is involved in the formulation and implementation of policy.

International governance, with or without a European dimension, requires facilitation. The three Benelux countries created the possibility for cross-border cooperation by public law. The Benelux Agreement of 1986, which has been in force since April 1991, allows local and regional layers of government to fulfill their tasks and exercise their authorities in international cooperation. This cooperation can take form in three levels of intensity, culminating in establishing a public body. In his dissertation, Antoine Kessen (1992) mentions these legal facilities in further detail. Perhaps it is good to point out that "form follows function": The creation of a relatively powerful public body can help realize cross-border initiatives, but it does not guarantee that actors are sufficiently motivated to meet and formulate joint policy. Public authorities continue to search for the relevant roles to play in cross-border policies and for ways to make themselves effective in such roles (Duijn et al. 2001).

Governance in a European Region

A change in the nature of policy programs for spatial investment has taken place. National programs aimed mainly at interregional equity, by means of which companies in relatively underdeveloped areas were subsidized, have been replaced by European and national programs aimed at competitiveness, in which cofunding and partnerships are most important (Halkier 2001). This change should give regional and local actors noteworthy opportunities for bottom-up regional economic policy. The Dutch ROM policy aims at mobilizing public and private actors within policy networks, and it involves within the ROM areas nonhierarchical steering by national government. In the already mentioned report *European Sustainable Cities* written by the Expert Group on the Urban Environment (1996), the European Commission adheres to the same principles. Peter John (2000) writes on the trend toward governance as follows:

> The emphasis on governance and management reflects a change in philosophy that rejected the old top-down approach of the 1970s and 1980s, with its emphasis on physical regeneration projects, and moved towards one that encourages more flexible and dynamic forms of policies targeted at economic renewal. (880)

According to John, the touch of European policy on local government stimulates a public administration of governance as network steering. In the case under scrutiny here, it can be observed that the broadening of the spatial and administrative orientation toward integration of a Gent-Terneuzen region created the opportunity for the Dutch ROM approach to be introduced in Flanders.

The cooperation of chambers of commerce, of institutions for higher education within the International Scheldt Faculty, and the cooperation concerning spatial planning and the environment in the canal zone are all mainly bottom-up and rather strictly confined to the Dutch-Flemish situation. The European context might be a motive, or at least an argument, for policy integration and joint action. But at present, the practical meaning of the European Union is that of attracting structural funds for the Euroregion. Cross-border cooperation within the Gent-Terneuzen region will consist of action by local actors in answer to policy demands from Flanders and the Netherlands respectively.

Gent-Terneuzen, and the existing maritime ties with Vlissingen can be understood as the west flank of the somewhat larger Rotterdam-Antwerp region, which is well-placed on the map of Europe. That larger region would comprise the Dutch provinces of South Holland, Zeeland, North Brabant, and the Flemish provinces of West Flanders, East Flanders, Antwerp, and Brabant. Public actors have met on this scale in the 1990s, but one might ask what the inland province of North Brabant and its city of Breda could mean for Gent-Terneuzen. An enlargement of the region to other territories alone will of course not bring about a European perspective for the further development of Gent-Terneuzen. That requires growing cross-border cooperative strategies with both the public and private sectors.

The International Scheldt Faculty is based in the provinces of Zeeland, East Flanders, and West Flanders. So that the larger Rotterdam-Antwerp region can be included, it is absolutely necessary that the provinces of South Holland and Antwerp also be involved.

CONCLUSIONS

The ROM policy in the Gent-Terneuzen canal zone demonstrates how governance as network steering may create developments toward policy integration and joint action. It is a challenge to extend the approach of this ROM project beyond the Gent-Terneuzen situation with its specific geography. The challenge includes the facilitation of the growth of a Gent-Terneuzen and perhaps even a Rotterdam-Antwerp regional awareness. Such an awareness can only arise if cooperation is based on more than a narrow or short-term approach. This does not seem to be the case at present. For instance, Rotterdam cooperates with ports in the southwest of the Netherlands, but this may be related to the fact that they want to avoid to be invited by the government to merge with all Dutch port organizations, including its main rival Amsterdam.

Promoting the region and its development ought to start with a network analysis—for instance, conducted by the Euroregion Scheldemond and the cities of Gent and Terneuzen—in order to identify all relevant actors, their potentials, and aims. Some sense of belonging and identity will be necessary for the involvement of citizens in the design of policy and in decision making and for achieving a lasting character of international regional cooperation.

NOTES

1. During the era of the Dutch Republic, the provinces that made up the confederation each appointed a chief civil servant: the stadholder or steward, in Dutch *stadhouder*. In practice there usually were only two stadholders, because each of these functionaries was employed by several provinces. The stadholders were always members of the Nassau-Orange family. Only after the Napoleonic era did this family gain its present-day royal status.

2. The Fifth Report on Spatial Planning was presented as a draft in early 2001 (Rijksplanologische Dienst 2001), but the Fourth Report on Spatial Planning remains in force. Several policy documents are listed among the references.

3. The Dutch Ministry of Transport, Public Works and Water Management has worked with a comparable process design, called InfraLab (see Matthijsen 2000).

4. It should be mentioned that the Dutch national policy aimed at solving social problems in the largest cities is also criticized for its lack of regional orientation.

REFERENCES

Allaert, G., L. Versluys, S. Boeckhout, D. Holt, and M. Westerweele. 2000. *Samenvatting "Dynamisch centrum in de Delta, strategische planvisie voor Terneuzen in het perspectief van de Westerscheldetunnel."* Gent: Rijksuniversiteit Gent Rotterdam: NEI.

Beleidsovereenkomst tot verbetering van leef- en omgevingskwaliteit voor de periode 2000–2002 tussen de Vlaamse Gemeenschap en de stad Gent en het OCMW van Gent. 1999. Brussels: Flemish government.

Drewe, P. 1999. Grensoverschrijdende kennisinfrastructuur: De Internationele Schelde Faculteit en haar toekomst. In *Grensoverschrijdende activiteiten in beweging, Grensregio's, onderzoek en beleid*, edited by F. Boekema and G. Allaert, pp. 141–50. Assen: Van Gorcum.

Duijn, M., D. J. Ginter, H. J. M. Puylaert, and W. J. Oosten. 2001. *Beargumenteerd afwegen in Grensregio's: Een systematiek, Leidraad voor Rijksacties bij het Oplossen van Grensregionale knelpunten.* Delft: TNO Inro.

Expert Group on the Urban Environment. 1996. *European sustainable cities.* Report, by Directorate General XI Environment, Nuclear Safety and Civil Protection. Brussels: European Commission.

Gelder, H. van. 2000. De kruipende fabriek. *Starters* 2 (19): 40–44.

Halkier, H. 2001. Regional policy in transition: A multi-level governance perspective on the case of Denmark. *European Planning Studies* 9 (3): 323–38.

Hall, P. 1995. A European perspective on the spatial links between land use, development and transport. In *Transport and urban development*, edited by D. Banister, pp. 65–88. London: E & FN Spon.

Houtum, H. van. 1999. The action, affection, and cognition of entrepeneurs and cross-border economic relationships: The case of Zeeland-Gent/Eeklo. In *Grensoverschrijdende activiteiten in beweging, Grensregio's, onderzoek en beleid*, edited by F. Boekema and G. Allaert, pp. 53–82. Assen: Van Gorcum.

Israel, J. I. 1995. *The Dutch Republic: Its rise, greatness, and fall 1477–1806.* Oxford: Clarendon Press.

John, P. 2000. The Europeanisation of sub-national governance. *Urban Studies: An International Journal for Research in Urban and Regional Studies* 37 (5/6): 877–94.

Kersbergen, K. van, and F. van Waarden. 2001. *Shifts in governance: Problems of legitimacy and accountability.* Den Haag: Netherlands Organization for Scientific Research.

Kessen, A. A. L. G. M. 1992. *Bestuurlijke vernieuwing in grensgebieden: Intergemeentelijke grensoverschrijdende samenwerking.* N.p. A. A. L. G. M. Kessen.

Matthijsen, M. I. 2000. Infralab. In *The border story*, edited by E. Bout, pp. 55-60. Amsterdam: Agora Europa.

Ministerie van Volkshuisvesting, Ruimtelijke Ordening en Milieubeheer. 1988. *Vierde nota over de ruimtelijke ordening, Op weg naar 2015, Deel a Beleidsvoornemen.* Den Haag: SDU uitgeverij.

Newman, P. 2000. Changing patterns of regional governance in the EU. *Urban Studies: An International Journal for Research in Urban and Regional Studies* 37 (5/6): 895–908.

Paasi, A. 1996. *Territories, boundaries and consciousness: The changing geographies of the Finnish-Russian border.* Chichester: John Wiley.

Rijksplanologische Dienst. 2001. *Ruimte maken, ruimte delen, Vijfde nota over de ruimtelijke ordening 2000/2020.* Den Haag: Ministerie van Volkshuisvesting, Ruimtelijke Ordening en Milieubeheer.

Sande, J. van de. 2000. Boren op de grenzen van het technisch vernuft. *Algemeen Dagblad*, August 26, p. 3.

Siraa, H. T. 1989. *Een miljoen nieuwe woningen, De rol van de rijksoverheid bij wederopbouw, volkshuisvesting, bouwnijverheid en ruimtelijke ordening (1940–1963).* Den Haag: SDU uitgeverij.

Slobbe, E. van. 2001. Nieuwe beleidsarrangementen: Externe integratie vergt andere stijl van opereren. Supplement to *Stedebouw & Ruimtelijke Ordening* 82 (2): 29–31.
Sociaal Impulsfonds. 1999. *Meerjarenplan 2000–2002.* Gent: Stad Gent and OCMW-Gent.
Spoormans, H. C. G., E. A. Reichenbach, and A. F. A. Korsten, eds. 1999. *Grenzen over: Aspecten van grensoverschrijdende samenwerking.* Bussum: Uitgeverij Coutinho.

Conclusion: Regional Governance in the European Union

Susan Hodgett, José M. Magone, Wouter-Jan Oosten, and Linze Schaap

This book intended to map out the complexity and diversity of regional governance within the framework of a multilevel Europe. Each chapter addresses different issues of regional governance, which clearly can be separated only analytically from the overall EU multilevel governance system. Liesbet Hooghe and Gary Marks, the main theorists of this new heuristic framework, have recently written a useful theoretical book on multilevel governance. One of their overall conclusions is that there is a need for further concrete empirical studies of how multilevel governance works in practice (Hooghe and Marks 2001). This was reinforced by a recent article by Markus Jachtenfuchs (2001) reappraising the governance approach within European integration theory. He concludes:

> The governance approach offers to integrate the European Union in the number of other theories beyond international relations. This is not a trivial exercise. But it is worth pursuing since the EU is the place where fundamental developments that are transforming the possibilities of effective and responsible governance are probably stronger than elsewhere. In

this respect, the EU constitutes a unique laboratory for enhancing our understanding of politics in the twenty-first century. To realize this promise is the great challenge of the governance approach. (259–60)

In this volume, we attempted to study the making of regional governance as well as how regional governance systems relate to other analytical distinctive tiers of the EU multilevel governance system such as the national, supranational, local, and functional governance tiers. It is naturally our point of departure that this analytical differentiation is used only to look more in detail at regional institutions and processes. In reality, the EU multilevel governance system has to be conceptualized heuristically as more than the sum of its parts. This means that the dynamics of multilevel governance system do not allow for such strong analytical distinction among the different tiers. On the contrary, the complexity and intertwinedness of governance processes within the levels and among the levels make it difficult to observe such analytical differentiation in the actual process of daily life. Nevertheless, many policy actors still think that such a differentiation is possible. And we have to admit that in some specific and concrete cases, daily life policy-making processes still are a one-level game instead of multilevel one. There are still examples of decisions that are made in a context of one-level autonomy and policy discretion. It may be that these are exceptions to the general rule of multilevel policy making, but one has to acknowledge their existence.

In spite of these heuristic-theoretical reservations, at least five conclusions about the role of regional governance within the multilevel European Union can be drawn.

First, regional institutions and governance in the European Union are not always related to endemic processes of institution building. As Norman O'Neill clearly states, regional institutions may matter, but they do not always do so. Aspects such as technological innovation may be more important for the creation of a full-fledged regional governance system within a globalized economy. Nevertheless, one may argue that regional institutions, governance, and subsidiarity are important political devices in strengthening civil society. They along with the implementation of the new European Social Model together support Europe's social cohesion. These concepts move forward the debate on the development of Europe in line with other international agencies and policies working at pushing forward the long-term agenda of development.

Our case studies clearly illustrate that the process of developing Europe, as well as being insitutional, may also be organizational, applied to communities and to individual citizens. Therefore, it may well be asserted that development itself is a multilevel process and that the

European Union has facilitated its implementation from the macro- to the microlevels through the implementation of multilevel governance.

Considering that the examples in this volume differ from case to case, in France we see that regionalization had more of an economic rationale of decentralization, and it was not related to existing cultural legacies. The great exceptions in the French case are Britanny, Occitania, the Basque regions, and naturally Corsica. Particularly, the latter case witnessed a revival of separatist tendencies, including the repertoire of political violence since the 1970s (Molas 2001) The growing demand for more devolution in Northern Italy is clearly linked to a cultural legacy that can be combined with aspects of economic advantage and technological innovation. In contrast, southern Italy has difficulties creating efficient institutions. The crucial variable of social capital based on long-term existence or lack of civic traditions has to be taken into account, although we should avoid a deterministic explanation for the emergence of regional consciousness and a virtuous cycle of regional governance building (Putnam 1993). We should limit ourselves, though, and try not to formulate too general a conclusion about the necessity of a regional government layer for pushing a long-term agenda and strengthening the civil society. The examples discussed here are without exception examples from countries with rather weak local government. The strength of local government seems to be an important factor. Countries with a long tradition of strong local government do not seem to need a regional layer of government. One could even argue that regional institutions might negatively influence the importance of local government and have a negative impact on civil society and citizen involvement. One could find such a dilemma in the excellent contribution offered by Linze Schaap in this volume.

Second, the whole process of the creation of regional governance is quite asymmetrical and different from member-state to member-state. On the one end of the spectrum, some unitary states have escaped the move toward a more genuine regional governance process.[1] This is the case of Portugal and Greece, where central administration still dominates aspects of regional development. The discontinuous and difficult development toward democracy may be referred as the main reason why both countries were unable to create strong regional civil societies, which would put the central administrations under pressure to allow for a more decentralized way of formulating, deciding, and implementing public policy. Although administrative regionalization was imposed on Greece by the European Union, the lack of a cultural legacy of regional civil societies makes it very difficult to make democracy work at this level (Paraskevopoulos 1998). In Portugal, Commissions for Regional Coordination (*Comissoes de Coordenacao Regional*—*CCRs*) are merely extended arms of central administration. A referendum on regionalization, which is enshrined in the constitution, was rejected by two thirds of the voters, although the overall turnout was below 50 percent (Magone 2000). The unitary nature of Portugal and Greece is different from that of the Netherlands. Although unitary, the Dutch system is quite decentralized. But as Linze Schaap tells us in this book, reforms related to devolution in the Netherlands accumulated over the years without leading to a new regional system. On the contrary, the Dutch system is quite confusing for any outsider who wants to classify the country in terms of regional governance. As was suggested in Chapter 8, the Netherlands somehow took a different road, although almost unaware and definitely hesitantly. Instead of creating a directly elected new regional layer of government, new forms of cooperation between the municipalities emerged, at least in metropolitan areas. In this process, some aspects were overlooked, though. Legitimacy is one of them—and certainly not the least important one. Another difficulty in the Netherlands is the role of European policies as factors in the debate on regional governance. Some policy actors have merely paid lip service. On the other hand, there are more countries where European policies are not the only, or even most important, factor in the region-alization process. Other factors—often political reasons—are at stake as well.

On the other end, countries such as Belgium, Spain, and Germany have developed strong regional governance systems that seek strong connections to the other tiers of governance. Quite well developed is such integration of regional governance in Belgium and Germany, with Spain catching up fast (Börzel, 2000). In this volume, we paid special attention to the devolution process in the United Kingdom. All of them moved toward devolution in a different pace. Again, the role of a strong regional civil society yearning for more decentralization and devolu-tion was the most important factor leading to a faster or slower integra-tion into the overall multilevel governance system. The Scottish case is quite salient in this book. The study by Elisa Roller and Amanda Sloat is quite crucial in this respect, because it shows clearly the asymmetrical transformation of Scotland and Catalonia toward decentralized re-gional governance systems. What unites the two cases is the strong regional consciousness in the two regions. Whereas nationalist-region-alist parties are hegemonic in Catalonia, in Scotland this constitutes a substantial challenge within the new Scottish party system. Alex Wright's study clearly shows that the ambition of Scotland goes beyond the borders of the European Union. Paradiplomacy may increase the international projection of Scotland at the international level. As J. Barry Jones stresses, Wales has achieved a strong regional consciousness that is sustained by strong links to the other tiers of the European Union multilevel governance system. In spite of that, devolution remained below the level of Scotland, showing clearly that regional civil societies are important in creating momentum to demand more devolution powers. The new institutions have only modestly added value to the previous efforts of central government to improve the social and economic situation of Wales. The case of Northern Ireland studied in this volume by Susan Hodgett and Elizabeth Meehan is probably the best example that solutions to regional governance can be achieved by a bottom-up approach with EU funding. The meaning of the division of the island clearly changes in the context of European integration. A culture of integration may actually lead in the long-term perspective to the overcoming of sectarian forms of behavior. This naturally can be achieved only if there is significant support for a new culture of integration within Northern Ireland itself. The positive developments since 1997 are precious pieces toward this culture of understanding and cooperation that is reinforced by the European Union multilevel governance system. Cooperation between Irish and British governments at the European Union level had spill-over effects upon the whole process of making regional governance—in spite of sectarian difficulties—work in Northern Ireland.

Third, the emergence of regional governance in the United Kingdom clearly shows that unitary states have to change their own established governance system. This means that devolution cannot be achieved over time. It takes some years to become a full-grown embedded reality. The study by Graham Pearce and Steve Martin is quite crucial to understand these transformations. Before regional governance or governances became a reality in the United Kingdom, local authorities were the second tier of governance in the United Kingdom. The relationship to Brussels was quite asymmetrical from local government to local government. Nevertheless, the center-periphery relations were limited to a dyadic central-local government structure. The devolution process led to a major transformation of governance within the United Kingdom and of the United Kingdom within the European Union. In this sense, the establishment of regional governance is not only asymmetrical, but requires the calculation of a time of transition to change the culture of governance within a country. Such a process may take more than one decade—as the Spanish example clearly shows—or become an integral part of the policy-making process, as can be observed in Belgium (Börzel 2000; Kerremans 2000).

Fourth, the creation of new regional political institutions is shaping the dialogue within a multilevel governance system. New regional parliaments symbolize the beginning of a new regional political culture that wants to differentiate itself from the national and the emerging supranational political culture. Aspects of transparency and accountability are strongly connected with the emergence of these new institutions. Indeed, regional parliaments in the German Bundesländer, Spanish autonomous communities, or the Belgian regions/communities are setting the pace in making regional political cultures visible. In this volume, the case study of the Flemish Parliament, written by Karen Celis and Alison Woodward, shows that new institutions are very concerned with the creation of a new distinctive identity in relation to other levels of the multilevel governance system. The European Union is not crucial for the development of a regional political culture in this first phase, although the Welsh Assembly and the Scottish Parliament clearly are stronger linked to the Europe of the Regions. In the Flemish case, the new parliament is trying to gain its space within the new devolved Belgian state. All three cases show that the first legislatures of new regional parliaments are dedicated to the establishment of the internal terms of references and the first steps towards institution building. In comparison to these newcomers, the parliaments of the German Länder are already moving toward a new stage of development by asking for stronger participation and information at the supranational level. The demand for a (EAC) for regional parliaments has been put forward recently by German regional parliaments (see Chapter 1).

A point of concern is whether the new identities will leave room for policy discretion at the level below the regional, the local level. As can be seen very clearly in Spain, the devolution to the autonomous communities has stopped at that level. The relative importance of Spanish local government has hardly altered over the years. The devolution might even result in a new centralization, a centralization at the regional level.

Fifth, the boundaries of regions may not be confined to the member-states. The proliferation of Euroregions across the European Union shows that cross-border cooperation may lead to new forms of regionalism and regional governance. This naturally makes the overall process of EU multilevel governance more complex and difficult to understand, but at the same time these forms of cooperation foster thrusts toward further integration (Christiansen and Jorgensen 2000, 66–70).

In this volume, Wouter-Jan Oosten explored the growing cooperation between Belgian Gent and Dutch Terneuzen in the prospect of creating a sustainable Euroregion. It seems that there is some cross-fertilization between Belgium and the Netherlands, but there is still a long way to go before Gent-Terneuzen can move to a similar level of integration as the Maas-Rhine Euroregion or the Saar-Lorraine-Luxembourg Euroregion. Positive developments can be registered on the Spanish-Portuguese border, where several border regions are cooperating. The highest level of integration can be found among the Galicia-North Portugal Euroregion. The role of Interreg funding cannot be underestimated in pushing border regions to cooperate (Magone 2001, 259–80). But here again one can find that the whole process is quite asymmetrical and uneven. There are problems related to different cultures of administration, different languages, and historical rivalries that prevent seeing the benefit of cooperation. The case study by Wouter-Jan Oosten highlights both the possibilities and the problems of cooperation.

This volume shows that regional governance and its relations to other tiers of the EU multilevel governance system is a crucial unit of analysis to understand European integration processes. In sum, these contributions are designed to stimulate more research and discussion on the nature of regional institutions and governance within a multilevel European Union. As such they represent a stepping-stone for producing more studies on regional institutions and governance so that the complex map of EU governance can be understood through a process of empirical thick description. This is crucial to understanding the potentialities of the subnational democratization of the European Union.

NOTES

1. It is important to make clear that the development toward regional governance does not have to be adopted or come inevitably to all countries. Small countries such as Denmark, Netherlands, Portugal, and Greece do not need a new tier, but rather an improvement of the present structure.

REFERENCES

Börzel, T. A. 2000. From competitive regionalism to cooperative federalism: The Europeanization of the Spanish state of autonomies. *Publius: Journal of Federalism* 30 (2): 17–42.

Christiansen, T., and K. Jorgensen. 2000. Transnational governance "above" and "below" the state: The changing nature of borders in the New Europe. *Regional Studies* 10, no. 2 (summer): 62-77.

Hooghe, L., and G. Marks. 2001. *Multi-level governance and European integration.* Oxford: Rowman and Littlefield.

Jachtenfuchs, M. 2001. The governance approach to European integration. *Journal of Common Market Studies* 39 (2): 245–64.

Kerremans, B. 2000. Determining a European policy in a multilevel setting: The case of specialized coordination. Belgium. In *Regional and Federal Studies* 10, no. 1 (spring): 36–61.

Magone, J. 2000. The transformation of the Portuguese political system: European regional policy and democratization in a small EU member state. *Europeanization and the Southern Periphery,* edited by Kevin Featherstone and George Kazamias. Special issue of *South European Society and Politics* 5 (2): 120–49.

———. 2001. *Iberian trade unionism: Democratization under the impact of the European Union.* New Brunswick: Transactions.

Molas, I. 2001. Partis nationalistes: Autonomie et clans en corse.Working paper
     number 181. Barcelona: Institut de Ciencies Politiques i Socials.
Paraskevopoulos, C. J. 1998. Social capital and the public/private divide in
     Greek regions. *West European Politics* 21, no. 2 (April): 154–77.
Putnam, R. 1993. *Making democracy work: Civic traditions in modern Italy.*
     Princeton: Princeton University Press.

Selected Bibliography

MULTILEVEL GOVERNANCE THEORY

Barata, M de Oliveira. n.d. Étymologie du terme "gouvernance." At http://www.europa.eu.int/com/governance.html

Christiansen, T., and K. E. Jorgensen. 2000. Transnational governance "above" and "below" the state: The changing nature of borders in the new Europe. *Regional and Federal Studies* 10, no. 2 (summer): 62–77.

Cram, L. 1997. *Policy-making in the European Union: Conceptual lenses and the integration process.* London: Routledge.

European Commission, Governance Team. 2001. Consultations conducted for the preparation of the white paper on democratic European governance. Report to the Commission. SG 8533/01, June.

European Commission. 2001. European governance. White paper, July 25, 2001, COM(2001), 428 final.

Hooghe, L., and G. Marks. 2001. *Multi-level governance and European integration.* Lanham, Md.: Rowman and Littlefield.

Jachtenfuchs, M. 2001. The governance approach to European integration. *Journal of Common Market Studies* 39 (2): 245–64.

Kohler-Koch, B., and K. Eising, eds. 2000. *The transformation of governance in the European Union.* London: Routledge.

König, T., E. Rieger, and H. Schmitt. 1996. (eds.) *Das europäische Mehrebenensystem.* Frankfurt a. M.: Campus.

Magone, J. M. 2000. La costruzione di una società civile Europea: Legami a più livelli tra comitati economici e sociali. In *Il comitato economico e sociale nella costruzione Europea*, edited by A. Varsori, pp. 222–42. Venice: Marsilio.

Marks, G. 1997. An actor-centred approach to multi-level governance. In *The regional dimension of the European Union*, edited by C. Jeffery, pp. 20–40. London: Frank Cass.

Marks, G., L. Hooghe, and K. Blank. 1996. European integration from the 1980s: Statecentric *v* multi level governance. *Journal of Common Market Studies* 34 (3): 341–78.

Marks, G., F. Scharpf, P. Schmitter, and W. Streeck. 1996. *Governance in the European Union.* London: SAGE.

Newman, P. 2000. Changing patterns of regional governance in the EU. *Urban Studies: An International Journal for Research in Urban and Regional Studies* 37 (5/6): 895–908.

Pollack, M. 1994. Creeping competence: The expanding agenda of the European community. *Journal of Public Policy* 14 (2): 95–140.

———. 2000. The end of creeping competence? EU policy making since Maastricht. *Journal of Common Market Studies* 38 (3): 519–38.

Rhodes, R. A. W. 1996. The new governance: Governing without government. *Political Studies* 44, no. 4 (September): 652–67.

———. 1997. *Understanding governance.* Buckingham: Open University Press.

Sbraglia, A. M. 2000. Governance, the state, and the market: What is going on? *Governance* 13, no. 2 (April): 243–50.

Scharpf, F. W. 1999. *Governing in Europe: Effective and democratic.* Oxford: Oxford University Press.

THE EUROPEAN UNION AND THE REGIONS

Anderson, J. 1990. Skeptical reflections on a "Europe of the Regions": Britain, Germany and the European Regional Development Fund. *Journal of Public Policy* 10: 417–47.

———. 1996. Germany and the structural funds: Unification leads to bifurcation. In *Cohesion policy and European integration: Building multi-level governance*, edited by L. Hooghe, pp. 163–94. Oxford: Oxford University Press.

Bache, I. 1998. *The politics of EU regional policy: Multi-level governance or flexible gatekeeping?* Sheffield: Sheffield Academic Press.

Bache, I., and R. Jones. 2000. Has EU regional policy empowered the regions? A study of Spain and the United Kingdom. *Regional and Federal Studies* 10, no. 3 (Autumn): 1–20.

Balme, R. 1999. Las condiciones de la acción colectiva regional. In *Nacionalidades y regiones en la Unión Europea*, edited by F. Letamendia, pp. 69–91. Madrid: Fundamentos.

Bassot, E. 1993. Le Comité des Régions: Regions Françaises et Länder Allemands face à un nouvel organe communautaire. *Revue du Marché Cummun et De l'Union Européenne*, no. 371 (September–October): 729–39.

Benz, A. 2000. Two types of multi-level governance: Intergovernmental relations in German and EU regional policy. *Regional and Federal Studies* 10, no. 3 (Autumn): 21–44.

Bomberg, E., and J. Peterson. 1998. European Union decision making: The role of subnational authorities. *Political Studies* 46, no. 2 (June): 219–35.

Börzel, T. 2001. *Nations and regions in Europe.* Cambridge: Cambridge University Press.

Bullmann, U., ed. *Die politik der dritten ebene: Regionen im Europa der Union.* Baden-Baden: Nomos Verlaggesellschaft.

Calussi, F. B. 1999. The Committee of the Regions: In an atypical influential committee? In *EU committees as influential policymakers,* edited by M. P. C. M. Van Schendelen, pp. 225–49. Aldershot: Ashgate.

European Commission. 1995. *Europe 2000+: Cooperation for European territorial development.* Brussels: Office of the Official Publications of the European Community.

———. 1996. *Europe at the service of regional development.* Luxembourg: Office of the Official Publications of the European Community.

———. 1997. Agenda 2000: For a stronger and wider Union. *Bulletin of the European Union.* Supplement 5/97.

———. 1997b. *European spatial development perspective.* First official draft, presented at the informal meeting of ministers responsible for spatial planning of the member-states of the European Union, Noordwijk, June 9–10, 1997.

———. 1999a. *European spatial development perspective: Towards balanced and sustainable development of the territory of the European Union.* Luxembourg: Office of the Official Publications of the European Community.

———. 1999b. *Sixth periodic report on the social and economic situation and development in the regions of the European Union.* Luxembourg: Office of the Official Publications of the European Community.

European Commission/Netherlands Economic Institute. 1993. *New location factors for mobile investment in Europe.* Luxembourg: Office of the Official Publications of the European Community.

Hooghe, L. 1998. EU cohesion policy and competing models of European capitalism. *Journal of Common Market Studies* 36 (4): 457–77.

Hooghe, L., ed. 1996. *Cohesion policy and European integration: Building multi-level governance.* Oxford: Oxford University Press.

Hooghe, L., and M. Keating. 1996. The politics of European Union regional policy. *Journal of European Public Policy* 1 (3): 367–93.

Hooghe, L., and G. Marks. 1995. Channels of subnational representations in the European Union. In *What model for the Committee of the Regions? Past experiences and future perspectives,* edited by R. Dehousse and T. Christiansen, pp. 6-33. EU working paper EUI No. 95/2. Florence: European University Institute.

Jeffery, C. 1997. Regional information offices in Brussels and multi-level governance in the EU: A UK-German comparison. In *The regional dimension of the European Union,* edited by C. Jeffery, pp. 183–203. London: Frank Cass and Co.

———. 2000. Subnational mobilization and European integration: Does it make any difference? *Journal of Common Market Studies* 38, no. 1 (March): 1–23.

Jeffery, C., ed. 1997. *The regional dimension of the European Union.* London: Frank Cass.

Jones, B., and M. Keating, eds. 1995. *The European Union and the regions.* Oxford: Clarendon Press.

Keating, M., and L. Hooghe. 1996. By-passing the nation-state? Regions and the EU policy process. In *European Union: Power and policy-making,* edited by J. Richardson, pp. 216–29. London: Routledge.

Keating, M., and B. Jones, eds. 1985. *Regions in the European community.* Oxford: Clarendon Press.

Laffan, B. 1983. Policy implementation in the European Community: The European social fund as a case study. *Journal of Common Market Studies* 21: 389–408.

Lang, J., F. Naschold, and B. Reissert. 1998. *Reforming the implementation of European structural funds: A next development step.* Paper of the Wissenschaftszentrum Berlin. Fs Ii 98–202.

Lang, J., and B. Reissert. 1999. Reform des implementationssystems der strukturfonds: Die neuen verordnungen vor dem hintergrund der leistungsfähigkeit des bisherigen systems. *WSI-Mitteilungen* 6: 380–89.

Loughlin, J. 1996. Representing regions in Europe: The Committee of the Regions. *Regional and Federal Studies* 6: 147–65.

Marks, G. 1993. Structural policy and multi-level governance in the EC. In *The state of the European Union. Volume 2: The Maastricht debates and beyond*, edited by A. Cafruny and G. Rosenthal, pp. 391–411. Boulder: Lynne Rienner.

———. 1996. Exploring and explaining variation in EU cohesion policy. In *Cohesion policy and European integration: Building multi-level governance*, edited by L. Hooghe, 388–422. Oxford: Oxford University Press.

Marks, G., F. Nielsen, L. Ray, and J. Salk. 1996. Competencies, cracks and conflict: Regional mobilization of the European Union. In *Governance in the European Union*, edited by G. Marks, F. W. Scharpf, P. C. Schmitter, W. Streeck, pp. 40–63. London: Sage

Mazey, S. 1995. Regional lobbying in the New Europe. In *The regions and the new Europe*, edited by M. Rhodes, pp. 78–104. Manchester: Manchester University Press.

Mazey, S., and J. Mitchell. 1993. Europe of the Regions: Territorial interests and European integration: The Scottish experience. In *Lobbying in the European Community*, edited by S. Mazey and J. Richardson, pp. 95–121. Oxford: Oxford University Press.

Munoa, J. M. 1998. El Comité de las Regiones y la democracia regional y local en Europa. In *Nacionalidades y regiones en la Unión Europea*, coordinated by F. Letamendia, pp. 51–68. Madrid: Fundamentos.

Prodi, R. 2000. Reshaping Europe. Speech to the Committee of the Regions, February 17, in Brussels.

Rhodes, R., I. Bache, and S. George. 1996. Policy networks and policy makers in the European Union: A critical appraisal. In *Cohesion policy and European integration: Building multi-level governance*, edited by L. Hooghe, pp. 294–379. Oxford: Oxford University Press.

Smyrl, M. E. 1997. Does European Community regional policy empower the regions? *Governance* 10, no. 3 (July): 287–309.

Tömmel, I. 1998. Transformation of governance: The European Commission's strategy for creating a "Europe of the Regions." *Regional and Federal Studies* 8 (2): 52–80.

COLLECTIVE ACTION OF EUROPEAN REGIONS

Balme, R. 1999. Las condiciones de la acción colectiva regional. In *Nacionalidades y regiones en la Unión Europea*, coordinated by F. Letamendia, pp. 69–91. Madrid: Fundamentos.

Hooghe, L. 1995. Subnational mobilisation in the European Union. *West European Politics* 18 (3): 175–98.

Marks, G., and D. McAdam. 1996. Social movements and the changing structure of political opportunity in the European Union. *West European Politics* 19, no. 2 (April): pp. 249–78.

Weyand, S. 1997. Inter-regional associations and the European integration process. In *The regional dimension of the European Union*, edited by C. Jeffery, pp. 166–82. London: Frank Cass.

REGIONALISM AND REGIONALIZATION

Balme, R., P. Garraud, V. Hoffmann-Martinot, and E. Ritaine. 1994. *Le territoire pour politiques:Variations européennes*. Paris: L'Harmattan.

De Winter, L., and H. Türsan, eds. 1998. *Regionalist parties in Western Europe*. London: Routledge.

Down, W. M. 1997. *Coalition government, subnational style: Multiparty politics in Europe's regional parliaments*. Columbus: Ohio State University Press.

Harvie, C. 1994. *The rise of regional Europe*. London: Routledge.

Keating, M. 1998. *The new regionalism in Western Europe: Territorial restructuring and political change*. Cheltenham: Edward Elgar.

Letamendia, F., ed. 1999. *Nacionalidades y regiones en la Unión Europea*. Madrid: Fundamentos.

———. 2000b. Regional autonomy and state paradigm shifts in Western Europe. *Regional and Federal Studies* 10 (2): 10–34.

Loughlin, J. 2000a. Regional and local democracy in the European Union. Oxford: Oxford University Press.

Loughlin, J., E. Aja, U. Bullman, and Hendriks. 1999. *Regional and local democracy in the European Union*. Luxembourg: Office for Official Publications of the European Community.

Rhodes, R. A. W., and V. Wright, eds. 1987. *Tensions in the territorial politics of Western Europe*. London: Frank Cass.

Rokkan, S., and D. W. Urwin. 1983. *Economy, territory, identity: Politics of west European peripheries*. London: SAGE.

Sharpe, J., ed. 1993. *The rise of meso government in Europe*. London: Sage.

Sharpe, L. J. 1987. The West European state: The territorial dimension. In *Tensions in the territorial politics of Western Europe*, edited by R. A. W. Rhodes and V. Wright, pp. 148–68. London: Frank Cass.

Weir, M. 2000. Coalition building for regionalism. In *Reflections on Regionalism*, edited by B. Katz, pp. 127–54. Washington: Brookings Institution Press.

REGIONAL POLITICAL ECONOMY

Ansell, C. 2000. The networked polity: Regional development in Western Europe. *Governance* 12 (3): 303–33.

Ansell, C., C. Parsons, and K. Darden. 1997. Dual networks in European regional development policy. *Journal of Common Market Studies* 35 (3): 347–75.

Gaffard, J. L 1986. Reconstruction de l'espace économique et trajectoires technologiques. In *Milieu innovateurs en Europe*, edited by P. Aydalot, pp. 17–27. Paris: GREMI.

Loughlin, J., ed. 1997. *The political economy of regionalism*. London: Frank Cass.

MacLeod, G., and M. Goodwin. 1999. Reconstructing an urban and regional political economy. *Political Geography* 18: 697–730.

Maillat, D., and J. C. Perrin. 1992. *Enterprises innovantes et developpement territorial.* Neuchâtel: EDES.

Maillat, D., A. Schoepfer, and F. Voillat, eds. 1984. *La nouvelle politique régionale: Le cas de l'arc jurassien.* Neuchâtel: EDES.

Maillat, D., and J. Y. Vasserot. 1986. Les milieux innovateurs: Le cas de l'arc jurassien Suisse. In *Milieux innovateurs en Europe*, P. Aydalot, pp. 217–46. Paris: GREMI.

Meyer-Krahmer, F. 1985. Innovation behaviour and regional indigenous potential. In *Regional Studies* 19 (6): 523–34.

Raines, P. 2000. Regions in competition: Inward investment and regional variation in the use of incentives. In *Regional Studies* 34 (3): 291–96.

Storper, M. 1995. The resurgence of regional economies, ten years later: The region as a nexus of untraded interdependencies. *European Urban and Regional Sudies* 2 (3): 191–221.

Storper, M., and A. J. Scott, eds. 1992. *Pathways to industrialisation and regional development.* London: Routledge.

———. 1997. *The regional world.* New York and London: Guilford Press.

REGIONAL PARADIPLOMACY

Keating, M., and F. Aldecoa, eds. 1999. Paradiplomacy in action: The foreign relations of subnational governments. Special issue of *Regional and Federal Studies* 9, no. 1 (Spring).

EUROREGIONS

Blatter, J. 2001. Netzwerkstruktur, Handlungslogik und politische Räume: Institutionenwandel in europäischen und nordamerikanischen Grenzregionen. *Politische Vierteljahresschriften* 42 (2): 193–222.

Cochrane, A. 1993. Beyond the nation-state? Creating Euro-Regions. In *Die politik der dritten ebene: Regionen im Europa der Union*, edited by U. Bullmann, pp. 393–405. Baden-Baden: Nomos Verlaggesellschaft.

Lerch, W. 1999. Neu in Europa: Der interregionale wirtschafts—Und Sozialauschuß in the Großregion Saar-Lor-Lux. *WSI Mitteilungen* 6: 396–406.

Letamendia, F. 1997. Basque nationalism and cross-border co-operation between the southern and northern Basque countries. *Regional and Federal Studies* 7, no. 2 (summer): 25–41.

Morata, F. 1995. L'Eurorégion et le Réseau C-6: L'Émergence du suprarégionalisme en Europe du Sud? *Pole Sud*, no. 3 (autumn): 117–27.

———. 1997. The Euro-region and the C-6 network: The new politics of subnational cooperation in the western Mediterranean. In *The political economy of regionalism*, edited by M. Keating and J. Loughlin, pp. 292–305. London: Frank Cass.

Paasi, A. 1996. *Territories, boundaries and consciousness: The changing geographies of the Finnish-Russian border.* Chichester: John Wiley.

Sodupe, K. 1999. La Unión Europea y la cooperación interregional. In *Nacionalidades Y Regiones En La Unión Europea*, coordinated by F. Letamendia, pp. 13–50. Madrid: Fundamentos.

Wolters, M. 1993. Euregios along the German border. In *Die politik der dritten ebene: regionen im Europa der Union*, edited by U. Bullmann, pp. 407–18. Baden-Baden: Nomos Verlaggesellschaft.

REGIONAL GOVERNANCE IN THE MEMBER-STATES OF THE EUROPEAN UNION

Austria

Falkner, G. 2000. How pervasive are Euro-politics? Effects of EU membership on a new member-state. *Journal of Common Market Studies* 38, no. 2 (June): 223–50.

Falkner, G., and W. C. Müller., eds. 1998. *Österreich im europäischen Mehrebenensystem*. Vienna: Signum.

Müller, W. C. 2000. Austria. In *The national co-ordination of EU policy: The domestic level*, edited by H. Kassim, B. G. Peters, and V. Wright, pp. 201–18. Oxford: Oxford University Press.

Benelux Countries

Celis, K. 2001. *Het Vlaams Parlement: Nieuwe politieke cultuur en het potentieel voor een valorisering van het maatschappelijk kapitaal van vrouwen in de politieke besluitvorming*. Brussels: Ministerie van de Vlaamse Gemeenschap/ Gelijke Kansen Wetenschappelijke monografie 5.

Celis, K., with A. Woodward. 2000. *Het Vlaams Parlement: Nieuwe politieke cultuur en het potentieel voor een valorisering van het maatschappelijk kapitaal van vrouwen in de politieke besluitvorming*. Brussels: Center for Women's Studies, Vrije Universiteit Brussel.

Fitzmaurice, J. 1996. *The politics of Belgium: A unique federalism*. London: Hurst and Company.

Hooghe, L. 1994. The dynamics of constitution building in Belgium. In *Contemporary political studies 1994*, edited by P. Dunleavy and J. Stanyer, pp. 314–24. Belfast: Political Studies Association.

Kerremans, B. 1996. The Belgian sub-national entities in the European Union: Second or third level players? *Journal of Regional and Federal Studies* 2 (4): 41–54.

———. 2000. Determining a European policy in a multilevel setting: The case of specialized coordination in Belgium. *Regional and Federal Studies* 10, no. 1 (Spring): 36–61.

Toonen, Th. A. J. 1990. The unitary state as a system of co-governance: The case of the Netherlands. *Public Administration* 68 (3): 281–96.

Woodward, A. 1998. Sterft de NPC door gebrek aan vrouwen? *Vrouwenraad*, no. 3, pp. 20–27.

France

Cole, A. 1998. *French politics and society*. Hemel Hempstead: Prentice-Hall.

Molas, I. 2001. *Partis nationalistes: Autonomie et clans en corse*. Working paper number 181. Barcelona: Institut de Ciencies Politiques i Socials.

Germany

Jeffery, C. 1997. Farewell to the third level: The German Länder and the European policy process, In *The regional dimension of the European Union*, edited by C. Jeffery, pp. 56–75. London: Frank Cass and Co.

Lenz, A., and R. Johne. 2000. Die Landtage vor der Herausforderung Europa: Anpassung der parlamentarischen Infrastruktur als Grundlage institutioneller Europafähigkeit. *Aus Politik und Zeitgeschichte*, B6: 20–29.

Wessels, W., and D. Römetsch. 1997. German administrative interaction and European Union: The fusion of public policies. In *Adjusting to Europe: The impact of the European Union on national institutions and policies*, edited by Y. Meny, P. Muller, and J. L. Quermonne, pp. 73–109. London: Routledge.

Greece

Featherstone, K. 1998. Europeanization and the center periphery: The case of Greece in the 1990s. In *South European Society and Politics* 3 (1): 23–39.

Featherstone, K., and D. Yannopoulos. 1995. The EC and Greece: Integration and the challenge to centralism. In *The European Union and the regions*, edited by B. Jones and M. Keating. Oxford: Clarendon.

Legg, K. R., and J. M. Roberts. 1997. *Modern Greece: A civilization on the periphery*. Boulder: Westview Press.

Paraskevopoulos, C. J. 1998. Social capital and the public/private divide in Greek regions. *West European Politics* 21, no. 2 (April): 154–77.

Verney, S. 1994. Central state-local government relations. In *Greece and EC membership evaluated*, edited by S. Theophanides, pp. 166–79. London: Pinter.

Italy

Ciaffi, A. 2001. Multi-level governance in Italy: The case of Marche. *Regional and Federal Studies* 11 (2): 115–46.

Desideri, C., and V. Santantonio. 1996. Building a third level in Europe: Prospects and difficulties in Italy. *Regional and Federal Studies* 6 (2): 96–116.

Koff, S., and S. Koff. 2000. *Italy: From the first to the second republic*. London: Routledge.

Putnam, R. 1993. *Making democracy work: Civic traditions in modern Italy*. Princeton: Princeton University Press.

Nordic Countries

Arter, D. 2001. Regionalization in the European peripheries: The cases of northern Norway and Finnish Lapland. *Regional and Federal Studies* 11, no. 2 (summer): 94–114.

Bache, I., and J. Olsson. 2001. Legitimacy through partnership? EU policy diffusion in Britain and Sweden. *Scandinavian Political Studies* 24 (3): 215–37.

Halkier, H. 2001. Regional policy in transition: A multi-level governance perspective on the case of Denmark. *European Planning Studies* 9 (3): 323–38.

O'Neill, N. 1995. *Economic development in North Sea regions*. Aberdeen: North Sea Commission.

Portugal and Spain

Baum, M. A., and A. Freire. 2001. Political parties, cleavage structures and referendum voting: Electoral behaviour in the Portuguese regionalization referendum of 1998. *South European Society and Politics* 6, no. 1 (summer): 1–26.

Börzel, T. A. 2000. From competitive regionalism to cooperative federalism: The Europeanization of the Spanish state of autonomies. *Publius: Journal of Federalism* 30 (2): 17–42.

———. 2001. *Nations and regions in Europe.* Cambridge: Cambridge University Press.

Brugué, Q., R. Gomà, and J. Subirats. 2000. Multilevel governance and Europeanization: The case of Catalonia. *South European Society and Politics* 5 (2): 95–118.

Conversi, D. 1997. *The Basques, the Catalans and Spain.* London: Hurst and Company.

Giordano, B., and E. Roller. 2002. Catalonia and the "idea of Europe": Competing strategies and discourses within Catalan party politics. *European Urban and Regional Studies* 9 (2): 99–113.

Guibernau, M. 2000. Nationalism and intellectuals in nations without states: The Catalan case. *Political Studies* 48 (5): 989–1005.

Held, G., and A. Sanchez-Velasco. 1996. Spain. In *Policy networks and European structural funds*, edited by H. Heinelt and R. Smith, pp. 227–56. Aldershot: Avebury.

Magone, J. 2000a. The transformation of the Portuguese political system: European regional policy and democratization in a small EU member-state. *South European Society and Politics* 5 (2): 119–40.

———. 2000b. EU territorial governance and national politics: Reshaping marginality in Spain and Portugal. In *Margins of European integration*, edited by N. Parker and B. Armstrong, pp. 155–77. Basingstroke: Macmillan.

Magone, J. M. 2001. *Iberian trade unionism: Democratization under the impact of the European Union.* New Brunswick, N.J.: Transactions.

Moreno, L. 1995. Multiple ethnoterritorial concurrence in Spain. *Nationalism and Ethnic Politics* 1 (1): 11–32.

———. 1997. *La federalización de España: Poder político y territorio.* Madrid: Siglo Veintiuno.

Newton, M. T., and P. J. Donaghy. 1997. *Institutions of modern Spain: A political and economic guide.* Cambridge: Cambridge University Press.

Pires, L. M. 1998. *A politica regional Europeia em Portugal.* Lisboa: Fundacao Calouste Gulbenkian.

Solozábal, J. J. 1996. Spain: A federation in the making? In *Federalizing Europe? The costs, benefits and preconditions of federal political systems*, edited by J. J. Hesse and V. Wright, pp. 241–65. Oxford: Oxford University Press.

United Kingdom and Ireland

Bache, I. 1999. The extended gatekeeper: Central government and the implementation of EC regional policy in the UK. *Journal of European Public Policy* 6 (1): 28–45.

Bache, I., S. George, and R. Rhodes. 1996. The European Union, cohesion policy, and subnational authorities in the United Kingdom. In *Cohesion policy and European integration: Building multi-level governance*, edited by L. Hooghe, pp. 294–319. Oxford: Oxford University Press.

Bache, I., and J. Olsson. 2001. Legitimacy through partnership? EU policy diffusion in Britain and Sweden. *Scandinavian Political Studies* 24 (3): 215–37.

Bentley, J., and J. Shutt. 1997. European regional policy in English regions: The West Midlands and Yorkshire and Humberside. In *The coherence of EU regional policy: Contrasting perspectives on the structural funds*, edited by J. Bachtler and I. Turok. London: Jessica Kingsley.

Bogdanor, V. 1999. *Devolution in the United Kingdom*. Oxford: Oxford University Press.

Bradbury, J., and J. Mawson. 1997. *British regionalism and devolution*. London: Jessica Kingsley.

Brown, A., D. McCrone, and L. Paterson. 1998. *Politics and society in Scotland*. 2nd ed. Basingstroke: Macmillan.

Brown A., D. McCrone, L. Paterson, and P. Surridge. 1999. *The Scottish electorate*. London: Macmillan.

Cole, M. 2001. Elections to the Welsh Assembly: Proportionality, continuity and change. *Regional and Federal Studies* 11 (summer): 147–63.

Elcock, H. 1997. The north of England and the Europe of the Regions, or, when is a region not a region. In *The political economy of regionalism*, edited by M. Keating and J. Loughlin, pp. 422–35. London: Frank Cass.

Goldsmith, M., and E. Sperling. 1997. Local government and the EU. In *European integration and local government*, edited by M. Goldsmith and T. Klaussen, pp. 95–120. Cheltenham: Edward Elgar.

Griffiths, D. 2000. Writing on the margins: Welsh politics. *The British Journal of Politics and International Relations* 2, no. 1 (April): 124–34.

Hodgett, S., and D. Johnson. 2001. Troubles, partnerships and possibilities: A study of the Making Belfast Work Development Initiative in Northern Ireland. *Public Administration and Development* 21 (4): 321–52.

Hughes, J., C. Knox, M. Murray, and J. Greer. 1998. *Partnership governance in Northern Ireland: The path to peace*. Dublin: Oak Tree Press.

John, P. 1994a. *The Europeanisation of British local government: New management strategies*. Luton: Local Government Management Board.

———. 1994b. UK sub-national offices in Brussels: Diversification or regionalization? *Regional Studies* 28, no. 7 (November): 739–46.

———. 1996. Centralisation, decentralisation and the European Union: The dynamics of triadic relationships. *Public Administration* 74: 293–313.

———. 1997. Europeanisation in a centralising state: Multi-level governance in the UK. In *The regional dimension of the European Union*, edited by C. Jeffery, 131–46. London: Frank Cass.

Jones, B., and D. Balsom. 2000. *The road to the National Assembly for Wales*. Cardiff: University of Wales Press.

Jones, J. B. 1985. Wales in the European Community. In *Regions in the European Community*, edited by M. Keating and B. Jones, pp. 89–109. Oxford: Clarendon Press.

———. 1995. Nations, regions and Europe: The UK experience. In *The European Union and the regions*, edited by B. Jones and M. Keating, pp. 89–115. Oxford: Clarendon Press.

———. 1997. Wales: A developing political economy. In *The political economy of regionalism*, edited by M. Keating and J. Loughlin, pp. 388–405. London: Frank Cass.

Kassim, Hussein. 2000. The United Kingdom. In *The national co-ordination of EU policy: The domestic level*, edited by H. Kassim, B. G. Peters, and V. Wright, pp. 22–53. Oxford: Oxford University Press.

Kay, A. 2000. Objective 1 in Wales: RECHAR redux? *Regional Studies* 34 (6): 581–85.

Kellas, J. G., and P. J. Madgwick. 1985. Territorial ministries: The Scottish & Welsh Offices. In *The territorial dimension in United Kingdom politics*, edited by P. Madgewick and R. Rose, pp. 9–34. London: Macmillan.

Klijn, E., J. Koppenjan, and C. Termeer. 1995. Managing networks in the public sector: A theoretical study of management strategies in policy networks. *Public Administration* 73 (3): 437–54.

Lanigan, C. 1997. The private sector and regionalism in North East England. *Regional and Federal Studies* 7 (3): 66–86.

Lynch, P. 2001. *Scottish government and politics*. Edinburgh: Edinburgh University Press.

Madgwick, P., and R. Rose, eds. 1985. *The territorial dimension in United Kingdom politics*. London: Macmillan.

Marr, A. 1992. *The battle for Scotland*. Harmondsworth: Penguin.

Martin, S. J. 1997. *EU capital funding and local authorities in England and Wales*. Luton: Audit Commission.

———. 1998. Managing local economic change: EU programmes and local economic governance in the UK. *European Urban and Regional Studies* 5 (3): 237–48.

———. 2000. Implementing best value: Local public services in transition. *Public Administration* 78 (1): 209–27.

Martin, S. J., and G. R. Pearce. 1993. Regional economic development strategies: Strengthening meso-government in the UK. *Regional Studies* 27 (7): 681–85.

———. 1994. The impact of Europe on local government: Regional partnerships in local economic development. In *Contemporary political studies*, edited by P. Dunleavy and J. Stanyer, pp. 962–72. Belfast: Political Studies Association of Great Britain.

———. 1999. Differentiated multi-level governance? The response of British sub-national governments to European integration. *Regional and Federal Studies* 9 (2): 32–52.

Mawson, J. 1996. The re-emergence of the regional agenda in the English regions: New patterns of urban and regional governance? *Local Economy* 10 (4): 300–26.

———. 1999. The English regions and the wider constitutional and administrative reforms. In *The new regional agenda*, edited by J. Dungey and I. Newman, pp. 85-98. London: Local Government Information Unit.

Mawson, J., and K. Spencer. 1997. The government offices for the English regions: Towards regional government. *Policy and Politics* 25 (1): 71–84.

Meegan, R. 1994. A Europe of the Regions: A view from Liverpool on the Atlantic Arc Periphery. *European Planning Studies* 4 (2): 59–80.

Meehan, E. 2000. Europe and the Europeanization of the Irish Question. In *A farewell to arms? From 'long war' to long peace in Northern Ireland*, edited by M. Cox, A. Guelke, and F. Stephen, pp. 199–213. Manchester: Manchester University Press.

Mitchell, J. 1997. Scotland: The Union state and the international environment. In *The political economy of regionalism*, edited by M. Keating and J. Loughlin, pp. 406–21. London: Frank Cass.

———. 2001. Review article: The study of Scottish politics post-devolution: New evidence, new analysis and new methods. *West European Politics* 24 (4): 216–23.

Murray, G. 2000. New relations between Scotland and Ireland. In *Scotland: The challenge of devolution*, edited by A. Wright, pp. 125–36. Aldershot: Ashgate.

Paterson, L. 1994. *The autonomy of modern Scotland*. Edinburgh: Edinburgh University Press.

Paterson, L., A. Brown, J. Curtice, K. Hinds, D. McCrone, A. Park, K. Sproston, and P. Surridge. 2001. *New Scotland, new politics?* Edinburgh: Edinburgh University Press.

Pearce, G. R. 1999. The West Midlands. In *Metropolitan planning in Britain: A comparative study*, edited by P. Roberts, K. Thomas and G. Williams, pp. 78–96. London: Jessica Kingsley.

Pearce, G. R., and S. J. Martin. 1996. The measurement of additionality: Grasping the slippery eel. In *Local Government Studies* 22 (1): 78–92.

Roberts, P., and T. Hart. 1996. *Regional strategy and partnership in European programmes: Experience in four UK regions.* York: Joseph Rowntree Foundation.

Roberts, P., and M. Lloyd. 2000. Regional development agencies in England: New strategic regional planning issues? *Regional Studies* 34 (1): 75–79.

Salmon, T. 2000. An oxymoron: The Scottish Parliament and foreign relations? In *Scotland: the Challenge of Devolution*, edited by A. Wright, pp. 150–67. Aldershot: Ashgate.

Scott, A., J. Peterson, and D. Millar. 1994. Subsidiarity: A "Europe of the Regions" *v* the British Constitution. *Journal of Common Market Studies* 32, no. 1 (March): 47–67.

Scott, P. H. 1992. *Scotland in Europe: Dialogue with a skeptical friend.* Edinburgh: Cannongate.

Sloat, A. 2000. Scotland and Europe: Links between Edinburgh, London and Brussels. *Scottish Affairs*, no. 31: 92–110.

———. 2002. *Scotland in Europe: A study of multi-level governance.* Bern: Peter Lang.

Stolz, K. 1994. The Committee of the Regions and Scottish self-government: A German perspective. *Scottish Affairs*, no. 9 (autumn): 13–23.

Tomaney, J., and P. Hetherington. 2001. *Monitoring the English regions.* Report No. 2. Center for Urban and Regional Development Studies, University of Newcastle on Tyne.

Wright, A. 1995. The Europeanisation of the Scottish Office. In *Region building*, edited by S. Hardy, pp. 81-85. London: Regional Studies Association.

———. 1996. Scottish fishermen and the EU: A choice between two Unions? *Scottish Affairs*, no. 14 (winter): 27–41.

———. 2000a. The Europeanisation of Scotland: A driver for autonomy. In *Europe united, the United Kingdom disunited?*, edited by M. Graves and G. Girrard, pp. 55–71. University of Brest.

———. 2000b. The 2002 review of the CFP. *Scottish Affairs*, no. 32 (summer): 59–74.

———. 2000c. Scotland and the EU: All bark and no bite? In *Scotland: The challenge of devolution*, edited by A. Wright, pp. 137–49. Aldershot: Ashgate.

———. 2002. A federalised polity: An alternative to Scottish independence in Europe? In *Modernising Britain: Central, devolved, federal?* edited by S. Henig, London: The Federal Trust.

Index

About the Editor and Contributors

Karen Celis is currently preparing her Ph.D. thesis at the Department of Political Sciences at the Free University of Brussels entitled "Substantive Representation: Investigating the Impact of Descriptive Representation on the Substantive Representation of Women in the Belgian Lower House during the 20th Century." For this purpose she is holder of a special doctoral grant from the Fund for Scientific Research, Flanders. She studied contemporary history at the Catholic University of Louvain before specializing in women's studies at the University of Antwerp. She has published on abortion, gender and socialism, women and war, women MPs in the Flemish Parliament, State Feminism and substantive political representation of women.

Susan Hodgett is codirector of the Centre of Canadian Studies at Queen's University, Belfast and a lecturer in lifelong learning. She is also an adjunct professor in public administration at Dalhousie University, Nova Scotia. Her research, on the role of the voluntary section in Northern Ireland, has emphasized the impact of the intervention of structural funds and European regional policy upon local communities. She contributed to the *Journal of Public Administration and Development* on the importance of the European Union and policy diffusion on implementing partnership models in the Making Belfast Work development initiative in Northern Ireland. Her most recent work for the *British Journal of Canadian Studies* has looked at *Conceptualising Community*. Susan has worked with governments of Canada and Northern Ireland on regional development as well as having been a special advisor to the Northern Ireland Assembly.

J. Barry Jones is reader in politics and director of the Welsh Governance Center in the School of European Studies, Cardiff University. He is the coordinator of the MScEcon in Welsh politics and government and lectures on European territorial politics, and public policy in the United Kingdom. His research interests include the Labour Party, European regionalism, and the politics of Welsh devolution. He is a recipient of several research grants from the Nuffield Foundation (to study European regionalism), the Rowntree Foundation (to track the operation of the National Assembly committees), and the ESRC (to compare Wales and Brittany in the development of language and industrial training policies). His publications include *Parliament and Territoriality*, with R. A. Wilford (1985); *The European Union and the Regions*, with M. J. Keating (1995); *The Road to the National Assembly for Wales*, with D. Balsom, (2000); and *Building a Civic Culture*, with J. Osmond (2002).

José M. Magone is a senior lecturer in European politics at the Department of Politics and International Studies, University of Hull. He was Robert Schuman scholarship holder in the European Parliament in 1990, visiting research fellow at the Center for Mediterranean Studies at the University of Bristol in 1990-1991, lecturer in political science and sociology at the Institute Jean Piaget in Lisbon in 1992-1993, guest researcher at the Juan March Center for Advanced Social Studies (Madrid) in 1997, and Karl W. Deutsch Guest Professor 1999 at the Wissenschaftszentrum Berlin für Sozialforschung (WZB). He has published extensively on the impact of European integration on the southern European states. He has published four books: *The Changing Architecture of Iberian Politics* (1996); *European Portugal (1997); Iberian Trade Unionism: Democratization under the Impact of the European Union* (2001); and *The Politics of Southern Europe* (Prager, 2003).

Steve Martin is professor of public policy and management, Cardiff Business School, and director of the local and regional government research unit at Cardiff University, where he leads a multidisciplinary team engaged in long-term research on public service improvement in local government. His research is focused on local government policy and management and the regulation of local public services. He has written widely about the implications of EU integration for UK local government, the policy and politics of the Best Value regime, and the development of inspection and audit within local government.

Elizabeth Meehan is the director of the Institute of Governance, Public Policy and Social Research at Queen's University, Belfast. Previously she was a professor in the school of politics and before that lecturer at Bath University. Her research and publications cover women and politics (United States, United Kingdom, European Union); citizenship in the European Union and the United Kingdom; British-Irish relations in the context of the European Union, with reference to freedom of movement of persons and to the Northern Irish peace process and devolution.

Norman O'Neill is director of the Centre for Regional Business Development at the Business School, University of Hull. He has published extensively on regional development and the European Union.

Wouter-Jan Oosten has been a Ph.D-researcher at the Centre for Public Management of the Erasmus University, Rotterdam, and at the Netherlands Research School for Transport, Infrastructure and Logistics since September 1999. He has studied law and political science at Leiden University. His research interests are political theory, urban planning, and public-private partnerships. His dissertation will suggest improvements in processes of spatial investment. Since February 2001, W. Oosten has been an editor of *Idee, Tijdschrift van het wetenschappelijk bureau van D66*. In 2002 Lemma (Utrecht, the Netherlands) published his *Politieke theorie ingeleid*, an introduction to political theory.

Graham Pearce is Jean Monnet Senior Lecturer at Aston Business School, Aston University, Birmingham. He has undertaken research on a range of public policy issues, including the impacts of EU integration on UK local government and EU information society policies for data protection and electronic commerce. He has written about the politics and policies of devolved approaches to local government in England and is presently investigating the emerging patterns of governance in the English regions as part of an ESRC program of research on devolution and constitutional change.

Elisa Roller is a lecturer in European Politics in the Department of Government, University of Manchester. She earned her Ph.D. from the London School of Economics. Publications include "Reforming the

Spanish Senate: Mission impossible?" in *West European Politics*, "The Basque Country and Spain—continuing the deadlock?" In *Mediterranean Politics*, "The 1997 Llei del Català: A Pandora's Box in Catalonia?" in *Regional and Federal Studies* and "The March 2000 general election in Spain" in *Government and Opposition*. Co-authored publications include "Catalonia and the 'idea of Europe': Competing strategies and discourses within Catalan party politics," *European Urban and Regional Studies*, and "A comparison of Catalan and 'Padanian' nationalism: More similarities than differences?" in *Journal of Southern Europe and the Balkans*.

Linze Schaap is a senior lecturer in the Department of Public Administration. He studied Juridical Public Administrative Sciences at Groningen University. In 1993 he became lecturer at Erasmus University Rotterdam. Since 1999 he also is a member of the Provincial Council of South-Holland. In 2000 he founded the Centre for Local Democracy at Erasmus University (together with Dr. H.H.F. Daemen). His main research areas are governance, sub-national government, citizen-government relations at the local level. His main publications are with R. J. Veld, C.J.A.M. Termeer, and M.J.W. van Twist, *Autopoiesis and configuration theory: New approaches to societal steering* (Dordrecht: Kluwer Academic Publishers, 1991); *The search for Inciting Governance: On autopoiesis, self-governance and city province* (Delft: Eburon, 1997); with H.H.F.M. Daemen (eds.), *Citizen and City: Developments in fifteen local democracies in Europe* (Delft: Eburon, 2000).

Amanda Sloat is a research fellow in the Institute of Governance, Public Policy and Social Research at Queen's University, Belfast. Her Ph.D. in Politics, which she obtained from the University of Edinburgh, analyzed elite expectations of Scotland's role in the European Union. She worked with the European Commission's governance team and served as an adviser to the Scottish Parliament's European Committee during its governance inquiry. She has published numerous articles on UK devolution and governance and recently published her first book, *Scotland in Europe: A Study of Multi-Level Governance* (2002). She is currently coordinating an EU-funded research project on the civic and political participation and representation of women in Central and Eastern Europe.

Alison Woodward (Ph.D., University of California at Berkeley) is professor and chair of the International Affairs and Politics Program of Vesalius College at the Free University of Brussels (VUB) and cofounder of the center for women's studies. She has held appointments at the universities of Uppsala, Antwerp, and Brussels; the Wissenschaftszentrum Berlin; and the Royal Institute of Technology in Stockholm, among others. She held the M. Jahoda Chair at the Ruhr University in 2001. Her primary research interest is in the field of comparative European public policy and organization, especially in the areas of equal opportunities policies for women, housing, and alternative energy. Recent publications include *Inclusions and Exclusions in European Societies* (edited with Martin Kohli) (2001) and *Going for Gender Balance* (2001).

Alex Wright is a lecturer at the Department of Politics, University of Dundee. His Ph.D. thesis was on Scotland's relations with the European Union. He has been elected to a visiting research fellowship at the Institute for Advanced Studies in the Humanities, the University of Edinburgh during 2002, where his research focused on Scotland's agenda in the EU following legislative devolution. He currently contributes to ESRC/Leverhulme Devolution report, where he is the rapporteur for Scottish/UK relations and Scottish/EU relations. He has been consulted by the European committee of the Scottish parliament on a number of occasions, and he has been interviewed by the committee as an expert witness on the proposal to regionalize the CFP. He is an independent assessor for ministerial appointments to public bodies in Scotland. Among his publications is *Scotland: The Challenge of Devolution* (2000), for which he was the editor and a contributing author.